STILL FIDDLING

IN THE KITCHEN

NATIONAL COUNCIL OF JEWISH WOMEN

ncjw

GREATER DETROIT SECTION

Still Fiddling In The Kitchen is the long awaited sequel to the popular **Fiddler In The Kitchen**. This is a collection of 400 recipes from approximately 750 submitted. We are most grateful to all NCJW members and friends who shared their ideas and recipes. Because of duplication and space limitations, not every recipe submitted could be included; nevertheless, we thank each and every one of you. All recipes have been tested, reviewed, and edited by the committee and a corps of volunteer cooks to assure the quality of the recipes. We thank them all. All proceeds from the sale of **Still Fiddling In The Kitchen** will help support the many projects and programs of the National Council of Jewish Women, Greater Detroit Section.

About The Artist

BEN KONSTANTIN, who grew up in Oak Park, Michigan, received a BFA from Wayne State University. He is currently an illustration student at The Center for Creative Studies in Detroit. His hope is to become an illustrator of children's books and editorial publications.

ISBN: 0-9633490-0-7

LCCN: 92-061040

1st Printing   10,000 copies   September, 1992

Printed in the USA by
WIMMER BROTHERS
A Wimmer Company
Memphis • Dallas

Table of Contents

 Denotes general cooking hints

ABOUT NCJW

The National Council of Jewish Women is a volunteer organization, which in the spirit of Judaism, is dedicated to furthering human welfare in the Jewish and general communities, locally, nationally, and internationally. Through an integrated program of education, service, social action, and advocacy, it provides essential services and stimulates the individual and the community toward their responsibility in advancing human welfare and the democratic way of life. Through their thrift shops, Fashion Spree, and contributions, the Greater Detroit Section supports the following local services:

ACCESS GUIDE
A directory of facilities for handicappers and the elderly.

ADOPT-A-SCHOOL
Tutoring and enrichment for students in special schools.

BALDWIN AVENUE HUMAN SERVICES PROJECT
Special programs for the homeless.

CALL POLICE BANNER
An aid for stranded motorists.

CASA-LEGAL GUARDIAN *(Court Appointed Special Advocates)*
Investigations and recommendations for the secure placement of children within the Probate Court system.

DOR L'DOR
A musical program that pairs seniors and sixth graders in song and friendship.

EDUCATION ASSISTANCE
Interest free loans and grants to Jewish undergraduate and graduate students.

FAMILY TO FAMILY
A matching of newcomers from the Soviet Union with American families for friendship and enriching Jewish experiences.

FEDERATION APARTMENT SHOPPING BUS
Weekly shopping transportation for apartment residents.

HIPPY USA
Training parents to teach the basic learning skills to their preschoolers.

THE JEWISH NEWS ON TAPE
Reading The Jewish News weekly on tape for the visually impaired.

MEALS ON WHEELS
Packing and delivery of kosher meals to the homebound.

SPACE
Support for the separated, widowed, and divorced and their families through peer groups, workshops, and retreats.

SPACE RAINBOWS FOR ALL CHILDREN
Support groups for children ages 4-18 who have experienced the loss of a parent through death or divorce.

UP AND OUT
Activities for seniors; transportation provided.

WICS
Recruitment of young men and women for the Federal Job Corps and related programs.

Special Interest Groups

BUSINESS AND PROFESSIONAL BRANCH

Meeting the needs of working women, adding Networking to NCJW goals of Community Service, Social Action and Education.

HAKOL
Capturing the voice of today's young women as volunteers reach out and raise social consciousness through programs emphasizing action and community service.

In Israel, NCJW supports the following projects:

HIPPY *(Home Instruction Program for Preschool Youngsters)*
Paraprofessionals train mothers to teach basic learning skills to their 3-6 year olds.

HATAF *(Home Activities for Toddlers and their Families)*
Teaches mothers to develop the intellectual abilities of their 1-3 year olds.

MANOF *(Residential Program for Unattached Adolescent Boys and Girls)*
Enables troubled adolescents to become productive members of society through education, work experience and support services.

YACHAD *(Children Tutoring Children)*
Fifth to eight graders aid second graders to achieve reading success.

RULES OF THE GAME
A program to familiarize Israeli and Arab youths with the concept of democracy and promote cooperation.

SHIP-A-BOX
Provides educational and therapeutic materials for disadvantaged children, senior citizens and veterans.

Cookbook Committee

COMMITTEE CO-CHAIRWOMEN

Wendy Wagenheim
Laurel Portner

STEERING COMMITTEE

Judy Blake
Lillian Chinitz
Ronni Cohen
Charlotte Edelheit
Carol Fogel
Rona Freedland
Sally Green
Sherry Haffner
Beth Hirsch
Kari Izu
Suzanne Kaine
Harriet Kanter
Gert Kershenbaum

Edythe Klein
Marjory Kurzmann
Sally Mayer
Janelle Miller
Louise Newman
Ruth Rosenthal
Joyce Rubenstein
Phyllis Schwartz
Lois Shiffman
Jackie Tepper
Elizabeth Warnick
Ruth Wayne

ILLUSTRATOR

Ben Konstantin

TYPIST

Erin Walz

PROOFREADERS

Henry Gordon
Marsha Gordon
Barbara Grant
Sondra Nathan

SPECIAL ASSISTANCE

Ricky Blumenstein
Randy Blumenstein

APPETIZERS

Chicken Liver Pâté

½ pound chicken livers
1 teaspoon salt
Pinch cayenne pepper
½ cup softened margarine
¼ teaspoon nutmeg
1 teaspoon dry mustard

⅛ teaspoon ground cloves
2 teaspoons finely minced
  onions
¼ cup currants, soaked in
  brandy or water and drained

In a saucepan, barely cover livers with water, bring to a boil, then simmer for 15 minutes. Drain and put through the finest blade of a food mill. Mix with remaining ingredients and blend well. Pack mixture into a crock or pretty bowl and chill well.

NOTE: This recipe can be doubled.

Joan Weil

Vegetarian Pâté

1 large onion, finely diced
1 minced garlic clove
¾ pound fresh mushrooms,
  finely chopped
½ teaspoon dried thyme
1 cup sliced almonds, toasted
  and ground

2 tablespoons olive oil
2 tablespoons balsamic vinegar
1 drop almond extract
Vegetable spray
Almonds and parsley for
  garnish

Spray saucepan with vegetable spray. At medium heat, sauté vegetables and thyme. Cook until liquid is gone, While vegetables are cooking, combine almonds, olive oil, and almond extract in a food processor using quick on/off (one pulse). Add vegetable mixture and process until smooth. With machine running, slowly add vinegar through the feed tube. Remove from bowl and chill. Garnish with sliced almonds and parsley.

NOTE: This pâté may be used to stuff mushrooms or may be made into a mold. Serve with sliced apples, crackers, crusty bread, and other vegetables.

Yield: Makes about 1 pound.

Sally Mayer

Party Pinwheel Hors d'Oeuvres

2 (8-ounce) packages cream
   cheese
1 package dry ranch dressing
   mix
2 green onions, finely chopped
½ cup finely chopped celery
½ cup finely chopped red
   pepper

1 (6-ounce) jar sliced olives
   with pimento or sliced black
   olives
4 large lavash or flour tortillas
Parsley or dill leaves for
   garnish

Mix first 3 ingredients in processor or by hand. Spreading with spatula or knife, completely cover lavash or tortilla. Sprinkle on remaining ingredients one at a time. Roll up tightly and wrap each roll separately with plastic wrap. Chill several hours. Slice into 1 inch thick pieces, cutting on the diagonal. Discard ends. Place on a platter so the filling will look like a pinwheel. Garnish with parsley or dill leaves.

NOTE: These can be rolled the day before, wrapped and refrigerated. This recipe works with chopped tomatoes, hommus and tabbouleh, chopped egg salad, and minced lox and cream cheese.

Yield: Serves 8 to 10.
                        Fran Levin & Lois Shiffman

Roasted Garlic Appetizer

6 whole garlic heads
Sprig of rosemary or dill
   (optional)

¼-½ cup olive oil
French bread, sliced and lightly
   toasted

Preheat oven to 350°. With sharp knife, cut ¼ inch from top of each garlic head. Lay a sprig of rosemary or dill over each head. Place in a baking dish and brush with oil. Bake 1 hour, basting frequently.

To serve: Give each guest 1 garlic head accompanied by slices of French bread. Provide a small knife or cocktail fork to remove softened cloves of garlic and to smear on the bread.

NOTE: This is also very good as a side dish, especially with a hearty soup or stew meal.

Yield: Serves 6.
                                  Laurel Portner

Marinated Tortellini and Broccoli Appetizer

1 (10-12-ounce) package fresh
   tortellini, uncooked
⅓ cup white wine vinegar
⅓ cup olive oil
½ teaspoon grated lemon peel
1 tablespoon fresh lemon juice

1 teaspoon sugar
½ teaspoon salt
¼ teaspoon dried basil leaves
4 cups fresh broccoli flowerets
   or cauliflowerets
2 cups cherry tomatoes

Prepare tortellini as directed on package. Rinse with cold water. Drain, set aside. In a 2 quart casserole, combine remaining ingredients except broccoli and tomatoes. Mix well. Stir in broccoli. Cover and microwave on high for 3-5½ minutes, or until tender crisp. Add tortellini. Toss to coat. Cover and chill at least 4 hours. Stir in tomatoes. Serve skewered on 3 inch wooden picks.

Yield: 8 servings.   Ronni Cohen

Tabbouleh

1 cup fine bulgar wheat
¾ cup finely chopped onions
½ cup finely chopped scallions
1½ cups finely chopped Italian
   parsley
1 teaspoon salt
¼ teaspoon freshly ground
   black pepper

½ cup finely chopped fresh
   mint leaves
½ cup lemon juice, about 2½
   lemons
½ cup olive oil
Skinned tomato wedges and
   Romaine lettuce leaves for
   garnish

Cover bulgar wheat with cold water and let stand one hour. Drain well, squeezing out any excess water. Add the remaining ingredients. Mix well. Pile into a serving dish and garnish with tomatoes and lettuce.

NOTE: Tabbouleh may be stored in the refrigerator in a covered container for 2 weeks.

Yield: 6-8 salad servings.   Josephine Weiner

Hommus-Chick Pea Spread

1 (9-ounce) can chick peas
2 cloves garlic
⅔ cup olive oil
½ cup tahini (sesame seed
   butter or paste)
6 tablespoons fresh lemon juice
1 teaspoon salt

Freshly ground pepper to taste
½ teaspoon cumin
3 tablespoons olive oil or less
   for garnish
Paprika and black olives for
   garnish

Place all ingredients, except the last 3 tablespoons of olive oil, in a food processor or blender. Process or blend to a smooth paste. Transfer to a serving dish and garnish with 3 tablespoons olive oil, paprika, and olives. Serve with pita, party bread, or crackers.

NOTE: This keeps well in the refrigerator for several days.

Yield: 1¼ cups.   Helen Levy

Spinach Dip

LOW CALORIE VERSION:
16 ounces frozen spinach
1 package vegetable soup mix
1½ cups sour cream substitute
1 cup light mayonnaise-type
   salad dressing

1 small onion, finely chopped
1 (8-ounce) can sliced water
   chestnuts

Thaw and squeeze out all water from frozen spinach. Mix all ingredients, except the spinach, until well blended. Add spinach and chill at least 2 hours before serving. Serve with raw vegetables and bread rounds.

Carol Harrison

 To keep parsley and dill fresh, wash with cold water, shake off excess. Place in covered jar and refrigerate.

Curried Egg Dip for Vegetables

¼ teaspoon red hot pepper
   sauce
½ teaspoon curry powder
¼ teaspoon dry mustard
½ teaspoon salt
½ cup mayonnaise-type salad
   dressing

1½ tablespoons finely chopped
   onion
1 teaspoon minced parsley
½ cup finely chopped celery
4 hard boiled eggs, finely
   chopped

Combine all the spices with the salad dressing. Combine the onion and parsley with the salad dressing mixture. Fold in the eggs. Chill until ready to serve.

Yield: 2 cups.   Judy Rosenberg

Guacamole

2 avocados
2 teaspoons salt
2 tablespoons lemon juice
2-3 drops red hot pepper sauce

1 bunch green onions, chopped
2 medium tomatoes, peeled and
   chopped

Mash the avocados, add the rest of the ingredients, and mix. Season with salt and hot sauce to taste. Serve in a bowl or a cut-out cabbage. Serve with tortilla chips.

Judi Schneider

Peanut Dip

⅔ cup crunchy peanut butter
6 tablespoons firmly packed
   dark brown sugar

½ cup lemon juice
4 tablespoons chili sauce
1 teaspoon soy sauce

Combine all ingredients. Refrigerate at least 24 hours. Serve with celery, carrot, cucumber, and zucchini strips.

NOTE: This is also a wonderful marinade for chicken or fish.

Yield: 1¾ cups.   Edie Klein

Smoked Salmon Spread

1 (8-ounce) package cream
   cheese
¼ cup sour cream
1 green onion, sliced

1 teaspoon fresh lemon juice
Dash of red hot pepper sauce
4 ounces smoked salmon,
   shredded

Blend sour cream and cream cheese together until smooth. Add the rest of the ingredients to the cheese mixture. Place in a serving bowl. Chill in refrigerator at least 1 hour or longer. Serve with bread rounds, pita, or crackers.

NOTE: Nova lox may be substituted for salmon.

Ellen Labes

Sun Dried Tomato Dip

1 cup mayonnaise
½ cup sour cream
2 tablespoons sun dried tomato
   paste
2 garlic cloves, minced
¼ cup chopped sun dried
   tomatoes, drained well

4 drops hot pepper sauce, more
   if desired
1 tablespoon Worcestershire
   sauce

Blend all ingredients together and let stand in refrigerator for at least 4 hours. When ready to serve, place in a serving dish and serve with cut up vegetables and crackers.

NOTE: Ketchup may be used if sun-dried tomato paste is not available.

Yield: 1¾ cups.

Janelle Miller

 Sour cream and cottage cheese will keep longer if stored in refrigerator upside down.

13

Super Vegetable Dip

¼ cup cream cheese
1 (8-ounce) carton plain nonfat
   yogurt
½ cup light mayonnaise
1 (4½-ounce) jar marinated
   artichoke hearts, drained
1 tablespoon anchovy paste

1 teaspoon chives
1 teaspoon dill weed
1 tablespoon red wine vinegar
1 tablespoon onion powder
1 tablespoon Dijon mustard
1 tablespoon grated Parmesan
   cheese

Combine all ingredients in food processor until smooth. Refrigerate. Serve with fresh vegetables and crackers.

NOTE: Flavors will improve if made one day in advance.

Yield: 1½ cups.

Sarah Kier

Vegetarian Chopped Liver

1 (15-ounce) can baby peas,
   drained
3 medium onions, chopped and
   sautéed
2 hard boiled eggs, sliced in
   half

¾ cup ground pecans or
   walnuts
Salt and pepper to taste

Put drained peas, sautéed onions, and hard boiled eggs in food processor and blend together well. Add ground nuts and blend again. Add salt and pepper to taste. Place in serving bowl and chill.

NOTE: For low fat diets, use 4 hard boiled egg whites instead of 2 whole eggs.

Bluma Schechter & Carole Sobel

 Instead of crackers, slice unpeeled zucchini into rounds. Use as a base for hors d'oeuvres.

Gefilte Fish Appetizer

1 (24-ounce) jar gefilte fish,
    drained
1 (14-ounce) jar artichoke
    hearts, drained
1 cup pitted black olives,
    drained

1 can sliced water chestnuts,
    drained
1 (9-ounce) jar horseradish
    sauce

Cut fish and artichokes into bite-size pieces. Cut olives in half. Toss all ingredients together and refrigerate overnight. Serve with pita or cocktail bread or on a bed of lettuce as a first course.

NOTE: Horseradish can be diluted with mayonnaise-type salad dressing if too strong for your taste.

Barbara Mayer & Rene Eisenberg

Herring Salad

1 (12-ounce) jar herring snacks
    in wine sauce, drained, juice
    reserved
1 green pepper
1 medium red onion

1 large can black olives
1 (6-ounce) jar marinated
    artichoke hearts, drained
1 (12-ounce) bottle chili sauce

Chop all ingredients. Do not over chop. Mix together, adding the jar of chili sauce to all of the other ingredients. Put in jar and refrigerate 24 hours before serving.

NOTE: Refrigerate for up to 6 weeks. In place of marinated artichoke hearts, use 1 large green apple, chopped.

Dorothy Haber & Marilyn Sobel

Chopped Herring Mold

1 (12-ounce) jar herring in wine,
  drained
1 cup finely sliced celery
2 tablespoons minced scallions
2 tablespoons minced parsley
½ cup mayonnaise

1 (3-ounce) package lemon
  flavored gelatin
½ cup hot water
¼ cup cold water
Pepper to taste

Finely chop first four ingredients and add mayonnaise. Dissolve lemon gelatin in hot water, add cold water and pepper. Blend in the herring mixture. Put in a pint size mold and chill. Serve with crackers or party rye.

NOTE: This recipe unmolds easily.

Yield: 1 pint mold.   Elaine Fish

Gefilte Fish Dip

1 (24-ounce) jar regular gefilte
  fish in broth
1 (8-ounce) package cream
  cheese

2-3 tablespoons horseradish
  (white or red)

Drain fish and put in the food processor with the rest of the ingredients. Process until smooth. Serve with pita triangles or crackers.

Debbie Iwrey

Appetizer Conserve

2 (10-ounce) jars pineapple
  preserves or apricot
  preserves
1 (10-ounce) jar apple jelly

1 (1-ounce) can dry mustard
1 (6-ounce) jar regular
  horseradish

Mix all ingredients together, adding horseradish gradually to taste and store in refrigerator.

NOTE: The conserve can be served as a relish with meat or chicken. It can also be served poured over a block of cream cheese with crackers for spreading. The conserve will keep in the refrigerator for 6 months.

Barbara Emery

Chinese Spiced Eggplant Dip

2 medium young eggplants,
   total weight 1¾ pounds
3 tablespoons light soy sauce
2 tablespoons red wine vinegar
2 teaspoons sugar
2 teaspoons dry sherry
1 tablespoon sesame oil

1 tablespoon peanut oil
1 tablespoon minced garlic
1 tablespoon fresh ginger
Few drops hot oil (optional)
1 tablespoon white sesame
   seeds

In a steamer, steam eggplant 30 minutes or until collapsed (this can be done in a microwave). Let cool. Combine soy sauce, vinegar, sugar, sherry, and sesame oil. In a small saucepan, heat sesame seeds until toasted, set aside. In the same saucepan, heat peanut oil and cook garlic and ginger until oil is fragrant. Add soy sauce mixture and optional hot oil. Shred eggplant, discarding tough seeds and stems. Mix with cooled sauce and sprinkle with sesame seeds.

NOTE: This is nice to serve in a hollowed whole eggplant and garnished with attractively cut carrot flowers or radish roses. Pita bread is nice to dip with this, as is romaine lettuce or endive.

Yield: 2½ cups.   Anita Sudakin

Artichoke Nibbles

2 (6-ounce) jars marinated
   artichoke hearts
1 clove garlic, minced
1 small onion, finely chopped
4 eggs
¼ cup fine bread crumbs

¼ teaspoon salt (optional)
⅛ teaspoon each: pepper,
   oregano, hot pepper sauce
½ pound Sharp Cheddar
   cheese, shredded
2 tablespoons minced parsley

Drain marinade from 1 jar of artichokes into frying pan. Drain the other jar, chop contents of both jars and set aside. Add onion and garlic to frying pan and sauté about 5 minutes. In a bowl, beat eggs with fork and add bread crumbs, salt, pepper, oregano, and hot pepper sauce. Stir in cheese, parsley, artichokes, and onion mixture. Turn into a greased 7 x 11 inch baking pan. Bake at 325° for 30 minutes or until set when lightly touched. Let cool in pan. Cut into 1 inch squares. Serve hot or cold.

NOTE: Freezes well.

Yield: 30 servings.   Fiddler Favorite-submitted by Sharon Leider

Hot Spinach Balls

2 (10-ounce) packages frozen
   spinach
2 cups herb stuffing mix, finely
   crushed in food processor
1 cup grated Parmesan cheese

½ cup melted butter
4 small green onions, chopped
3 eggs
Dash of grated nutmeg
Dijon mustard or hot mustard

Preheat oven to 350°. Combine all ingredients except mustard. Form into balls. Bake for 10-15 minutes on a cookie sheet. Serve with Dijon or hot mustard.

NOTE: Balls can be made and frozen on a cookie sheet before baking. When frozen, put into a freezer bag. Bake frozen balls 20-25 minutes.

Yield: 20 balls.   Anna Levin

Vegetable Nachos

1 cup diced tomatoes
¼ cup diced green peppers
2 tablespoons sliced green
   onions
2 tablespoons chopped green
   chilies
2 tablespoons chopped ripe
   olives

2 teaspoons white vinegar
¼ teaspoon garlic powder
⅛ teaspoon ground pepper
26 corn tortilla chips
¼ cup (1-ounce) shredded 40%
   less fat Sharp Cheddar
   cheese

Combine first 8 ingredients. Spoon 2 teaspoons vegetable mixture on each chip. Divide cheese evenly among chips. Broil 6 inches from heat for 1 minute or until cheese melts.

Yield: 26 appetizers, 18 calories each.   Rose Weintraub

Potato Latkes Appetizer

2 large potatoes
1 egg
½ medium to large onion
¼ cup flour

1 teaspoon salt
Pepper to taste
Corn oil

Grate potatoes in food processor, leaving skins on, and place in a glass bowl. Grate the onions. Using a fork, stir onions into the potatoes, then add the remaining ingredients. Heat ⅛ inch of corn oil in a large non-stick skillet over medium-high heat. Using a slotted spoon, drop level spoonfuls of the potato mixture into the hot oil. Sauté them until golden brown on both sides, about 1½ to 2 minutes per side. Drain the pancakes on brown paper bags and keep them warm. Add more oil to skillet as needed for additional batches. Serve the pancakes immediately, piping hot.

Jackie Tepper

Greek Cheese and Spinach Triangles

1 package phyllo dough,
   defrosted

½ pound butter, melted

FILLING:

2 (10-ounce) boxes frozen
   chopped spinach, defrosted
1 large onion, chopped
1-2 tablespoons cooking oil

½ pound cottage cheese
¼ pound feta cheese
2 large eggs
Salt and pepper to taste

Defrost spinach in strainer overnight. Drain well. Sauté onions in oil. Remove from skillet and add spinach. Add the remaining ingredients and set aside.
Assembly: Follow directions on phyllo package. Keep dough covered with damp towel. Cut sheets into 3 inch strips. Take 2 sheets at a time and brush each strip with melted butter. Place 1 teaspoon of filling at edge and fold up "flag style". Place on cookie sheet and brush top with butter. Bake for 20 to 25 minutes or until golden brown.

NOTE: This may be made into squares, if desired, by placing whole sheets in a 9 x 13 inch baking pan. Layer 3 or 4 sheets on bottom, middle and top, placing filling between each layer and buttering the top. Bake until golden brown, about 35-40 minutes. This recipe freezes well.

Yield: 40-50 triangles.

Charlotte Edelheit

Sesame Chicken Wings Phillips

3½ tablespoons light soy sauce
½ garlic clove, minced
½ teaspoon fresh ginger root, minced and peeled
1 tablespoon honey
Freshly ground black pepper to taste

2 pounds chicken wings, wing tips cut off
1 tablespoon oriental sesame oil
2 tablespoons sesame seeds, toasted lightly

In a bowl, whisk together the soy sauce, garlic, ginger root, honey and pepper. Add the wings, coat well, and let marinate, covered and chilled, for 2 hours. Line a baking pan with foil. Drain wings, reserving the marinade, and arrange in one layer on the foil. Brush the wings with the oil, sprinkle with the sesame seeds, and bake them in the middle of a preheated 400° oven, basting occasionally with the reserved marinade, for 30-35 minutes, or until they are browned.

Phyllis Welling

Roasted Salami Appetizer

1 (1-2 pound) salami
3 tablespoons apricot jam
1 teaspoon yellow mustard

1 tablespoon Dijon mustard
1 tablespoon honey mustard

Remove skin from salami. Score with ¼-inch deep x's along the top of the salami, leaving ½ inch on each end. The x's should connect with each other. Put salami on a rack. Place on a baking pan sprayed with vegetable spray. Mix the remaining ingredients together to make glaze. Put glaze into x's of salami. Bake at 400° for 1 hour. Baste continually. Serve warm on tray with sharp knife to slice.

Sally Green

20

Stuffed Grape Leaves

1 (16-ounce) jar grape leaves,
 rinsed and drained (set
 aside small and torn leaves
 for layering)

FILLING:

1 cup long grain rice, uncooked
⅓ cup olive oil
1 cup chopped yellow onions
¼ cup chopped parsley
1 tablespoon dried dill weed

Juice of 1 lemon
1 pound ground lean lamb
1 teaspoon allspice
2 cloves garlic, minced
Salt and pepper to taste

BROTH:

2 cups chicken broth

Juice of 1 lemon

Mix all ingredients together for the filling. Spread a leaf on the counter, bottom side up, stem side toward you. Place one tablespoon of the filling in the center of the leaf. Fold stem end over the filling, then fold the sides over to secure the filling and roll from you toward the tip of the leaf, forming a small cigar or cylinder. Do not wrap too tightly as the rice needs room for expansion as it cooks.

Using a 2 quart heavy lidded kettle, place a single layer of unrolled leaves on the bottom of the pot. Place rolled leaves on top, rolled against each other rather tightly so that they will not come undone while cooking. Cover them with a layer of unrolled leaves and then add another layer of rolled leaves. Continue until all rolled leaves are in the pot. Top with remaining unrolled leaves. Mix chicken broth and lemon juice and pour over the leaves in the pot. Place an ovenproof plate over the top of the leaves as a weight. Cover and bring to a light simmer. Cook one hour. Remove the pan from the heat and allow to cool one more hour. Do not remove the lid or the leaves will darken. Drain on paper towels.

NOTE: This may be made in advance and warmed in a microwave oven.

Yield: 30-40 pieces.   Beth Hirsch

Swedish Meatball Appetizer

MEATBALLS:

½ cup chopped onions
Vegetable oil
1 pound ground beef

1 pound ground veal
½ cup bread crumbs
½ cup water

Brown chopped onions lightly in a small amount of vegetable oil. Combine onions with the rest of the ingredients and refrigerate overnight. Form small balls and fry in a small amount of vegetable oil until done.

SAUCE:

1 (8-ounce) jar currant jelly   1 (8-ounce) jar mustard

Combine currant jelly and mustard and heat in a double boiler. Add meatballs to sauce. Heat through and serve.

NOTE: Ground chicken or turkey may be substituted for meat. This recipe also makes a good main course by serving it over rice or pasta.

Yield: 10 servings or more.   Ilse Schloss

Smoked Turkey on Endive

½ pound smoked turkey,
    julienned
8 dried apricot halves, diced
½ red pepper, slivered
3 tablespoons sweet, creamy
    style, mustard

6 tablespoons mayonnaise
2 heads endive
Chopped fresh coriander or
    Chinese parsley for garnish

Mix all ingredients together except coriander. Stuff small amount of mixture onto each endive leaf, up to 3 hours in advance of serving. Sprinkle with coriander to garnish.

Yield: 2 cups.   Anita Sudakin

Brie en Croute

½ cup pine nuts
2 tablespoons butter
½ pound phyllo dough

1 (1-2 pound) wheel of Brie
½ cup butter, melted

Preheat oven to 400°. Sauté pine nuts in 2 tablespoons butter until browned. Drain on paper towels. Brush 2 layers of phyllo with some of the remaining butter. Place the wheel of Brie, skin removed, in the center. Place pine nuts on the top of the cheese and gently press in. Enclose the cheese in the dough. Brush 2 more layers of phyllo with butter. Place the wheel in the center, seam side down, and enclose. Repeat this process until all the dough has been used. Place on a baking sheet, seam side down, and refrigerate for 10 minutes. Brush the top with butter and bake for 15-20 minutes depending on the size of the cheese, or until golden brown. Transfer to a serving platter and let cool for at least 30 minutes. Serve at room temperature.

Yield: Serves 10-12.

Judi Schneider

Brie with Cranberry Topping

3 cups fresh cranberries
¾ cup brown sugar
⅓ cup dried currants or ⅓ cup currant jelly
⅓ cup water
⅛ teaspoon each of: dried mustard, ground cloves, ground ginger, cinnamon, ground allspice

1 large wheel of Brie (2 kilos) or 2 small wheels of brie (1 kilo each)

Place all ingredients, except cheese, in a heavy 2 quart saucepan. Cook until berries pop. Cool to room temperature (this may be prepared in advance). Peel rind off top of brie, leaving rind on the sides. Spread fruit mixture on top of cheese. Bake at 300° for 12 minutes. Serve with crackers

NOTE: If using currant jelly, omit water.

Yield: 24 servings.

Bobbie Stone

Cheese Puffs

3 ounces cream cheese
¼ pound Cheddar cheese
½ cup butter

2 egg whites
1 loaf unsliced white bread

Melt cheeses slowly with the butter in a double boiler, stirring constantly until completely blended. Remove from heat. Beat egg whites until stiff and fold into the cheese mixture. Cut bread into 1 inch cubes, crust removed. Spear cubes with a skewer and dip into mixture, covering all sides. Place on cookie sheet and chill overnight or freeze. Place in preheated 400° oven and bake 10-12 minutes or until lightly browned. If frozen, defrost about 30 minutes before baking.

Yield: Approximately 50.

Frances Quint

Crispy Cheese Twists

½ cup grated Parmesan cheese
¾ teaspoon seasoned pepper
  or lemon pepper
½ teaspoon garlic powder

½ teaspoon parsley flakes
1 (17¼-ounce) package frozen
  puff pastry, thawed
1 egg white, lightly beaten

Combine Parmesan cheese with seasonings in a small bowl. Unfold pastry onto cutting board. Brush lightly with egg white. Sprinkle each sheet with ¼ of the cheese mixture and lightly press into pastry. Turn over and repeat. Cut each sheet into 12 one inch strips, then cut strips in half. Twist and place on a greased cookie sheet. Bake at 350° for 15 minutes or until golden brown.

NOTE: Twists may be frozen before baking. They may also be cut to any length.

Yield: 24 twists.

Barbara Charlip

Grilled Cheese Pie

1 egg
¾ cup flour
½ teaspoon salt
½ teaspoon pepper

1 cup milk, divided
1 cup (4-ounces) shredded
  Muenster cheese

In small bowl, combine egg, flour, salt, pepper, and ½ cup milk. Using rotary beater, beat until smooth. Add remaining milk, beat until well blended. Stir in ½ of the cheese. Pour into well greased 8 inch pie plate. Bake at 425° for 30 minutes. Sprinkle remaining cheese on top and bake until cheese is melted, about 2 minutes.

Variation: Olives, mushrooms, onions, or peppers can be added, if desired.

NOTE: Batter may be prepared ahead and stored in refrigerator before baking.

Yield: 24 small appetizers or 4 main course servings.   Marilyn Friedman

Spicy Cheese Squares

1 pound sharp Cheddar cheese,
  grated
1 pound Monterey Jack cheese,
  grated
2½ jalapeño peppers, seeded
  and finely chopped

1 (5½-ounce) can evaporated
  milk
6 eggs

Mix both cheeses together and place half into a glass 9 x 13 inch pan. Sprinkle jalapeño peppers on top of cheese. Spread remaining cheese over the top. Mix together 1 can evaporated milk and eggs and pour over cheese. Bake for 35 minutes until brown. Cut into small squares or spread on bread or crackers.

Lynne Loren

Fresh Basil Cheesecake

1 tablespoon soft butter
¼ cup grated Parmesan cheese
½ cup fine, dry breadcrumbs
2½ cups fresh basil leaves, packed
½ cup parsley leaves
¼ cup olive oil
½ teaspoon salt
¼ teaspoon cayenne pepper

1 large garlic clove
1 pound ricotta cheese, room temperature
2 pounds cream cheese, room temperature
½ pound grated Parmesan cheese
5 large eggs
½ cup pine nuts

Preheat oven to 350°. Butter bottom and sides of a 10-inch springform pan. Mix breadcrumbs and ¼ cup Parmesan cheese. Sprinkle mixture into pan, turning to coat completely. Mix basil leaves, parsley, oil, salt, pepper, and garlic in food processor until smooth paste forms, about 2 minutes, scraping sides occasionally.

Place ricotta, cream, and Parmesan cheeses in a mixer bowl and beat until smooth and lightened, about 5 minutes. Scrape sides of bowl. Fold in eggs, one by one, and continue beating for another 2 minutes. Remove about ⅓ of this mixture to a small bowl. Into the original ⅔ cheese mixture, fold in the basil mixture until well blended. Pour this basil/cheese combination into the springform pan, and carefully spread (or pipe) an even layer of the cheese mixture on top. Sprinkle with pine nuts.

Set on baking sheet. Bake 1½ hours. Turn oven off and cool cheesecake about 1 hour with the oven door slightly ajar. Transfer to a rack and cool completely. Serve at room temperature, or slightly warmed.

NOTE: To make a thinner pie, use half the ingredients. Using the same size pan, adjust cooking time to 40 minutes and allow to cool in oven for 30 minutes. This can also be served as a luncheon dish.

Yield: 12-16 servings.   Beth Hirsch

Layered Tomato Pesto Cheese Mold

2 (8-ounce) packages cream
    cheese, room temperature
2 cups butter, room
    temperature

½ cup sun-dried tomatoes,
    drained
1 cup sunflower seed pesto
    (see recipe below)

Mix cream cheese and butter in processor or large bowl of electric mixer, stopping occasionally to scrape down sides of bowl. Spread ⅓ of cheese mixture in bottom of a 7 cup mold. Layer tomatoes over cheese. Cover with ⅓ of cheese mixture, spreading evenly. Spread with pesto. Add remaining cheese mixture, spreading evenly. Refrigerate at least 2 hours, or over-night. Unmold onto platter. Serve at room temperature.

SUNFLOWER SEED PESTO:

4 garlic cloves
3 cups firmly packed fresh basil
    leaves
1 cup freshly grated Parmesan
    cheese

1 cup olive oil
1 cup sunflower seeds

With processor running, drop garlic through feed tube and mince finely. Add remaining ingredients and process until smooth, about 1 minute. Transfer to a small bowl. Cover and chill until ready to use.

NOTE: This is easier to unmold if an unsculptured glass mold is used, instead of a heavy metal one.

Yield: Serves 12-14, or more.

Penny Blumenstein

Gougere Crust Pizza

DOUGH:

½ pound unsalted butter
2 cups water
½ teaspoon salt
Pinch of pepper
1 teaspoon dried herbs of
  choice (e.g. parsley, dill,
  chervil)

2 cups all-purpose flour
8 eggs
1 cup grated mixed cheeses
  (Cheddar, Swiss, Parmesan)

Preheat oven to 425°. Combine the butter and water in a saucepan, heat until the butter melts and bring to a low boil. Add salt, pepper, and dried herbs. Add the flour and mix until mixture is smooth and dry (about 15 minutes on medium heat). Transfer mixture to the bowl of the mixer. Add the eggs, one at a time, mixing well after each addition. Add the cheeses and mix. Wet an ice cream scoop and place scoopfuls of dough on a baking sheet. Re-wet scoop and make a depression in each gougere with the back of the scoop. Bake at 425° for 10-15 minutes, or until fluffy-crispy, puffed, and golden. Remove from oven and cool on rack to room temperature. Top with favorite toppings. To rewarm after topping, place in oven at 325° for about 10 minutes.

NOTE: Suggested toppings: trio of roasted sweet peppers with tomato salsa; fresh tuna and Montrachet cheese with sun-dried tomatoes and olives; Oriental vegetables.

Yield: 8-10 servings.   Elwin Greenwald

Super Snack Mix

¾ cup margarine
¼ cup grated Parmesan cheese
½ teaspoon onion powder
½ teaspoon garlic powder

1 (16-ounce) box oat squares
2 cups crunchy cheese puffs
2 cups small pretzels

Preheat oven to 325°. Melt margarine in roaster pan. Stir in cheese, onion, and garlic powder. Add the rest of ingredients and toss until coated with mixture. Bake a total of 24 minutes, tossing every 8 minutes. Cool and store in air-tight container. Can be frozen.

NOTE: This recipe can be doubled. Freezes well.

Yield: 6 cups.   Debbie Iwrey

Mini Corn Meal Muffins

2 (8½-ounce) cans creamed
  corn
4 cups grated Cheddar cheese
  (reserve 1 cup)
2 cups yellow cornmeal
1 cup sour cream

1 (4-ounce) can chopped green
  chilies
4 eggs
4 teaspoons baking powder
½ teaspoon salt
Jalapeño jelly for garnish

Blend all ingredients, except for reserved grated cheese. Pour into greased mini muffin tins. Bake at 350° for 15 minutes. Sprinkle tops of muffins with reserved cheese and continue baking for 15 minutes or until cheese is melted. Serve with jalapeño jelly, if desired.

NOTE: Batter can also be baked in two 8 x 11 inch pans. Bake 45-60 minutes. Cut into squares. These freeze very well.

Yield: 4-8 dozen, depending on muffin size.   Beth Hirsch

Onion Pizza

2 cups flour
3 tablespoons oil
½ teaspoon salt
1 package dry yeast
½ cup warm water

4 large onions, finely diced
4 tablespoons butter
Paprika
Vegetable spray

Spray cookie sheet with vegetable spray and set aside. Preheat oven to 375°. Put flour in mixing bowl. Stir in oil and salt. Mix dry yeast in warm water and add to flour mixture. Knead dough until firm and smooth. Refrigerate until dough is firm (about ½ hour). Roll out dough on a slightly floured surface until dough is very thin, about the size of a cookie sheet. Put dough on prepared pan. Brown onions in butter and spread on the dough. Sprinkle with paprika and bake for 25 minutes or until golden brown. Cool and cut.

Yetta Dubin

Pita Toasts

¾ cup butter or margarine,
  softened
2 tablespoons minced parsley
1 tablespoon snipped chives
1 tablespoon lemon juice

1 large garlic clove, crushed
  and minced
Salt and pepper to taste
6 pita loaves

Preheat oven to 450°. In bowl, cream butter or margarine. Mix the remaining ingredients, except for the pita, into the butter. Let stand, covered, for at least one hour. Halve pita breads horizontally. Separate each half into 2 pieces. Spread inside of each piece with mixture. Arrange pita on baking sheet in one layer. Bake on top rack of oven for 5 minutes, until brown and crisp.

Yield: 24 pieces.   Ronni Cohen

Aunt Helen's Puffed Crackers

Soda crackers
Water

Melted Butter
Caraway or dill seed

Grease cookie sheet. Do not use vegetable spray. Preheat oven to 400°. Soak soda crackers in cold water for 20 minutes. Lift carefully from water with slotted pancake turner. Place on greased cookie sheet. Put a few drops of melted butter on each and sprinkle with caraway or dill seeds. Bake for 30 minutes until brown and crisp. DO NOT OPEN OVEN DOOR. First batch takes a little longer. Can be stored and reheated.

NOTE: There are no exact amounts because Aunt Helen said you didn't need the exact amounts.

Phyllis Welling

 Crescent roll dough makes a flaky pastry to fill for a quick hors d'oeuvre.

SOUPS

Barley Mushroom Soup

1 ounce dried mushrooms,
   soaked, drained, and
   chopped
¼ pound fresh mushrooms,
   sliced
2 quarts water plus 3
   tablespoons chicken soup
   mix or 2 quarts chicken
   broth

1 cup chopped onions
1 cup chopped carrots
1 cup chopped celery, including
   leaves
1 cup barley
Salt and pepper to taste

Soak dried mushrooms in 1 cup of boiling water until soft, about 30 minutes. Drain mushrooms, passing the liquid through a fine sieve or linen cloth. Reserve ½ cup liquid to add with broth. Chop drained mushrooms. Bring broth and mushroom liquid to a boil, reduce to a simmer and add the vegetables and barley. Simmer one hour. Add salt and pepper to taste and serve.

Yield: 8 servings.

Mary Mirvis & Audrey Zupmore

Vegetarian Chili

1 green pepper, diced
1 onion, diced
8 ounces fresh mushrooms,
   sliced
1 medium zucchini, diced
2 cans kidney beans, drained
1 (28-ounce) can tomatoes and
   liquid

1 (6-ounce) can tomato paste
2 tablespoons chili powder
½ teaspoon cumin
½ teaspoon oregano
1 teaspoon garlic powder

Place all ingredients in a 2½ or 3 quart glass bowl. Cover and microwave on high, 40-45 minutes or insert temperature probe so tip rests on center bottom of dish and microwave temperature reaches 190°. Let stand 10 minutes before serving.

NOTE: This can also be prepared on stove in a 4 quart pot. Simmer for one hour or until thickened and zucchini is tender. Freezes well.

Audrey Saperstein

Cabbage Soup

3 tablespoons vegetable oil
2 medium onions, halved and
    sliced crosswise
½ cup golden raisins
⅓ cup lemon juice, freshly
    squeezed
2 tablespoons brown sugar
1 tablespoon honey
1 medium cabbage, cored,
    quartered and sliced into ¼
    inch strips (about 8 cups)

1½ teaspoons minced garlic
1 tablespoon Kosher salt
1 teaspoon paprika
1 (2 pound 3 ounce) can of
    tomatoes with juice
3-4 short ribs or flanken
3½ cups water
¼ cup ginger snaps, crumbled
Freshly ground pepper to taste
Fresh lemon juice to taste
Chopped parsley to garnish

Heat oil in heavy saucepan and cook onions 10-15 minutes until tender. Stir together raisins, lemon juice, brown sugar, and honey and reserve. Add cabbage to pan and toss to coat with oil. Steam cabbage covered over medium heat until wilted, about 6 minutes. Add garlic, salt, paprika, and tomatoes. Tuck in meat, add water to just cover ingredients. Heat to boiling and skim off foam. Reduce heat and simmer, partially covered, for 1-1½ hours. Remove meat and bones. Shred meat and return to pot. Stir in gingersnaps and simmer 5-10 minutes. Add pepper and extra lemon juice to taste. Garnish with chopped parsley, if desired.

Yield: Serves 4-6.   Arlene Redfield

Chicken Soup

5-6 pounds Kosher stewing
    chicken, quartered
1 large leek, washed well
1 parsnip
4-5 carrots, peeled and cut into
    serving-size pieces

3 stalks celery
1 tablespoon salt
4-5 peppercorns
Fresh dill, optional

Cover chicken, vegetables, and seasonings with water in an 8 quart soup pot bringing water level 3-4 inches above the chicken. Cook 3-4 hours until chicken falls apart. Strain into large bowl using a linen dish towel as a strainer. Return carrots to soup and serve.

Wendy Wagenheim

Black Bean Vegetable Chili

1 medium eggplant, cut into ½ inch cubes
1 tablespoon Kosher salt
½ cup olive oil
2 medium yellow onions, diced
2 zucchini, diced
1 red bell pepper, seeded, cored, and diced
1 yellow bell pepper, seeded, cored, and diced
4 large garlic cloves, peeled and coarsely chopped
8 ripe plum tomatoes, cut into 1 inch cubes
1 cup vegetable broth, using a vegetable bouillon cube
1 cup chopped Italian parsley
½ cup slivered fresh basil leaves

1 tablespoon chili powder
½ tablespoon ground cumin
1 tablespoon dried oregano
1 teaspoon freshly ground black pepper
Salt to taste
2 cups cooked black beans
1½ cups fresh corn kernels removed from 2 cobs
½ cup chopped fresh dill
¼ cup lemon juice
Sour cream, optional garnish
Grated Monterey Jack cheese, optional garnish
3 thinly sliced scallions, optional garnish

Place eggplant in colander and toss with Kosher salt. Let sit for 1 hour to remove moisture. Pat dry. Heat ¼ cup olive oil in a large casserole. Sauté onions, zucchini, peppers, and garlic for 10 minutes. Place remaining ¼ cup olive oil in a skillet over medium-high heat, cook eggplant until just tender, about 10 minutes. Remove with slotted spoon to casserole. Add tomatoes, broth, ½ cup parsley, basil and spices. Cook over low heat for 30 minutes, stirring occasionally. After 30 minutes, add black beans, corn, dill, and lemon juice. Cook 15 minutes more. Adjust seasonings and add remaining ½ cup parsley. Serve hot, garnished with a generous dollop of sour cream and/or grated Monterey Jack cheese and some scallions.

Yield: Serves 8.

Lauren Cohen

 If you do not have time to soak dried beans overnight, cover and bring them to a boil. Boil for 2 minutes, remove from heat, and let them soak covered in the cooking water for 1 hour.

Brunswick Stew

1 chicken, skinned and cut into
   serving-size pieces
3 teaspoons salt, divided
Paprika to taste
¼ cup vegetable oil
2 medium onions, chopped
1 medium green pepper, diced
3 cups water
1 (28-ounce) can tomatoes,
   undrained

2 tablespoons chopped parsley
½ teaspoon hot pepper sauce
1 tablespoon Worcestershire
   sauce
2-3 packages frozen mixed
   vegetables
3 tablespoons flour

Wash chicken and pat dry. Sprinkle with salt and paprika. Heat oil in a deep pot over medium-high heat. Brown chicken, then add onions and green peppers. Cook until onions are transparent. Add water, tomatoes and liquid, parsley, remaining salt, hot sauce, Worcestershire sauce, and bring to a boil. Cover and reduce heat. Simmer 30 minutes. Add vegetables and cook 20 minutes longer. Blend flour with a little cold water and gradually stir into stew. Cook, stirring, 10 minutes longer.

NOTE: Serve in flat soup plate.

Yield: Serves 4-6.   Lauren Cohen

Garlic Soup

1 onion, medium diced
1 carrot, medium diced
1 celery rib, medium diced
¼ cup margarine or oil
¾ cup peeled garlic cloves
1½ quarts chicken stock

1 pound redskin potatoes,
   medium diced
2 tablespoons chopped fresh
   parsley
1 tablespoon chopped fresh
   thyme

In a heavy-bottomed soup pot, sauté the onion, carrot, and celery in butter. Add the garlic cloves and cook until garlic is soft and onion is transparent. Add the 1½ quarts chicken stock and bring to a boil. Add the potatoes and simmer until all ingredients are soft. Place half the mixture in the bowl of the food processor and purée. Add back to the soup pot, add the parsley and thyme. Keep warm.

Yield: 6-8 servings.   Elwin Greenwald

Gazpacho

1 large garlic clove, peeled and split

4 cups tomato juice or spicy tomato drink mix

2 large tomatoes, seeded and chopped

⅓ cup onion, peeled and chopped

1 large cucumber, peeled and chopped

2 small green peppers, seeded and chopped

2 tablespoons olive or vegetable oil

2 tablespoons red wine vinegar, or more to taste

1½ teaspoons salt, or more to taste

Pepper to taste

Impale garlic on a wooden toothpick. Mix remaining ingredients in a bowl. Taste, add more vinegar, salt, or hot sauce, if desired. Add garlic. Cover and chill several hours. Stir before serving and discard garlic.

Serves 4.

Phyllis Welling

Beverly Brandwine's Hamburger Soup

1 pound ground beef, browned and drained

3 cups sliced carrots

4 medium potatoes, diced

2 cups celery, diced

4 small onions, diced

1 (8-ounce) can stewed tomatoes and juice

6 cups water

5 beef bouillon cubes or 5 teaspoons dried beef soup mix

½ teaspoon dried basil

½ cup barley

1 cup ketchup

½ teaspoon garlic powder or to taste

Salt and pepper to taste

Instant potato flakes, as needed to thicken

Combine all ingredients except potato flakes and simmer in a soup pot until vegetables are soft. Thicken with potato flakes and serve.

NOTE: This soup freezes beautifully!

Yield: Serves 6-8.

Lois Granader

Heart Cuisine Lentil Soup

1 (12-ounce) bag of lentils
1 cup barley
2½ quarts water
1 large onion, chopped
2 ribs celery, chopped
1 or more large carrots,
    chopped

2 medium tomatoes, chopped
2 teaspoons salt
2 small bay leaves
¼ teaspoon pepper

Combine lentils, barley, and water in a large soup pot. Add the rest of the ingredients and bring to a boil. Cover and reduce to a simmer and cook until lentils and barley are softened, about 1-1½ hours. Stir more frequently as the soup thickens to prevent scorching. Add water as needed. Taste and adjust seasoning as desired.

NOTE: This soup freezes well. Gradually add more water to the soup when reheating. Reseason to taste.

Yield: Serves 8-10.   Dorothy Welber

Lentil and Brown Rice Soup

5 cups chicken broth
3 cups water
1½ cups lentils, rinsed
1 cup brown rice
1 (32-ounce) can chopped
    tomatoes with juice
3 carrots, cut into quarters
1 onion, chopped
2 ribs celery, chopped

3 garlic cloves, chopped
½ teaspoon dried thyme
½ teaspoon dried basil
½ teaspoon dried oregano
1 bay leaf
½ cup chopped parsley
2 tablespoons cider vinegar
Salt and pepper to taste

In a heavy soup pot, combine broth, water, lentils, rice, tomatoes, carrots, onions, celery, garlic, thyme, basil, oregano, and bay leaf. Cover and simmer for 45-55 minutes until lentils and rice are tender. Stir in parsley, cider vinegar, salt, and pepper to taste and discard bay leaf. This soup will be quite thick and will thicken as it stands. Thin with additional broth or water as desired.

NOTE: This soup freezes well.

Lois Shiffman

Healthful Minestrone Soup

½ cup chopped onion
½ cup chopped celery
1 garlic clove, finely chopped
2 tablespoons vegetable oil
1 (16-ounce) can undrained
   whole tomatoes, cut into
   chunks
2 cups water
1 cup shredded green cabbage

2 medium carrots, sliced
¾ teaspoon dried basil
¼ teaspoon dried oregano
¼ teaspoon salt
⅛ teaspoon pepper
½ cup elbow macaroni, or other
   pasta
1 (16-ounce) can kidney beans,
   undrained

Sauté onion, celery, and garlic in the vegetable oil in a heavy soup pot. When the vegetables are soft, stir in all the ingredients except macaroni and kidney beans. Bring to a boil. Cover and simmer for 25 minutes. Add pasta and simmer for 15 minutes. Stir in beans and liquid. Simmer for five minutes. Serve when thickened.

NOTE: This soup freezes well. You can add your own touches, like grated Parmesan cheese and/or croutons.

Yield: Serves 4-6.   Dorothy Welber

Parmesan Corn Chowder

2 cups water
2 cups chopped potatoes
½ cup sliced carrots
½ cup sliced celery
¼ cup chopped onion
1½ teaspoons salt

¼ teaspoon pepper
¼ cup margarine
¼ cup flour
2 cups milk
1 cup grated Parmesan cheese
1 (17-ounce) can creamed corn

In a medium saucepan, bring water to a boil. Add potatoes, carrots, celery, onions, salt, and pepper. Simmer for 10 minutes. While vegetables are cooking, make a white sauce by melting the margarine in a small saucepan over medium heat. Add flour and blend. Add milk and cook until slightly thick. Add the cheese and stir until melted. Add the sauce to the vegetables along with the can of undrained creamed corn. Heat—do not boil—and serve.

Yield: Serves 6.   Louise Neifeld

Potato & Leek Soup

3 tablespoons margarine
4 medium potatoes, thinly
    sliced
1 bunch leeks, white parts only,
    carefully washed and thinly
    sliced
1 medium onion, thinly sliced

1 (46-ounce) can chicken broth,
    fat removed
Salt and freshly ground white
    pepper to taste
1 tablespoon fresh dill or 1
    teaspoon dried dill

Melt the margarine in a large, heavy skillet over medium heat. When foam subsides, add potatoes, leeks, and onions. Stir until coated with margarine. Cut a circle of wax paper to fit over potato, leek, and onion mixture, and rest paper on top of mixture to sweat vegetables. Reduce heat to medium low. Sweat about 20 minutes, or until mixture is tender-cooked.

Remove the paper and add chicken broth. Simmer mixture for 10 minutes and add salt and freshly ground white pepper to taste.

Run mixture through a food mill or process in a food processor to medium consistency. Reheat before serving and top with chopped dill if desired.

Yield: Serves 4.   Kari Izu

Grandma Alice's Potato Soup

1-2 onions, peeled and diced
2 large potatoes, peeled and
    diced into ½ inch cubes
2 cups milk

⅓-½ cup kasha
Salt and pepper to taste
½ cup sour cream or plain
    yogurt

Put onions and potatoes in a soup pot and cover with cold water. Bring to a boil and cook over medium heat for 20 minutes, stirring occasionally. Add water as needed. Stir in milk, kasha, salt, and pepper. Continue to cook over low heat, stirring often, for 10-15 minutes. Remove from heat. Stir in sour cream or yogurt. Do not let this boil or it will curdle.

Variation: Barley can be used instead of kasha.

Yield: Serves 4.   Harriet Kanter

Salmon Chowder

Vegetable cooking spray
½ cup chopped onion
½ cup chopped celery
½ cup chopped green pepper
1 garlic clove, minced
¼ cup all-purpose flour
1½ cups clear broth
1 cup diced unpeeled red
   potato
1 cup diced carrot
¾ cup water

½ teaspoon pepper
¼ teaspoon dried thyme
1 (6½-ounce) can pink salmon,
   packed in water, drained and
   flaked
1 (12-ounce) can evaporated
   skim milk
1 (8¾-ounce) can cream-style
   corn
½ cup frozen peas

Coat a large saucepan with cooking spray; place over medium-high heat until hot. Add onion, celery, green pepper, and garlic; sauté until tender. Sprinkle with flour, stirring until well blended. Add broth, potatoes, carrots, water, pepper, and thyme and stir well. Reduce heat and cook, uncovered, for 20 minutes, or until potatoes are tender, stirring occasionally. Stir in flaked salmon and remaining ingredients. Cook until thoroughly heated.

Yield: 7 cups.

Marsha Zucker

Sweet Red Pepper Soup

2 large onions, chunked
4 large red peppers, seeded,
   deveined, diced
6 tablespoons unsalted butter
½ baking potato, peeled and
   grated

2½ cups clear broth
½ cup heavy cream or
   evaporated skim milk
2 tablespoons fresh lemon juice
2 tablespoons fresh snipped dill
Salt and pepper to taste

Combine onions, red pepper, and butter. Cover and cook over low heat for 30 minutes, stirring occasionally. Add potatoes and broth; bring to a boil, cover and simmer for 15 minutes, stirring to make sure it does not stick. Purée mixture in a blender or processor. Return to pot and add cream or milk, lemon juice, salt and pepper, to taste. Heat carefully. Serve hot or cold, garnished with dill.

Yield: Serves 4.

Harriet Kanter

Soup From The Sea

1 large onion, chopped
½ cup chopped celery with
    leaves
2 large garlic cloves, crushed
2 tablespoons margarine or oil
2 cups chopped tomatoes
1-2 cups dry white wine
½ cup minced parsley
1 teaspoon salt
¼ teaspoon pepper
¼ teaspoon thyme
2 pounds fish fillets, cut into 1
    inch cubes; flounder, sole,
    halibut, or orange roughy
    can be used

Optional addition: French bread
    with garlic aioli sauce
2-3 garlic cloves, minced
⅔ cup nonfat plain yogurt or
    sour cream
1-2 tablespoons low fat
    mayonnaise
1 French bread, cut into rounds
    and lightly toasted

Sauté onion, celery, and garlic in margarine or oil until tender. Stir in tomatoes, wine, parsley, salt, pepper, and thyme. Cover and simmer for about 30 minutes. Add fish and simmer for 10-12 minutes until fish flakes.

For Bread: For optional addition to soup, combine the garlic, yogurt, and mayonnaise in a small bowl. Cover and let stand for at least 30 minutes in refrigerator. Spread the mixture on toasted French bread rounds and float in the soup.

Yield: Serves 4.   Shary Cohn

Tortellina Soup

4 garlic cloves, minced
1 tablespoon olive oil
3½-4 cups clear broth
9 ounces tortellini
1 (14½-ounce) can stewed
    tomatoes

½ bag fresh spinach
1 teaspoon basil
Salt and pepper to taste
Chopped fresh tomatoes,
    optional
Parmesan cheese, optional

Sauté garlic in olive oil on medium heat in heavy saucepan for 2 minutes. Stir in broth. Add tortellini and cook about 5 minutes until done. Add tomatoes, spinach, and basil; simmer 2 minutes. Add salt and pepper. Top, if desired, with chopped fresh tomatoes and Parmesan cheese. Serve. Yummy!

Yield: 6 servings.   Lee Franklin

Soup Hints

 To reduce an excessively salty taste in stews, soups or casseroles, add several slices of raw potato and cook for about 10 minutes. Remove potato slices before serving.

 Stocks may be conveniently frozen in ice cube trays — also use to freeze portions of gravy, milk, cream, etc. Store the frozen cubes in plastic bags and use as needed.

 To remove fat from soup, refrigerate soup until fat congeals or place ice cubes in warm soup; discard cubes with hardened fat.

 Save skin and bones from chicken breast when recipe calls for boneless breasts. Store in freezer until you have enough to make a soup. Use the carcass from roasted turkey or bones from rib roast to enhance the flavor of your soup or stock.

 Another garlic trick: Get the full benefit of the herb in stews and soups without the hassle. Pierce a whole peeled clove with a toothpick and drop into the mixture. It will be easy to locate and remove.

 Adding one teaspoon each of vinegar and sugar will remove excess salty taste from foods while cooking.

BREADS & MUFFINS

Beer Bread

3 cups self-rising flour
3 tablespoons light brown
  sugar
1 tablespoon dried dill

1 (12-ounce) can light beer
4 tablespoons unsalted
  margarine

Mix all ingredients well, except margarine, and pour into greased loaf pan. Melt margarine and pour over the top of the loaf. Bake in glass loaf pan at 350° or in metal loaf pan at 375° for 55-60 minutes.

Jody Sack

Irish Soda Bread

2 cups all-purpose flour
2 tablespoons sugar
1 teaspoon baking powder
1 teaspoon baking soda
½ teaspoon salt

4 tablespoons butter or
  margarine, divided
½ cup dark raisins
1 cup buttermilk

Sift dry ingredients into a large bowl. Add 3 tablespoons softened margarine and cut into flour mixture, until it looks like fine crumbs. Add raisins and toss thoroughly. Add buttermilk, all at once, and toss with a fork until just moistened. Do not over mix. Shape into ball. Knead gently on lightly floured board until dough is smooth. Shape in a smooth round ball and place onto a greased baking sheet. Flatten to a 7-inch circle, 1½ inches thick. Press a large floured knife onto center of loaf, halfway through, to slit dough into quarters. Bake 30-40 minutes, until golden brown and hollow sounding when tapped. Place on a wire rack to cool. Brush top with melted butter and later dust with flour. Serve warm or toasted.

Kitty Hirsch

 French or Italian bread and hard rolls can be freshened by sprinkling with a few drops of water and then heating in a 350° oven for 15 minutes in a brown paper bag.

Food Processor Challah

1 package dry yeast (1 level
    tablespoon)
2¾ cup flour
1 teaspoon Kosher salt
¼ cup plus 1 teaspoon sugar,
    divided

¾ cup lukewarm (110-115° F)
    water, divided
¼ cup oil
1 egg, lightly beaten
¼ cup golden raisins, optional

EGG WASH:
1 egg yolk
Few drops of water

Sesame or poppy seeds

In 2 cup glass bowl, dissolve one package dry yeast in ¼ cup lukewarm water and one teaspoon sugar. Let stand for five minutes until bubbly. In processor bowl, with plastic blade, combine 2¾ cups flour, 1 teaspoon Kosher salt, and ¼ cup sugar. Blend for one second. To bubbly yeast mixture, add ¼ cup oil, ½ cup warm water, and 1 egg. With the processor running, pour liquid mixture through the feed tube and blend until it forms a ball, about 45 seconds. Add ¼ cup raisins, if desired, pulse 3-4 times.

With lightly floured hands, remove the dough from the processor. Place in uncovered bowl in warm place to rise until double in bulk, about 1 hour. Remove from the bowl and shape. Braid, make round balls, be as creative as you like. Let rise again, about 30 minutes. Glaze with egg wash and sprinkle with seeds. Bake at 350° for about 45 minutes until golden brown. If making 2 challahs, use lightly greased loaf pans or if making one challah, use a cookie sheet.

Variation: To make rolls, shape dough like pencils and tie in bow knot. Bake for 25-30 minutes.

Frieda Leemon

 To provide a warm place for yeast dough to raise, turn oven onto 400° for 1 minute, turn off oven. Place bowl of dough on center rack, close oven door; or place pan of very hot water on lower rack of unheated oven; place bowl of dough on center rack.

 To test when dough is properly risen, make an indentation in it with two fingers. It is ready if the indentation remains.

Oatmeal Bread

1 cup oatmeal (not quick-
    cooking type)
2 cups scalded milk
1½ packages dry yeast
1 egg
½ cup water

1 teaspoon salt
¼ cup molasses
¼ cup honey
4 tablespoons margarine
4½ cups flour (approximately)

Scald milk and pour over oats in a large bowl. Allow to stand until luke-warm. Dissolve yeast in ½ cup warm water. Let stand 5 minutes and then stir until dissolved. Add yeast, salt, molasses, honey, egg, and margarine to oat mixture. Stir in 4½ cups of flour. Cover and allow to rise for 1 hour. Knead for 8-10 minutes, adding flour if necessary. Divide in half and place in 2 greased metal loaf pans. Allow to rise for 45 minutes. Bake for 45-50 minutes at 350°.

Audrey Sobel

Six Week Muffins

1 cup boiling water
3 large biscuits shredded wheat
1½ cups raisins
6 tablespoons margarine
1¼ cups sugar
2 eggs

2½ cups flour
2 cups buttermilk
1 teaspoon salt
2½ teaspoons baking soda
2 cups 100% bran cereal

Pour boiling water over shredded wheat and raisins, set aside. Cream together margarine and sugar. Add remaining ingredients, including the shredded wheat and raisin mixture. Blend well. Spoon into greased muffin tins and bake at 400° for 20-25 minutes. Refrigerate remaining batter in covered container and bake when desired.

NOTE: This batter will keep for weeks and improves with age.

Yield: 3 dozen muffins.

Harriet Salzberg

Bran Muffins

¾ cup orange juice
½ cup milk
½ cup raisins
1 cup flour
¾ cup sugar
3 teaspoons baking powder
1 teaspoon cinnamon

½ teaspoon salt
1½ cups raisin bran cereal
½ cup uncooked quick-cooking
  oats
⅓ cup vegetable oil
2 eggs

Mix orange juice, milk, and raisins. Heat for 1 minute in microwave oven or in a saucepan until mixture simmers. Stir together flour, sugar, baking powder, cinnamon, and salt. Set aside. Add orange juice mixture to raisin bran and oats. Add flour mixture. Add oil and eggs. Stir all ingredients until combined. Grease muffin tins or use paper liners. Pour in batter and bake at 400° for 25 minutes.

Yield: 12 muffins.

Ann Zousmer

Morning Glory Muffins

2 cups unbleached flour
2 cups whole wheat flour
2½ cups sugar
4 teaspoons baking soda
1 teaspoon cinnamon
1 teaspoon salt
4 cups grated carrots
1 cup raisins

1 cup shredded coconut
1 cup chopped pecans
2 apples, peeled, cored, and
  grated
6 large eggs
2 cups vegetable oil
4 teaspoons vanilla

Preheat oven to 350°. Sift together flours, sugar, baking soda, cinnamon, and salt. Stir in carrots, raisins, pecans, coconut, and apples. In another bowl, beat eggs with oil and vanilla and stir into the flour mixture until the batter is just combined. Spoon the batter into well-greased muffin tins, filling to the top. Bake at 350° for 35 minutes. Cool in tins for 5 minutes and then turn out onto rack to cool completely.

NOTE: Raisins can be plumped in brandy, if desired. Cool in refrigerator before using.

Yield: 30 muffins.

Harriet Salzberg

The Best Oat Bran Muffins

1½ cups oat bran or oatmeal
¼ cup flour
2 teaspoons cinnamon
1 teaspoon baking powder
¾ teaspoon baking soda
½ teaspoon salt

1 cup unsweetened applesauce
½ cup brown sugar
⅓ cup oil
1 egg white
1 teaspoon vanilla
½ cup raisins

Put all ingredients, except raisins, in food processor. Process until blended. Add raisins and pulse 3-4 times. Fill greased muffin tins with batter. Bake at 375° for 20-25 minutes. Remove from pan and cool on a rack.

Yield: 12 muffins.

Margie Kurzmann

Peanut Butter Bran Muffins

½ cup peanut butter
2 tablespoons butter or
    margarine
¼ cup brown sugar, packed
    firmly
1 egg
1 cup 100% bran cereal

1 cup milk
¾ cup flour
1 tablespoon baking powder
½ teaspoon salt
½ cup raisins
¼ cup chopped unsalted
    peanuts, optional

Cream peanut butter, butter or margarine, sugar, and egg in a mixer. Stir together flour, baking powder, and salt. Add cereal and milk to peanut butter mixture. Blend well. Add flour mixture and blend until lightly combined. Stir in raisins and peanuts. Spoon into greased muffin tins. Bake at 400° for 20-25 minutes.

Yield: 12 muffins.

Karen Freedland

Banana Chocolate Chip Loaf

½ cup melted butter or
    margarine
2 eggs
4 tablespoons sour milk
3 very ripe bananas
1½ cups sugar

2 cups flour
½ teaspoon baking powder
1 teaspoon baking soda
Pinch of salt
8 ounces chocolate chips

Combine margarine, eggs, milk and bananas. Add all the dry ingredients, adding chocolate chips last. Pour into greased loaf pan. Bake at 350° for 45 minutes. Cool in pan for 5 minutes before popping out onto cake rack to complete cooling.

Variation: Make muffins or mini-muffins by cutting down on the baking time; 20-25 minutes for muffins, 10-12 minutes for mini-muffins.

NOTE: To sour milk, add 1 tablespoon white vinegar to 1 cup milk. Let stand for 10 minutes.

Sandi Matz

Banana Bread

3 bananas, mashed
½ cup margarine or butter
1 cup sugar
2 eggs

2 cups flour
1 teaspoon baking soda
½ cup chopped pecans

In a small bowl, whip bananas until light and set aside. Cream margarine and sugar. Add eggs. Sift flour and baking soda and add to creamed mixture. Add chopped pecans. Add mashed bananas. Pour into lightly greased loaf pan. Bake at 350° for 1 hour.

Rachel Rubinstein

 Quick bread loaves are easier to slice if cooled completely; flavors improve if made 1-2 days ahead, keep wrapped in foil.

Deluxe Banana Quick Bread

3 large ripe bananas
¼ cup sugar
2 tablespoons vegetable oil
¼ cup liquid (milk or juice)
1 whole egg or 2 egg whites
1½ cups whole wheat flour (or any flour desired)
1 teaspoon baking soda

½ teaspoon baking powder
¼ cup chopped nuts (walnuts, pecans, sunflower seeds, etc.)
1 cup dried fruits (any combination - dates, raisins, apricots, etc.)

In a large bowl, mash bananas. Add sugar, oil, liquid, and egg. Using a hand mixer, mix until well blended. Slowly add one cup of flour, mixing after each addition (no sifting is needed - lightly spoon flour into measuring cup). When blended, add remaining ¼ cup flour into which baking soda and powder have been stirred. Add fruit and nuts, blending until thoroughly combined. Pour into a lightly greased loaf pan. Bake at 350° for about 45 minutes or until sides pull away from pan and an inserted toothpick comes out dry.

NOTE: This recipe freezes well — so double the recipe and freeze one loaf. Also, ¼ teaspoon cinnamon is a welcome addition stirred into the flour.

Sylvia Druckman

Date And Nut Bread

¾ cup chopped dates
½ cup raisins
1 cup chopped nuts
3 tablespoons butter or margarine
½ teaspoon salt

½ teaspoon baking soda
1 cup boiling water
1½ cups flour
1 cup sugar
1 teaspoon vanilla
2 eggs, well beaten

In a medium mixing bowl, place chopped dates, raisins, nuts, butter or margarine, salt, and baking soda. Pour boiling water over and let stand to cool. In large bowl, beat eggs well, add sugar gradually and continue beating. Add flour and vanilla. Combine with date-nut mixture and blend well. Bake in greased and floured loaf pan at 375° for 1 hour, 15 minutes.

NOTE: Freezes well.

Mary Steffin

Lemon Tea Bread

½ cup butter, room temperature
1 cup sugar
2 eggs, room temperature
1½ cups all-purpose flour
1½ teaspoons baking powder
½ teaspoon salt

½ cup milk
½ cup chopped walnuts or
  pecans
3 tablespoons grated lemon
  peel

Preheat oven to 350°. Butter and flour loaf pan. Cream butter and sugar in large bowl with electric mixer. Beat in eggs, one at a time. Sift in flour, baking powder, and salt. Beat at low speed until smooth. Blend in milk. Fold in nuts and lemon peel. Pour into prepared pan. Bake about 40 minutes, until toothpick comes out clean from center. Cool in pan on rack for 10 minutes. Invert onto rack and cool completely before slicing.

NOTE: Freezes well.

Barbara Kuhlik

Milk And Honey Bread

1 cup milk
⅔ cup honey
¼ cup butter
2 eggs
1½ cup white flour

1 tablespoon baking powder
1 teaspoon salt
½ cup toasted wheat germ
1 cup walnut halves or chunks

Heat the milk and honey together until the honey is dissolved, then stir in the butter. When the milk and honey mixture is somewhat cooled, beat in the eggs. Sift together the flour, baking powder, and salt. Add the wheat germ and gradually stir the dry mixture into the liquid. Stir in the nuts, mix well, and turn into buttered loaf pan. Bake at 325° for 1 hour. Serve with cream cheese.

Jody Sack

No Cholesterol Pumpkin Bread

1½ cups sugar
1 cup safflower oil
1 cup egg substitute
3½ cups flour
4 teaspoons cinnamon
2 teaspoons nutmeg

2 teaspoons baking soda
1 teaspoon salt
2 cups puréed pumpkin
1 cup raisins
1 cup chopped dates
½ cup chopped almonds

Preheat oven to 350°. Spray two loaf pans with vegetable spray. In a large mixing bowl, cream sugar and oil. Add egg substitute and beat well. In another bowl, combine dry ingredients. Add to creamed mixture. Mix well. Add remaining ingredients. Divide batter evenly between the two pans. Bake one hour or until a toothpick comes out clean.

Marsha Zucker

Zucchini Bread

2 cups sugar
3 eggs
1 cup oil
3 cups flour
1 teaspoon cinnamon
1 teaspoon baking soda
1 teaspoon salt

½ teaspoon baking powder
½ teaspoon nutmeg
¼ teaspoon ground cloves
2 teaspoons vanilla
½ cup golden raisins
½ cup chopped nuts
2 cups grated zucchini

Beat sugar, eggs, and oil. Add all dry ingredients and mix well. Add vanilla and beat. Stir in, by hand, raisins, nuts, and zucchini. Divide evenly between two greased loaf pans. Bake at 350° for 1 hour.

Variation: 1 cup crushed pineapple, drained, can be added if desired.

NOTE: This freezes well.

Molly Ryback

SALADS

Broccoli Salad

2 bunches fresh broccoli (bite-size only flowerets)
½ medium red onion, sliced thin
½ cup golden raisins

1 cup mayonnaise type salad dressing
½ cup sugar
2½ tablespoons cider vinegar

Combine broccoli, red onion, and raisins. Set aside. In small bowl, mix salad dressing, sugar, and cider vinegar. Add to broccoli mixture and toss. Chill for four to six hours, not overnight.

Yield: 8 servings.

Janet Perlman

Broccoli or Asparagus Salad

1½-2 pounds broccoli or asparagus

Parboil vegetables. Rinse in colander under cold water to retain color. Drain well; chill. Peel stem and cut into 1 inch pieces. If using broccoli, separate flowers.

SAUCE:

4 teaspoons soy sauce
2 teaspoons oil, preferably sesame oil

1 teaspoon sugar

Mix soy sauce, oil, and sugar well. Pour over vegetables before serving.

Yield: 6-8 servings.

Helen Levy

Which asparagus is more tender ... thick stalks or skinny ones? although the width of the stalks has no relationship to tenderness, the length does — short spears (about 7 inches) are more tender than longer ones (8 or 9 inches) because they're younger when cut. To buy the best: Look for firm, straight stalks, compact tips, rich green color. Be sure stalks are uniform in size so they all cook in the same time.

Carrot Salad

2 pounds carrots, sliced in ¼ inch rounds, cooked

1 large onion, coarsely chopped
1 green pepper, cut in chunks

Cook carrots about 3 minutes, or until slightly tender. Drain and add onion and green pepper.

SAUCE:

1 cup sugar
½ cup salad oil
¾ cup white vinegar

1 (10½-ounce) can tomato soup
1 teaspoon salt
1 teaspoon pepper

Bring sugar, oil, and vinegar to a boil. Add soup, salt, and pepper. Cool slightly and pour over vegetables. Keep covered in refrigerator overnight.

NOTE: Keeps 2 weeks.

Yield: 8 servings.   Lenore Miller

Corn and Olive Salad

1 (16-ounce) package frozen corn
3 hard cooked egg whites
½ cup sliced pimento-stuffed olives
2 tablespoons chopped fresh chives

1 teaspoon chili powder
¼ teaspoon salt
¼ teaspoon cumin
Dash black pepper
2 tablespoons non-fat mayonnaise
Black olives for garnish

Cook corn according to package directions, drain, and refrigerate for several hours. Coarsely chop egg whites and combine with corn, olives, and chives. Mix well. In small bowl, combine chili powder, salt, cumin, black pepper, and mayonnaise; mix well. Add to corn mixture and stir until well blended. Cover and chill for several hours. Garnish with black olives.

Yield: 6-8 servings.   Esther Becker

Green Beans and Tomato Vinaigrette

¾ pound fresh green beans,
 cooked
2 teaspoons Dijon mustard
½ teaspoon minced garlic
2 tablespoons red wine vinegar
4 tablespoons olive oil

Freshly ground pepper
⅛ teaspoon cumin
1 tablespoon dried basil
1 pound tomatoes, sliced
¼ cup chopped red onion
Lettuce leaves

Cook green beans until crisp and tender; drain and cool. In a bowl, combine Dijon mustard, minced garlic, and red wine vinegar; slowly add olive oil with a wire whisk and add pepper, cumin, and basil. Add beans, tomatoes, and onion. Toss and serve on lettuce leaves.

Yield: 4 servings.

Annette Leckart

Israeli Salad

3 tomatoes
3 cucumbers
3 green onions
⅓ bunch parsley

1 teaspoon garlic, minced
¼ cup olive oil
5 tablespoons lemon juice
Salt and pepper to taste

Cube tomatoes, cucumbers, and onions. Chop parsley. Mix all together with garlic. Mix olive oil, lemon juice, salt, and pepper. Pour over salad just before serving and toss. If not tart enough, use more lemon juice.

Yield: 4 servings.

Maureen Shapiro

When adding tomato to a salad, slice vertically so they weep less.

Salad Extraordinaire

1 medium or 2 small zucchini,
   unpeeled
½ teaspoon salt
1 large leek
1 (16-ounce) can julienned
   beets, drained thoroughly

1 (13¾-ounce) can artichoke
   hearts
Romaine leaves

VINAIGRETTE:
¾ cup vegetable oil
2 tablespoons olive oil
¼ cup red wine vinegar
4 teaspoons Dijon mustard

2 teaspoons dried dill weed
2 teaspoons salt
Fresh pepper

Cut zucchini in julienne strips, place in colander with ½ teaspoon salt and let set for 30 minutes. Cut leeks in thin slices. Select 3 mixing bowls. In one, place the zucchini and leeks combined, in a second, the beets, and in the third, the artichokes. Sprinkle one-third of well mixed vinaigrette over each bowl. Stir slightly and allow at least 15-30 minutes for vinaigrette to take effect. Make a bed of Romaine on platter in a sun-spoke design. Mound the beets in the center. Cover the mound with zucchini-leek mixture, obscuring the red color. Circle the base of the mound with artichokes.

NOTE: Salad may be arranged 1-2 hours before serving.

Yield: 6-8 servings.

Ruth Lefkowitz

Mushroom Salad

4 tablespoons tarragon vinegar
¾ cup oil
1½ teaspoons salt
2 cloves garlic, crushed
½ pound fresh mushrooms,
   sliced

1 red onion, sliced
2 bunches Romaine lettuce,
   torn into bite-size pieces
½ green pepper, chopped
1 tablespoon chopped parsley

Combine vinegar, oil, salt, and garlic. Pour over mushrooms and onions, and marinate at least one hour. Add lettuce, green pepper, and parsley. Toss well.

Yield: 10 servings.

Phyllis Schwartz

Marinated Mushrooms and Vegetables

MARINADE:

⅔ cup white vinegar
½ cup corn or safflower oil
¼ cup chopped onion
1 teaspoon sugar or equivalent
  substitute

½ teaspoon salt (optional)
1 teaspoon dried basil
1 teaspoon crushed oregano

Combine marinade ingredients in a container with a screw-top, and shake well.

SALAD:

1 (10-ounce) package frozen
  baby carrots, cooked and
  drained
1 (14-ounce) can artichoke
  hearts, drained and
  quartered

8 ounces fresh mushrooms,
  halved
1 cup pitted ripe olives, halved
1 cup sliced celery
¼ cup chopped pimento,
  drained

Combine salad ingredients and place in a covered container. Pour marinade over vegetables; stir gently with a rubber spatula. Cover. Chill 6 hours or overnight.

NOTE: Keeps well for about 1 week. Add or substitute chick peas, baby corn, or blanched peapods. Serve drained as a salad on lettuce leaves or as an appetizer or relish.

Yield: 5 cups.

Merilyn Schwartz

Pickled Green Peppers

4 quarts green peppers,
  quartered
2 cups sugar

2 quarts cider vinegar
2 tablespoons plus 2 teaspoons
  uniodized salt

Combine green peppers, sugar, cider vinegar, and salt in stainless steel pot. Bring to a boil, cover, and boil for 3 minutes (over boiling makes peppers soggy). Pack into sterilized pint canning jars. Seal, sterilize, and use canning process.

Gayle Hirsch

Dee's Marinated Mushroom Salad

1 pound fresh mushrooms,
  sliced, or 2 (8-ounce) cans
  mushrooms, drained,
  reserving liquid
¾ cup salad oil
½ cup white vinegar
¼ cup water or mushroom
  liquid

1 tablespoon garlic salt
¼ teaspoon black pepper
1½ cups sliced carrots
1 cup diced green pepper
½ cup onions, sliced in rings
1 (4-ounce) jar pimentos,
  drained and sliced
2 tablespoons basil

In a large saucepan, combine oil, vinegar, water (or mushroom liquid), garlic salt, and black pepper. Bring to a boil, reduce heat, and add carrots. Return to a boil, reduce heat, cover, and simmer for 5 minutes. Add mushrooms, green pepper, and onions; cover and simmer 3 minutes longer. Add pimentos and basil. Chill in glass container for 1 day before serving. Serve as a relish.

Yield: 5 cups.   Gayle Hirsch

Tomatoes Toccata

8 firm ripe tomatoes, peeled
½ cup chopped parsley
1 clove garlic, minced
1 teaspoon salt (optional)
1 teaspoon sugar

¼ teaspoon pepper
¼ cup olive or vegetable oil
2 tablespoons tarragon vinegar
  or wine vinegar
2 teaspoons Dijon mustard

Cut stem ends from tomatoes. Cut vertical ½ inch slices partially through tomatoes and stuff 1 tablespoon parsley between slices. Place tomatoes in shallow dish. Combine remaining ingredients. Mix well. Pour over tomatoes. Cover lightly and refrigerate. Let stand at room temperature 20 minutes before serving.

NOTE: May be made 2 days ahead.

Yield: 8 servings.   Karen Marks

 Brush dirt off mushrooms ... with a soft brush or cloth. If very gritty, rinse as quickly as possible under running cold water so they don't soak up liquid.

No-Mayonnaise Potato Salad

4 large potatoes, cooked
½ cup snipped parsley
3 green onions, chopped
¼ cup olive oil or other oil

¼ cup lemon juice
1 teaspoon salt
Dash pepper
Dash garlic powder

Cut cooled potatoes into small cubes. Add the rest of the ingredients and toss. Chill thoroughly. Best when prepared ahead of time.

Margie Ansell

Carrot Slaw

3 pounds carrots
1½ cups raisins
1 (20-ounce) can crushed
    pineapple, drain and reserve
    juice
½ cup orange juice concentrate

¾ cup low-calorie mayonnaise
¾ cup plain, low-fat yogurt
½ medium lemon
1 teaspoon salt
¼ teaspoon pepper

Shred carrots, add raisins and pineapple. Set aside. Mix orange juice concentrate, mayonnaise, and yogurt. Add to carrot mixture. Squeeze lemon over the slaw. Add salt and pepper and mix well. Taste and if too sweet, add more lemon juice. If too tart, add pineapple juice. Let sit for several hours.

Yield: 12-15 servings.

Ina Egnater

Fancy Farmers Chop Suey

1½ bunch radishes, sliced
2-3 large tomatoes, coarsely
    diced or 1 box cherry
    tomatoes, each cut in half
1½ bunches scallions, cut into
    ¼ inch slices

2 cucumbers, diced and drained
3 pints sour cream
Salt and pepper to taste

Combine radishes, tomatoes, scallions, and cucumbers in a large bowl, covered with a paper towel. Refrigerate overnight. When ready to serve, drain well in colander and pat dry. Add all three pints of sour cream and season to taste with salt and pepper. Mix well with a wooden spoon and transfer to serving bowl. Garnish with cherry tomato halves.

Yield: 40 servings - Serves a large crowd.   Melvy Erman Lewis

Cole Slaw

1 small cabbage, shredded or
    sliced
1 small Spanish onion, sliced
2-3 carrots, shredded

1 green pepper, thinly sliced
¼ tablespoon dill weed
1 tablespoon prepared mustard
¼ tablespoon celery seed

DRESSING:
½ cup sugar
2 teaspoons salt

½ cup white vinegar
5 tablespoons oil

Bring dressing ingredients to a boil and cool. Soak cabbage in water for 30 minutes, drain and dry thoroughly. Place cabbage in large bowl and add onion, carrots, green pepper, dill weed, mustard, and celery seed. Pour dressing over vegetable mixture and let marinate several hours or overnight.

Yield: 6 servings.   Fran Fetter

Creamy Cole Slaw

1 head cabbage, shredded
4 radishes, sliced
1 stalk celery, chopped
1 carrot, shredded

1 red pepper, chopped
⅓ cup sliced scallions or 1 red
   onion, chopped
Fresh parsley for garnish

DRESSING:

1 cup sour cream or light sour
   cream
2 tablespoons cider vinegar or
   white wine vinegar
2 tablespoons fresh lemon juice

3 tablespoons sugar
½ teaspoon salt
1 teaspoon Dijon mustard
1 teaspoon celery seed
1 teaspoon herb seasoning

Chop and shred vegetables and place in a large bowl. Mix all dressing ingredients together in a small bowl. Pour dressing over vegetables early in the day and mix thoroughly. Stir well again before serving. Garnish with chopped fresh parsley.

NOTE: Vegetables can be prepared a day ahead. Dressing can be made a day ahead and stored in a covered jar.

Yield: 8 servings.   Sue Kaine

Fritzel Salad Variation

9 lettuces, mixed Romaine,
   Head and Bibb
4 avocados, sliced
2 (13¾-ounce) cans hearts of
   palm, quartered

2 (13¾-ounce) cans artichokes,
   halved or quartered
4 hard cooked eggs, sliced

DRESSING:

1½ cups olive oil
2 teaspoons salt
½ teaspoon freshly ground
   pepper

1 cup wine vinegar
1 teaspoon prepared mustard
Garlic powder (optional)

Mix torn lettuce with avocados, hearts of palm, artichokes, and eggs. Combine dressing ingredients and add a little at a time to desired taste.

Yield: 50 servings.   Bluma Schechter

Andrea's Salad

4-6 bunches Romaine lettuce,
   chilled
1 (16-ounce) can chick peas
4-6 ounces feta cheese,
   crumbled

2 (18¾-ounce) cans artichoke
   hearts, quartered
Black olives, sliced (optional)
Parmesan cheese for garnish

DRESSING:

1 teaspoon salt
2¼ teaspoons sugar
½ teaspoon black pepper
1½ teaspoons dry mustard
3 large cloves garlic, crushed
1 cup plus 3 tablespoons
   vegetable oil

3 tablespoons olive oil
6 tablespoons red wine vinegar
6 drops hot sauce
3 teaspoons lemon juice
4 ounces Parmesan cheese
3 raw eggs
6 drops Worcestershire sauce

Place all ingredients for dressing in blender, except eggs, and blend. Add eggs very slowly, with blender on. Blend until thick (3 minutes). Sprinkle additional Parmesan cheese over chilled lettuce. Add remaining salad ingredients just prior to serving; toss with dressing.

Yield: 15-20 servings.

Andrea Silberg

Baroque Salad

3 heads Belgian endive
2-3 bunches watercress

1 (16-ounce) can sliced beets,
   drained

DRESSING:

¼ cup red wine vinegar
¾ cup olive oil
¾ teaspoon sugar

Dash salt
Dash pepper

Wash and pat dry endive and watercress. Cut endive in half lengthwise and slice into 1½ inch pieces. Divide endive among 6 plates. Trim tough stalks from watercress and divide among plates. Place 3 to 4 beet slices on top to decorate. Drizzle with salad dressing that has been mixed in a small bowl.

Yield: 6 servings.

Harriet Kanter

Crunchy Salad

2 heads small Napa cabbage
6 green onions, diced
½ pound fresh pea pods, sliced
¼ cup butter or margarine

½ cup sesame seeds
½ cup slivered almonds
1 (5-ounce) can wide Chinese
    noodles

DRESSING:
1 cup oil
2 teaspoon soy sauce

⅓ cup sugar
⅔ cup white vinegar

Shred cabbage very fine into a large bowl. Add onions and pea pods and set aside. Sauté sesame seeds and slivered almonds in butter or margarine. Drain nuts well and add to salad mixture. Add noodles. Immediately before serving, combine all dressing ingredients and slowly pour over salad until well coated.

NOTE: Sugar substitute may be used in place of sugar.

Yield: 8 servings.   Janelle Miller

Romaine Salad with Lemon Herb Dressing

½ pound fresh mushrooms,
    sliced
1 large avocado, sliced
3 medium tomatoes, cut into
    wedges

½ pound Romaine lettuce, torn
    into pieces

DRESSING:
⅔ cup vegetable oil
⅓ cup fresh lemon juice
2 tablespoons red wine vinegar
2 teaspoons chopped fresh
    parsley

½ teaspoon basil
½ teaspoon tarragon
½ teaspoon chervil

Combine mushrooms, avocado, and tomatoes in a large shallow dish. Mix dressing ingredients and pour over mixture. Chill at least one hour. Mix lettuce in a large salad bowl with marinated vegetables and dressing. Toss and serve.

Yield: 6-8 servings.   Barbara Kuhlik

Spinach Salad

1 pound spinach
½ bunch leaf lettuce

Croutons, optional

DRESSING:
½ cup mayonnaise
½ cup sour cream
1 (2-ounce) tin anchovies
3 green onions

1½ teaspoons parsley flakes
1½ tablespoons lemon juice
½ clove garlic

Combine all dressing ingredients in blender and mix well. Toss dressing with spinach and leaf lettuce. Garnish with croutons if desired.

Gert Kershenbaum

Spinach Salad with Honey Dijon Dressing

2 cups torn spinach leaves
2 cups torn red leaf lettuce

¼ cup thinly sliced radishes

DRESSING:
1 teaspoon water
1 teaspoon olive oil
1 tablespoon white wine
    vinegar

1 teaspoon Dijon mustard
1 teaspoon honey

Combine spinach leaves, lettuce and radishes in a large bowl. Combine water, olive oil, vinegar, Dijon mustard, and honey; stir well. Drizzle over salad and toss well.

Yield: 2 servings.

Esther Langer

 Washing spinach ... or other sandy greens in tepid water will remove grit more easily than cold water.

Spinach Pear Salad

1 (10-ounce) package fresh
   spinach
¼ cup dried cherries or raisins

2 medium ripe pears, cut into
   thin slices
¼ cup pecan halves

DRESSING:
½ cup olive oil
1 tablespoon grated Parmesan
   cheese
½ small onion
½ teaspoon Dijon mustard

2 tablespoons cider vinegar
½ teaspoon Worcestershire
   sauce
½ teaspoon each: dried basil,
   oregano, sugar, and salt

Whirl all dressing ingredients in a food processor or blender until smooth. Pour over salad. When ready to serve, add pears and nuts.

NOTE: Dressing can be made in advance and refrigerated. Salad can be made and mixed in advance, except for pears and nuts.

Yield: 6-8 servings.

Lois Shiffman

Spinach and Strawberry Salad with Lemon Dressing

1 (10-ounce) package fresh
   spinach, washed, drained,
   and coarsely torn

1 pound fresh strawberries

Chill washed and torn spinach. Arrange strawberries on top and chill.

DRESSING:
¼ cup sugar
Juice of 1 large lemon

1 egg yolk
6 tablespoons vegetable oil

Place sugar in mixing bowl. Add lemon juice and whisk. Add yolk, whisk. Add oil and continue to whisk until dressing is thick and creamy. Cover the dressing and refrigerate. Before serving, whisk dressing if necessary. Serve cold.

Yield: 6-8 servings.

Ann Zousmer

Artichoke Pasta Salad

4 ounces medium shell
   macaroni
4 ounces rotini pasta
1 (6-ounce) jar marinated
   artichokes
¼ pound mushrooms,
   quartered

1 cup cherry tomatoes, halved
1 cup medium-size pitted ripe
   olives
1 tablespoon chopped parsley
½ teaspoon oregano
½ teaspoon dry basil leaves
Salt and pepper to taste

Cook shells and rotini according to package instructions until al dente. Drain well and rinse with cold water several times. Place in salad bowl.

Add artichokes and liquid, mushrooms, tomatoes, olives, parsley, oregano, and basil. Toss gently. Cover and refrigerate for at least 4 hours or overnight. Before serving, season with salt and pepper to taste.

Yield: 6-8 servings.

Carol P. Fogel

Italian Vegetable Salad

1½ cups medium macaroni
   shells
2 cups fresh broccoli flowerets
1 cup fresh cauliflower
   flowerets
1 cup fresh sliced mushrooms
1 (6-ounce) can artichoke
   hearts, drained, rinsed, and
   chopped

½ cup chopped green onions
1 cup sliced pitted black olives
⅔ cup Italian salad dressing
1 medium avocado, peeled and
   sliced
1 medium tomato, seeded and
   sliced

Cook macaroni according to package directions. Drain, rinse in cold water, and drain again.

In large bowl, combine macaroni, broccoli, cauliflower, mushrooms, artichoke hearts, green onion, and black olives. Toss with Italian dressing. Cover and chill. Just before serving, toss vegetable mixture with avocado and tomatoes.

NOTE: Can be prepared a day ahead.

Yield: 8 servings.

Gayle Hirsch

Harvest Pasta Salad

MARINADE:

¾ cup vegetable oil
½ cup fresh lemon juice
4 large garlic cloves, crushed
4 teaspoons freshly cut chives
4 teaspoons fresh dill, or 1
    teaspoon dried dill weed
1 tablespoon minced fresh
    basil, or 2 teaspoons dried
    basil

½ teaspoon cracked black
    pepper
1 teaspoon salt
¼ teaspoon red pepper flakes

SALAD:

1 pound rotini or curly pasta
1 (6⅛-ounce) can tuna
2 cups broccoli flowerets
¼ pound snow peas
½ cup julienned carrots
1 large red pepper, cut in ⅛
    inch strips

½ cup chopped fresh parsley
½ pint cherry tomatoes
¼ cup freshly grated Parmesan
    cheese

Combine marinade ingredients in a quart jar. Shake well. Cook pasta according to package directions until just tender. Drain and toss with tuna and ½ cup of marinade. Cover bowl and refrigerate several hours or overnight. Blanch broccoli, snow peas, and carrots in lightly salted boiling water for 1-2 minutes. Drain well and chill. Just before serving, toss vegetables with pasta mixture, peppers, parsley, and remaining marinade.

NOTE: Garnish with cherry tomatoes and cheese.

Yield: 8 servings.

Barbara Grant

Whitefish Pasta Salad

1 (14-ounce) box pasta ruffles
  or shells, cooked
½ cup coarsely chopped
  scallions
½ cup coarsely chopped green
  pepper
½ cup coarsely chopped red
  pepper

1 pound smoked whitefish or
  sable (bite-size pieces)
3 tablespoons vinaigrette
  dressing
2 tablespoons cholesterol-free
  mayonnaise
Leaf lettuce, optional

Place cooked and drained pasta, scallions, green pepper, red pepper, and fish in a large bowl. Add vinaigrette dressing and mayonnaise. Gently toss to coat thoroughly. Serve immediately in a serving bowl lined with leaf lettuce. May be chilled, but tastes best at room temperature.

Yield: 6-8 servings.

Sherry Haffner

Spicy Rice and Kidney Bean Salad

1 cup cooked rice
1 (15-ounce) can red kidney
  beans
1 green pepper, chopped
1 yellow or red pepper,
  chopped

1 tablespoon minced parsley
1 teaspoon crushed red
  peppers

DRESSING:

⅓ cup balsamic vinegar
1 cup virgin olive oil
2 teaspoons dried tarragon or
   1½ tablespoons fresh
½ teaspoon salt

½ teaspoon cayenne pepper
1 teaspoon garlic powder
1 teaspoon Dijon mustard
1 teaspoon sugar

Mix rice, beans, peppers, parsley, and crushed red peppers in a bowl. Blend all dressing ingredients in a blender and pour over rice. Mix well.

NOTE: It is better if it sits at least 4 hours or overnight.

Yield: 6-8 servings.

Janelle Miller

Marinated Chicken Salad

SALAD:

2 whole chicken breasts,
skinned, boned, and cut into
chunks
1 large tomato, cut into wedges
¼ pound mushrooms, sliced
1 medium onion, sliced thin

1 green pepper, sliced in
rounds
1 red pepper, sliced in rounds
2-3 stalks celery, sliced
diagonally

DRESSING:

½ cup Italian dressing

Pepper to taste

Combine all salad ingredients. Pour dressing over ingredients and marinate overnight. Season with pepper. Shake or stir contents occasionally.

Yield: 4 servings.

Lee Bernstein

Southwest Chicken Salad

SALAD:

1 pound cooked, shredded
chicken
½ cup fresh corn kernels
¼ cup jicama, cut in thin strips

1 medium red pepper, cut in
thin strips
¼ cup chopped scallions
½ cup diced avocado

DRESSING:

¼ cup lime juice
¼ cup lemon juice
2½ cups olive oil (can use less)
Dash of each: oregano, garlic,
marjoram, salt, and pepper

1 tablespoon toasted sesame
seeds

Mix dressing ingredients and let sit for at least 1 hour. Combine salad ingredients and toss with some of the dressing until well coated. Serve on lettuce leaves or in a large bowl.

NOTE: Extra salad dressing should be refrigerated.

Yield: 6 servings.

Alma Burdick Rand

Wild Rice Grilled Turkey Salad

2 pounds turkey breast,
   skinned and boned

MARINADE:

¾ cup bottled Italian dressing   2 tablespoons soy sauce

Combine Italian dressing and soy sauce in a glass dish and marinate turkey for 2-3 hours, turning often. Grill over high heat, 10-12 minutes on each side, basting often with marinade. Cool and slice in small pieces.

SALAD:

1 package long grain and wild
   rice mix, cooked and cooled
2-2½ cups sliced grilled turkey
½ cup sliced scallion
1 ounce slivered almonds

¼ cup cholesterol-free or fat-
   free mayonnaise
1 (11-ounce) can mandarin
   orange sections
Leaf lettuce

Combine turkey, rice, scallions, almonds, mayonnaise, and ½ of mandarin oranges. Serve in large bowl lined with leaf lettuce and garnish with remaining oranges.

NOTE: Turkey may also be broiled. Grapes may be substituted for oranges; grilled tuna may be substituted for turkey.

Yield: 12 servings.   Sherry Haffner

Raspberry Mold

2 (3-ounce) packages raspberry
   gelatin
1½ cups boiling water
1 (4-ounce) can crushed
   pineapple

1 (16-ounce) package frozen
   raspberries, slightly thawed
1 mashed banana
½ pint sour cream

Dissolve gelatin in hot water. Add undrained raspberries, pineapple, and mashed banana. Pour ½ mixture into an oiled 6-cup mold. Refrigerate until firm. Spread sour cream onto mold and add remaining gelatin. Refrigerate until firm.

Yield: Serves 10-12.   Terran Leemis

Chinese Tuna Salad

DRESSING:

⅔ cup light sour cream
⅔ cup light mayonnaise

2 tablespoons lemon juice
1½ tablespoons sugar

SALAD:

1 head iceberg lettuce,
    shredded
1 (6⅛-ounce) can tuna, flaked
½ red onion, sliced thin

1 cup seedless grapes, red or
    green
1 (3-ounce) can Chinese chow
    mein noodles

In small bowl, combine dressing ingredients, mix well and set aside. In a large serving bowl, combine lettuce and tuna. Add onions and grapes. Add noodles last. Toss with dressing and serve immediately.

Yield: 4 servings.

Myra Wasser

Tart Gelatin Mold

2 (3-ounce) packages lemon
    gelatin
3 cups boiling water
1 (6-ounce) can frozen
    lemonade concentrate,
    thawed

1 (8-ounce) container frozen
    whipped topping

Dissolve gelatin in boiling water. Add lemon concentrate and stir until gelatin is dissolved. Refrigerate until partially set. Beat in frozen whipped topping using hand beater or whisk. Pour into oiled or sprayed 6-cup mold container. If desired, add ½ cup peaches or cherries between or on bottom, using small amount of gelatin to hold fruit securely. Refrigerate until set.

Yield: 8-10 servings.

Fran Cook

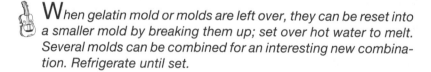 *When gelatin mold or molds are left over, they can be reset into a smaller mold by breaking them up; set over hot water to melt. Several molds can be combined for an interesting new combination. Refrigerate until set.*

Salad Niçoise

SALAD:

1 head Bibb lettuce, torn (2 cups)
1 head Romaine lettuce, torn (3 cups)
1 (7-ounce) can tuna, drained
1 (10-ounce) package frozen or fresh cut green beans, cooked, drained, and chilled
1 cup halved cherry tomatoes
1 small pepper, cut into rings
1 small onion, sliced and separated into rings
3 hard cooked eggs, chilled and cut into wedges
1 medium potato, cooked, chilled, and sliced
½ cup sliced pitted black olives
1 (2-ounce) tin anchovy fillets, drained (optional)

Line a large salad bowl with Bibb and Romaine lettuce. Break tuna into chunks, mound in center of torn lettuce. Arrange chilled green beans, tomatoes, green pepper, onion rings, egg wedges, potatoes, olives, and anchovy fillets (optional) on top of the lettuce. Cover and chill. Just before serving, add desired amount of dressing to coat vegetables.

DRESSING:

1 cup olive or salad oil
⅓ cup vinegar
⅓ cup lemon juice
2-3 teaspoons sugar
1½ teaspoons salt
1½ teaspoons paprika
1½ teaspoons dry mustard
½ teaspoon crushed dried oregano
Dash cayenne pepper

Pour all ingredients in a screw-top jar and shake well; chill. Shake again before serving.

NOTE: Salad can be made ahead and tossed just before serving. Additional dressing may be refrigerated.

Yield: 4 servings, dressing: 1⅔ cups.   Phyllis Schwartz

 Anchovies Hint ... If you find anchovies too salty for your taste, you can partially desalt them by soaking in cool water for 10 minutes; remove and pat dry with a paper towel and then immerse them in olive oil again.

No-Oil Salad Dressing from Canyon Ranch

½ cup red wine vinegar
¼ teaspoon freshly ground
   pepper
½ teaspoon salt
1 tablespoon fructose
2 cloves garlic, minced

2 teaspoons Worcestershire
   sauce
1 tablespoon Dijon mustard
Juice of ½ lemon
1 cup water

Combine all ingredients, except the water, in a jar with a tight fitting lid. Shake well. Add the water and shake well again. Refrigerate.

NOTE: Each serving contains 5 calories; 1 calorie from fat.

Yield: 32 servings of 2 tablespoons each.

Sandy Schwartz

Balsamic Vinaigrette Dressing

1 clove garlic, minced
1 tablespoon Dijon mustard

3 tablespoons balsamic vinegar
1 cup olive oil

In processor, mince clove of garlic. Add mustard and vinegar. With machine running, slowly add olive oil in small amounts. This will result in a creamy-type dressing.

Yield: 8-10 servings.

Beth Shapiro

Vinaigrette Salad Dressing from Sedona

⅔ cup olive oil
⅓ cup red wine vinegar

⅛ cup soy sauce
Salt and pepper to taste

Mix all ingredients and shake well. Store at room temperature.

Yield: 1⅛ cups.

Krana Grossman

74

BRUNCH

Blintz Soufflé with Blueberry Sauce

"LOW CHOLESTEROL"

½ cup margarine, melted
12 frozen cheese blintzes
2 cups low-fat cottage cheese
¼ cup skim milk

1 teaspoon lemon juice
1½ cartons egg substitute
2 teaspoons vanilla

BLUEBERRY SAUCE:

1 (8 -ounce) jar blueberry
   preserves

1 (12-ounce) package fresh or
   frozen blueberries

Pour melted butter into baking pan. Arrange blintzes in the pan. In blender, mix cottage cheese, skim milk, and lemon juice. Blend well. Add egg substitute and vanilla. Pour over blintzes and refrigerate at least 12 hours. Bake in 350° oven for 1 hour. Mix preserves and blueberries together and heat through. Serve with soufflé.

Yield: Serves 6-8.

Gertrude Kasle

Top Hat Cheese Soufflé

⅓ cup margarine or butter
⅓ cup flour
1½ cups milk
1 teaspoon salt

Dash of cayenne pepper
2 cups shredded sharp natural
   Cheddar cheese
6 eggs, separated

Melt butter or margarine in saucepan and stir in flour. Gradually stir in milk. Bring mixture to a boil, stirring constantly. Stir in salt, pepper, and cheese. Stir until cheese is melted. Remove from heat. Beat egg yolks slightly and gradually add to cheese mixture. Allow to cool. After cheese mixture has cooled, beat egg whites until stiff, but not dry. Fold cheese mixture into egg whites. Turn into 2-quart soufflé dish or casserole. With tip of spoon make a slight indentation around top of soufflé, one inch from the edge. Bake at 300° for 1¼ hours. Serve immediately.

NOTE: Be aware—this soufflé is beautiful when it rises, but collapses quickly.

Yield: Serves 6.

Lillian Finkelstein-Falick

Low Cholesterol Blintz Casserole

DOUGH:

½ pound margarine, melted
4 egg whites
3 teaspoons baking powder
¼ cup skim milk

½ cup sugar
1 cup flour
Pinch of salt
1 teaspoon vanilla

Mix all of the dough ingredients into a blender. Mix well. Pour half of the dough into a greased 9 x 13 inch pan.

FILLING:

2 pounds dry cottage cheese
½ cup sugar
Juice of one lemon
Pinch of salt

4 egg whites
1 (8½-ounce) can crushed
   pineapple

In a mixing bowl, blend all of the filling ingredients together and pour over the dough in the pan. Spread the remaining dough mixture on top of the filling. Bake for 1 hour at 325°.

NOTE: This can be served with any fruit sauce desired.

Yield: 8-10 servings.   Hilda Shapiro

Grits with Cheese

"A SOUTHERN FAVORITE":

6 cups boiling water
2 teaspoons salt
¾ cup margarine

1½ cups grits
1 pound sharp Cheddar cheese
4 eggs, well-beaten

Bring water, salt, and margarine to a boil. Add grits gradually. Cook until thick, stirring constantly. Add cheese and stir until melted. Add eggs and stir rapidly. Pour into a greased casserole and bake 1 hour at 250°-300°.

NOTE: Chopped spinach can be added; egg substitute can be used. This can be prepared ahead and baked before serving. Keeps well in oven.

Yield: Serves 8-10.   Jackie Tepper

Egg Challah Soufflé

6 eggs
2 cups of milk
1 teaspoon salt
½ teaspoon pepper
3 tablespoons margarine,
 melted

9 slices challah, crust removed
 and cubed.
1 (8-ounce) package grated
 sharp Cheddar cheese

Prepare the day ahead. Mix eggs, milk, salt, and pepper with electric beater. Add melted margarine. In a 9 x 13 inch greased glass baking pan, add ⅓ of bread cubes, ⅓ of egg mixture, ⅓ of the cheese and repeat for two more layers. Cover with foil and refrigerate overnight, or at least for several hours. Remove foil and bake at 350° for 1 hour.

Yield: 6-8 servings.

Liz Warnick

Danish Pancakes

½ cup flour
½ cup milk
2 eggs, lightly beaten
Pinch of nutmeg

4 tablespoons butter
2 tablespoons powdered sugar
Juice of ½ lemon

Preheat oven to 425°. Combine flour, milk, eggs, and nutmeg. Beat lightly, leaving batter a little lumpy. Melt butter in oven-safe 8-9 inch skillet or pie plate. When butter is bubbling, pour in batter. Bake 15-20 minutes or until pancake is golden. Sprinkle with powdered sugar and lemon juice. Serve with jelly or marmalade.

Ronni Cohen

French Toast Casserole-Praline Brunch Toast

8 eggs
1½ cup milk
1 tablespoon brown sugar
2 teaspoons vanilla
8 slices French or Italian bread,
   ¾ inch thick

¼ cup butter
½ cup brown sugar
¼ cup maple syrup
½ cup chopped pecans

Mix eggs, milk, 1 tablespoon brown sugar, and vanilla. Pour half of the egg mixture into a 13 x 9 inch pan. Place bread slices in pan and pour remaining egg mixture on top. Cover and refrigerate several hours or overnight. Preheat oven to 350°. Melt butter in serving casserole. Stir in ½ cup brown sugar, syrup, and nuts. Carefully place soaked bread on top of nut mixture and pour remaining egg mixture on top. Bake 30-45 minutes or until puffed and brown.

Yield: 4-6 servings.   Ann Zousmer

Spinach Pie

1 large onion, chopped
8 ounces sliced mushrooms,
   more if desired
1 tablespoon oil or vegetable
   spray for browning

1 (8-ounce) package shredded
   Cheddar cheese
Deep-dish pie crust
2 packages frozen spinach
   soufflé, thawed

Brown onion and mushrooms in oil. Drain. Spread cheese in bottom of unbaked pie shell. Spread onions and mushrooms on top. Mix up thawed soufflé and spread on top. Bake for 1 hour at 350°. Let stand for 10 minutes before cutting or mixture will run.

NOTE: This can also be made in a pie plate without the crust.

Yield: 6 servings.   Marsha Mitnick

Favorite Spinach Frittata

1 (10-ounce) package frozen
   spinach, cooked, drained,
   and squeezed dry
1 cup skim milk
3 eggs
2 tablespoons lemon juice
1 cup shredded Mozzarella
   cheese

1 teaspoon basil
1½ teaspoons oregano
2 teaspoons onion powder
2 tablespoons grated Parmesan
   cheese
½ teaspoon pepper

Preheat oven to 375°. Food processor method: mix eggs with milk and lemon juice for 10 seconds. Combine remaining ingredients, except Parmesan, and process for 8 seconds. Mixer method: combine eggs, milk, and lemon juice and beat until fluffy. Add spinach and Mozzarella and beat until well blended. Add seasonings and blend. Pour into greased 9 inch pie plate. Sprinkle with Parmesan and bake for 25-35 minutes until puffed and golden.

Variation: Add 1 cup cottage cheese and bake in 10 inch pie plate.

NOTE: This freezes well if cooled first. Thaw and warm in 350° oven.

Yield: 6-8 servings.   Carol Fogel

Oven-Baked Vegetable Omelet

Non-stick vegetable spray
2 eggs
8 egg whites
1 (10-ounce) frozen chopped
   broccoli, thawed and
   drained
⅓ cup finely chopped onion
½ cup chopped mushrooms

¼ cup grated Parmesan cheese
2 tablespoons skim milk
½ teaspoon dried basil
¼ teaspoon garlic powder
Salt and pepper, to taste
1 medium tomato, seeded and
   sliced

Preheat oven to 325°. Spray 11 x 7 inch baking dish with non-stick vegetable spray. In a 2½ quart bowl, beat eggs and egg whites until light and fluffy. Stir in broccoli, onion, mushrooms, cheese, milk, basil, garlic powder, salt, and pepper. Pour mixture into pan. Arrange tomato slices on top. Bake uncovered until set, 30-40 minutes. Serve immediately.

Yield: 4-6 servings.   Joyce Sherman

Vegetable Frittata

2 tablespoons olive oil
1 onion, thinly sliced
2 small cooked potatoes, sliced
1 small zucchini, sliced
1 small red pepper, sliced
6 black olives, sliced

¼ cup grated Gruyère cheese
1 tablespoon chopped parsley
6 eggs, slightly beaten
Salt
Pepper

Preheat oven to 450°. Pour olive oil in 10-12 inch round baking dish and arrange onion slices on bottom. Bake for 5 minutes. Remove baking dish from oven; onion should be slightly cooked. Arrange potatoes, zucchini, red pepper, and olives on top of onion. Sprinkle with cheese and parsley. Season with salt and pepper. Reduce oven to 400°. Pour eggs over vegetables and cheese. Bake for approximately 20 minutes, until eggs have puffed and center is set. Do not over cook. Serve in wedges.

NOTE: 12 egg whites can be substituted for 6 whole eggs; reduce cooking time.

Yield: 6-8 servings.   Rona Freedland

Lox and Tomato Quiche

4 tablespoons margarine
1 large tomato, chopped
3 ounces lox, diced
2 tablespoons instant onion
1 tablespoon flour

4 ounces Swiss cheese, grated
1 cup light cream
Dash of pepper
4 eggs

In a large skillet, melt margarine and add tomato. Cook several minutes until tomato is soft. Cool. Stir in lox and onions. In a bowl, stir together flour and cheese and sprinkle into quiche pan. Spoon lox mixture over cheese. Beat eggs with cream and pepper. Pour into quiche pan. Bake at 350° for 40-45 minutes.

NOTE: Sautéed onions can be used in place of instant onions.

Yield: 8 servings.   Ann Baruch

Salmon Quiche

9 inch pastry shell (baked at
　400° for 5 minutes)
1 (7¾-ounce) can salmon,
　flaked and drained
1 cup shredded cheese of
　choice
2 tablespoons flaked onions

⅛ teaspoon salt
½ teaspoon pepper
3 eggs
1 cup milk
¼ cup grated Parmesan cheese
Lemon and parsley, for garnish

Preheat oven to 350°. Distribute flaked and drained salmon over the bottom of the prepared pastry shell. Sprinkle grated cheese, then onions over salmon. Beat eggs well, add milk, salt, and pepper. Pour over salmon. Sprinkle with Parmesan cheese. Bake at 350° for 35-40 minutes until center is firm when gently shaken. Let stand 10 minutes before serving. Garnish with lemon wedges and parsley.

Variation: Tuna can be substituted for salmon.

Yield: 6 servings.   Rose Weintraub

Tuna Bake

1 (16-ounce) package frozen
　mixed vegetables
2 large onions, chopped
1 green pepper, chopped
　(optional)
4 (6½-ounce) cans tuna
4 ounces slivered almonds

¼ cup liquid non-dairy creamer
　or milk
White bread, crust removed
½ pound Gouda cheese, grated
½ pound American or American
　Swiss cheese, grated

Cook frozen vegetables according to directions on package. Sauté onions and green pepper and combine with mixed vegetables. Add tuna, almonds, and non-dairy creamer. Line 9 x 13 inch glass baking pan with bread and top with tuna mixture. Top with cheese. Bake at 350° for 30 minutes.

Yield: 10 servings.   Rochelle Sable

Tuna Quiche

3 tablespoons margarine
6-8 Challah slices
1 (6½-ounce) can tuna, drained
   and flaked
1 cup sour cream

3 eggs
1 cup shredded Cheddar
   cheese
½ cup canned onion rings

Preheat oven to 325°. Melt margarine in a 9 x 9 inch or 7 x 11 inch pan and layer with challah slices. Combine all other ingredients in mixing bowl and pour over the challah. Bake for 40 minutes or until top is lightly browned.

Yield: 4-6 servings.   Bess Moss

Zucchini Kugel

4 cups thinly sliced zucchini
1 small onion, grated
2 tablespoons chopped parsley
½ cup grated Parmesan cheese
1 cup biscuit mix

½ cup oil
4 eggs, slightly beaten
Salt, pepper, and oregano, to
   taste

Grease 9 x 13 inch pan. Mix all ingredients, blend well, and pour into pan. Bake at 350° for approximately 45 minutes or until golden brown.

Yield: 10 servings.   Shirley Siegal

 When you chop onions, prepare several cups more than you need and freeze them in a plastic bag for future use.

VEGETABLES

Asparagus with Shiitakes and Parmesan

2 pounds thin asparagus
8 ounces fresh Shiitake
  mushrooms
¼ cup unsalted margarine
¼ cup minced shallots
1 tablespoon chopped parsley
1 tablespoon chopped basil

1 tablespoon chopped chives
1 teaspoon fresh ground
  pepper
Dash of salt
5 ounces shaved Parmesan
  cheese

Add asparagus to 1 inch boiling water in large skillet. Simmer 1 minute, drain, and pat dry. Discard mushroom stems, slice mushroom into ¼ inch strips. Melt margarine in skillet, add shallots, cook and stir until golden brown. Add asparagus and mushrooms, cook 2 minutes. Add herbs, salt and pepper, cook 1 minute. Transfer to oven proof gratin dish keeping Shiitakes on top of asparagus. Top with Parmesan cheese, place under boiler until cheese melts—2 minutes. Serve immediately.

Yield: 6 servings.

Stephanie Bernstein

Evy's Baked Bean Casserole

2 (12-ounce) cans lima beans
2 (16-ounce) cans vegetarian
  baked beans
1 can red kidney beans
2 cans pear halves, drained,
  juice reserved

⅛ cup lemon juice
½ bottle chili sauce
Brown sugar to taste
¼ cup margarine

Drain beans and mix with 1 cup pear juice, add chili sauce and lemon juice—mix well. Add brown sugar. Place pears on top of beans. Sprinkle with brown sugar and margarine. Bake at 300° for 3 hours.

NOTE: Can be fixed ahead. The longer you bake it, the better it tastes—you won't ruin it!

Yield: 10-12 servings.

Carol Sue Coden

Green Bean Casserole

2 tablespoons margarine
2 tablespoons flour
1 teaspoon salt
¼ teaspoon pepper
¼ teaspoon minced onion
1 teaspoon sugar

1 cup sour cream
2 (8-ounce) boxes frozen
   French green beans, cooked
2 cups or ½ pound grated
   Swiss cheese

Melt margarine in sauce pan, add flour, onions, salt, pepper, sugar, and sour cream over low heat. Mix together. Increase heat until mixture is soft, bubbly, and thickened. Cool cooked beans, drain and add to mixture. Grease 11 x 7 inch casserole and add bean mixture. Sprinkle grated Swiss cheese on top.

TOPPING:
½ cup cornflake crumbs   1 tablespoon margarine

Melt margarine and add cornflakes to make cornflake topping. Spread evenly on top. Bake at 400° for 20 minutes.

NOTE: To double recipe, use 9 x 13 inch pan and double everything but the cheese. You need a little more cheese, but not double. Jarlsburg cheese is very good in the recipe. Doubled recipe is good to use for "potluck" dinners. You can use unsalted butter instead of margarine.

Yield: 6-8 servings, 11 x 7 inch pan; 14-16 servings, 9 x 13 inch pan.

Geraldine Palmer

Sesame Green Beans

1-1½ pounds green beans
¼ cup butter or margarine
2 tablespoons sesame seeds

1 teaspoon dry mustard
½ teaspoon salt
½ teaspoon garlic powder

Steam green beans. Melt butter or margarine, add remaining ingredients, stir. Blend well and pour over beans.

NOTE: Seasoning may be used on any vegetable of your choice.

Julie Meltzer & Dee Fishman

Greek Style Green Beans

1 pound whole green beans,
   fresh or frozen
1 teaspoon salt
2½ tablespoons olive oil

1 cup beef or chicken broth
2 tablespoons tomato sauce
Dash of: oregano, basil, garlic
   powder, onion powder

Bring all ingredients, except green beans, to a boil. Add green beans. Cover and cook until tender.

NOTE: This may be prepared earlier in the day.

Yield: 4 servings.

Sandra Leshman

Greek String Beans

1 cup chopped or sliced onions
2 tablespoons olive or canola
   oil
1 (8-ounce) can tomato sauce

2 pounds fresh or frozen string
   beans
½ teaspoon cinnamon

Sauté onions in oil. Add tomato sauce, string beans, and cinnamon. Add enough water to cover. Stir well and cook, covered, until tender, about 30 minutes.

Barbara Mayer

Baked Lima Beans

1 pound large California lima
   beans
½ cup minus 1 tablespoon
   margarine

6 tablespoons dark corn syrup
1 (14-ounce) bottle ketchup
Salt to taste

Wash beans thoroughly. Soak beans overnight in enough water to cover. Discard water. Add salt and fresh water to cover beans. Cover and cook until just tender (30-60 minutes). Be careful not to boil water. Drain. In 2 or 3 quart casserole, layer margarine, syrup, and beans. Pour bottle of ketchup over top. Bake at 350° for 1½ hours covered. Stir occasionally. Uncover last ½ hour.

NOTE: Freezes very well.

Yield: 10 servings.

Ethel Lappin

Curried Lentils

1 cup lentils
3 cups broth or water
2 large onions, finely chopped

1 tablespoon oil
1 garlic clove, minced
1 teaspoon curry powder

Combine lentils, broth, and half of onion. Bring to a boil; reduce heat, cover, simmer 30-40 minutes. Drain. Meanwhile, sauté remaining onion and garlic in the oil. Combine garlic and onion mixture with cooked lentils. Add curry powder and combine well.

Yield: 4-6 servings.   Hilary Langer

Carrots with Grapes

2 pounds carrots, peeled and
    cut into thick diagonal slices
2 tablespoons butter or
    margarine
⅛ teaspoon sugar

½ cup water
1 tablespoon vodka
1½ cups purple grapes (seeds
    removed)
Salt to taste

Sauté carrots in butter or margarine for a few minutes. Sprinkle sugar over carrots and cook for 2-3 minutes. Add water and vodka and cook until carrots are almost tender. Add grapes, cover pan, and cook until carrots and grapes are both tender. Add salt to taste.

Yield: 8 servings.   Phyllis Schwartz

Festive Carrots and Pineapple

1 (8-ounce) can pineapple
    chunks, drained
¼ cup brown sugar, packed
1 tablespoon butter
2 teaspoons cornstarch

½ teaspoon ground cinnamon
1 (16-ounce) can sliced carrots
    or 1 (16-ounce) package
    frozen baby carrots

Combine pineapple juice, sugar, butter, cornstarch, and cinnamon in saucepan. Cook and stir until clear and thickened. Add pineapple chunks and carrots. Heat and serve immediately.

Yield: 4-6 servings.   Ruth Savage

Carrot Ring

1 cup shortening	1½ cups cake flour
¾ cup brown sugar	½ teaspoon baking soda
1½ cups grated carrots	1 teaspoon cinnamon
2 egg yolks, beaten	½ teaspoon nutmeg
2 tablespoons lemon juice	1 teaspoon baking powder
1 tablespoon lemon rind	2 egg whites, stiffly beaten

Cream shortening and brown sugar. Add grated carrots, egg yolks, lemon juice and lemon rind, mix well. Add dry ingredients which have been sifted twice. Fold in stiffly beaten egg whites. Bake in greased 6-cup metal ring mold for 45 minutes in a 350° oven. Unmold and fill center with peas, brussel sprouts, or vegetable of your choice.

Yield: 6 servings.

Lucille Cassel

Very Rich Carrot Ring

4 eggs, separated	1 teaspoon baking powder
1 cup brownulated sugar	2 teaspoons baking soda
1 cup white sugar	½ teaspoon salt
2 cups butter	2 cups finely grated carrots
2 teaspoons vanilla	3 tablespoons lemon juice
2½ cups flour	

Separate eggs. Beat egg whites until stiff, set aside. Cream butter with brown sugar and white sugar; add 4 egg yolks (one at a time) and vanilla; set aside. Sift together: flour, baking powder, baking soda, salt. Add flour mixture to creamed mixture and mix thoroughly. Add carrots and lemon juice. Fold beaten egg whites into mixture. Pour carrot mixture into greased bundt pan. Bake for 1 hour at 350°. Cool.

NOTE: Can use regular brown sugar.

Yield: 10-12 servings.

Ina Egnater

 Peas become more than ordinary with the addition of crushed mint leaves, slivers of orange rind, nutmeg, or sautéed mushrooms during cooking.

Holiday Carrots with Caramelized Pecans

CARAMELIZED PECANS:

3 tablespoons butter
6 tablespoons corn syrup
3 tablespoons sugar

Pinch of salt
¾ teaspoon cinnamon
1½ cups pecans (halved)

Preheat oven to 250°. In heavy saucepan, melt butter and stir in corn syrup, sugar, cinnamon, and pinch of salt. Bring to a boil, then reduce to simmer for 5 minutes. While syrup is simmering, place pecans on a baking sheet and put into preheated oven for 5 minutes. Pour syrup over pecans and bake mixture for 1 hour, stirring every 20 minutes. Turn nuts onto buttered baking sheet and cool 3 minutes. Cool. Separate nuts with 2 forks and let cool completely (this may be made day before serving).

CARROTS:

2 pounds carrots, thinly sliced
   (⅛ inch)
2 teaspoons freshly grated
   orange peel (orange part
   only)

4 tablespoons butter
4 teaspoons sugar
½ cup water
White pepper and salt to taste

In a large skillet, melt butter, sugar, water, white pepper, and salt. When it boils, add carrots and stir. Reduce heat to medium and cover for 4 minutes. Stir in orange rind and cook, uncovered, until crisp and tender. Place in heated serving dish and cover with pecans.

NOTE: This recipe can be multiplied easily. If you want to serve only 4-6 people, reduce amount of carrots by ½ and pecans by ⅓.

Yield: 10-12 servings.   Kari Izu

Stovetop Eggplant Casserole

1 large eggplant, peeled, and
  cut into ¼ inch thick slices
Salt water for soaking eggplant
3 eggs, separated
1 tablespoon milk
1 cup flour
1-2 tablespoons olive oil
1 medium onion, chopped
1 clove garlic, crushed

5-6 mushrooms, sliced
  (optional)
1½ cups tomato sauce
½ cup water (mix with tomato
  sauce)
1 teaspoon seasoned salt
Juice of one lemon
2 teaspoons sugar

Put eggplant in a large bowl of salted water. Let soak for one-half hour. Towel dry slices.

Separate eggs. To the yolks, add milk, and beat well. Beat egg whites until slightly stiff. Dip eggplant slices in yolks, then dip in flour, and then in the egg whites. Sauté the eggplant in oil over medium heat until golden brown on both sides. Drain on paper towels. Sauté onion, garlic, and mushrooms until soft.

In an ungreased Dutch oven or 4-quart pot, layer eggplant slices, tomato and water mixture, salt and sautéed onion, garlic, and mushrooms. Continue layering until all eggplant is used.

Mix juice of lemon and sugar in a glass bowl. Pour over the eggplant. Simmer on top of stove for 1-1½ hours.

Yield: 4 servings.   Geraldine Palmer

Yummy Potatoes

6 medium Idaho potatoes
½ cup margarine
Kosher salt to taste

Dash of: basil and garlic
  powder

Parboil unpeeled potatoes. Dice potatoes. Melt margarine in a 9 x 13 inch pan, add diced potatoes. Sprinkle with Kosher salt, basil, and garlic powder. Bake at 450° for 45-60 minutes.

NOTE: For a dairy meal, sprinkle top with Parmesan cheese near end of baking.

Yield: 6-8 servings.   Ann Brasch

Yam Apple Casserole

2 (16-ounce) cans yams,
   drained
½ cup butter or margarine
½ cup dark corn syrup
⅓ cup and 2 tablespoons brown
   sugar

2 tablespoons dry sherry
1 teaspoon cinnamon
⅛ teaspoon salt
2 large Granny Smith apples,
   peeled, cored, and sliced

Combine all ingredients, except apples. Place in food processor and process. Layer in pie plate beginning with yam mixture, alternating with apples, ending with apples on top. Brush top with butter or margarine. Bake at 350° for 1 hour.

NOTE: This may be made day ahead.

Yield: 8 servings.   Sally Schottenfels

Thanksgiving Medley

3 large sweet potatoes (or
   yams)
¼ cup margarine or butter
½ cup brown sugar

½ bag (6-8 ounce) fresh
   cranberries
½ cup yellow raisins
Pecans, if desired

Peel and quarter sweet potatoes, lengthwise. Place in greased 9 x 12 inch glass dish. Top with margarine and brown sugar. Bake ½ hour at 400°. Add cranberries and raisins. Reduce to 350°. Bake until potatoes are tender. Top with pecans, if desired.

Yield: 4-6 servings.   Sally Green

Red Skin Casserole

6-8 red skin potatoes, unpeeled
½ cup margarine

1 package onion soup mix

Melt margarine and stir in onion soup. Cut potatoes in chunks and place in 2 quart glass baking dish. Pour soup mix and margarine over top. Bake, covered, at 350° for 1 hour, or until potatoes are tender.

Yield: 6-8 servings.   Sally Green

Seasoned Potatoes

1½ pounds unpeeled baking
　　potatoes
½ teaspoon onion powder
½ teaspoon paprika

¼ teaspoon salt
¼ teaspoon garlic powder
¼ teaspoon pepper
Vegetable cooking spray

Cut potatoes into ¼ inch thick slices, pat dry with paper towels. Combine onion powder, paprika, salt, garlic powder, and pepper in a large zip-top plastic bag. Add potatoes and shake well to coat. Coat baking sheet with vegetable spray and arrange potatoes in a single layer. Bake at 425° for 20 minutes.

Yield: 5 (½-cup) servings.

Marsha Zucker

Accordion Potatoes

6 medium Idaho potatoes,
　　peeled
⅔ cup melted butter or
　　margarine
1½ tablespoons vegetable oil

1¼ teaspoons salt
⅛ teaspoon pepper
⅔ cup grated Cheddar cheese
　　(optional)

Thinly slice each potato three-fourths of the way through vertically, leaving bottom of the potato intact. Roll potatoes in combined butter and oil. Place potatoes in shallow roasting pan. Pour remaining butter mixture over potatoes. Season with salt and pepper. Bake in preheated 375° oven for 2 hours, basting frequently. If desired, sprinkle Cheddar cheese over tops of baked potatoes and bake an additional 5 minutes or until cheese melts.

NOTE: Butter substitute can be used in place of butter or margarine.

Yield: 6 servings.

Karen Marks & Rosie Schlussel

Spinach Ring

3 cups cooked spinach (about 3
(10-ounce) packages frozen
spinach or 4½ pounds fresh
spinach)
½ cup margarine
3 tablespoons chopped onions

9 tablespoons flour
3 cups cream substitute or half
and half
9 eggs, separated
Salt, fresh pepper, nutmeg to
taste

Preheat oven to 325°. Cook and drain spinach very thoroughly and finely chop in blender. Melt margarine in large skillet and sauté onions until golden. Blend in flour and slowly add the cream substitute while stirring. Cook, stirring, until smooth and thickened. Reduce heat to low. Beat egg yolks and stir a little of hot mixture into them. Return to the hot mixture and cook 1 minute, stirring constantly. Add spinach and season to taste. Remove mixture from heat. Beat egg whites until stiff and fold into mixture. Pour into greased 9 x 13 inch pan or large greased ring mold. Set in a pan of hot water. Bake until set, about 40 minutes. If using a mold, invert onto a heated platter. Center of ring mold may be filled with mushrooms or steamed carrots.

Yield: 12-16 servings.

Doreen Hermelin

Stuffed Zucchini

4 medium zucchini
3 tablespoons butter
¾ cup onion, finely minced
3 cloves garlic, crushed
Salt and pepper to taste
3 eggs, beaten
½ cup feta cheese, crumbled

¾ cup grated Swiss cheese
2 tablespoons fresh chopped
parsley
1 tablespoon fresh chopped dill
1½ tablespoons flour
Paprika for the top

Scoop out the insides of the zucchini to leave ½ inch rim. Chop the insides into little bits and cook in butter with onions, garlic, salt, and pepper until onions are soft. Combine eggs, cheeses, herbs, and flour and add to onion mixture. Fill the zucchini cavities and dust the tops with paprika. Bake at 375° for 30 minutes or until the filling solidifies.

Yield: 4 (2 halves per serving).

Fran Wigod

Acorn Squash Purée

¼ cup margarine
4 acorn squashes, halved and
  seeded
Salt substitute and black
  pepper to taste

2 tablespoons brown sugar or
  honey

Preheat oven to 325°.

Lightly oil baking sheet with margarine. Season squash halves with salt substitute and place face-down on baking sheet. Bake for about 30 minutes. Flip halves up on the sheet, and cook another 5 minutes. Remove squash from oven, let cool enough to touch, and scoop flesh into food processor (add the skin of one of the squash halves as well, if desired). Process until puréed and blend in the brown sugar or honey. Keep warm until ready to serve.

NOTE: If you prefer, you can use purée as base for squash soup: blend 1 quart of de-fatted chicken stock (or ¾ cup stock plus 1 cup apple cider) into the purée and garnish before serving with fresh-ground nutmeg and chopped parsley.

Yield: 6-8 servings.   Elwin Greenwald

Easy Spaghetti Squash

1 medium spaghetti squash
⅓ cup each: diced red and
  green bell peppers
⅓ cup sliced mushrooms

½ cup each: broccoli and
  cauliflower flowerets
1 (24-ounce) jar spaghetti sauce

Pierce whole squash with fork 6 to 8 times. Place in 12 x 8 x 2 inch glass baking dish. Put in microwave oven, add just enough water to cover bottom of dish. Cover dish with plastic wrap, cook for 12 minutes on high. Remove from microwave and cut squash in half, remove seeds, scrape flesh with fork until it resembles spaghetti. Steam all vegetables and combine with spaghetti sauce. Pour vegetable and sauce mixture over squash in glass dish and bake in microwave for 4 minutes on high.

NOTE: This can be easily re-heated in microwave. A variety of vegetables can be used. Sprinkle with Parmesan cheese on top for extra flavor.

Yield: Main course-3 servings, Side dish-6 servings.   Maureen Shapiro

Zucchini with Basil

¾ pound small zucchini
1 tablespoon flour
Salt and freshly ground pepper
2 tablespoons olive oil
1 garlic clove, minced

3 tablespoons chopped fresh basil
3 tablespoons freshly grated Parmesan cheese

Preheat oven to 400°. Trim off and discard ends of unpeeled zucchini. Cut zucchini into ¼ inch slices. Toss slices in flour mixed with salt and pepper to taste. Heat oil and add zucchini, tossing occasionally and taking care not to break up the slices. When golden brown, slide zucchini into 8 inch pie plate. Sprinkle with garlic, basil, and cheese, and bake 5 minutes.

Yield: 4 small servings.   Ronni Cohen

Zucchini Baked with Cheese

3 pounds zucchini, washed
6 tablespoons flour
1 garlic clove, peeled and split
½ cup olive oil
3 tablespoons grated Parmesan cheese

1 cup tomato sauce
½ pound Mozzarella cheese, sliced thin
Salt to taste

Slice stem and tip off each zucchini. Put into a large pot of boiling water. Boil slowly, uncovered, until flesh yields slightly to pressure. Remove one by one as they are done, plunging them into cold water. Drain, cover, and refrigerate.

Cut zucchini into 1 inch slices and sprinkle with flour. Sauté garlic in the oil until brown and discard garlic, add zucchini and fry in batches until light brown. Drain well.

In a greased 2 quart glass casserole, place 1 layer of zucchini, sprinkle with salt and Parmesan cheese. Add several dots tomato sauce, cover with thin layer of Mozzarella cheese. Repeat process until all ingredients are used, ending with Mozzarella. Bake for 30 minutes at 350°.

NOTE: Can boil zucchini a day ahead. Salt may be eliminated for a healthier dish.

Yield: 6 servings.   Marcie Freedland

Ratatouille

½ cup olive or salad oil
1 large onion, diced
1 large garlic clove, minced
1 medium eggplant, cut into
   1 inch chunks
1 large green pepper, cut into
   1 inch pieces
3 medium zucchinis, cut into
   1 inch slices

½ cup water
1 tablespoon salt
2 teaspoons oregano leaves
1 teaspoon sugar
2 large tomatoes, cut into
   wedges

In a 6 quart saucepan over medium heat, heat olive oil and cook onion and garlic until tender, about 10 minutes, stirring occasionally. Add eggplant and green pepper, cook for 5 minutes, stirring the mixture frequently. Stir in zucchini, water, salt, oregano, and sugar; heat to medium-low, cook 30 minutes or until vegetables are tender, stirring occasionally.

Stir in tomato wedges; heat through; serve hot or cold.

Yield: 8 servings.

Phyllis Schwartz

Vegetarian "Meat" Balls

2 hard boiled eggs
1 small chopped onion
Salt and pepper to taste
½ cup wheat germ
½ cup ground walnuts
   (2¾ ounce package)

⅓ cup bread crumbs
2 raw eggs
Corn oil to cover bottom of pan
16 ounces tomato sauce
1 tablespoon water

Finely grate hard boiled eggs. Add all ingredients except oil, tomato, and water. Mix well. Form into small balls. Brown in hot corn oil in 10 inch glass pan. Add tomato sauce and water. Simmer covered for 30 minutes.

Yield: 4 servings.

Jacqueline Rogers

Purée of Vegetables

6 carrots (about 1 pound), peeled
4 parsnips (about 1 pound), peeled
6 potatoes, (½ pound), peeled
8 tablespoons butter or margarine
4 tablespoons finely chopped parsley

Ground pepper and salt, to taste
¼ teaspoon freshly ground nutmeg
Cinnamon and sugar for sprinkling

Cut each carrot into ½ inch thick rounds. Cut parsnips crosswise into 1 inch lengths. Cut potatoes into 1 inch rounds. Put all vegetables into saucepan, add water to cover and salt. Bring to a boil. Simmer about 15 minutes, covered, or until tender. Drain. Put vegetables and all other ingredients into food processor or blender. Mix until smooth. Bake at 325° about 30 minutes in 2 quart pan until heated through. Sprinkle top with cinnamon and/or sugar.

NOTE: Can prepare recipe in advance of baking; will be fine if refrigerated 1 or 2 days.

Yield: 12 servings.   Ruth Share

 Use greased muffin pans as molds for baking stuffed green peppers, tomatoes, onions, etc.

 For flavor variation, cook vegetables, rice and grains in chicken or beef bouillon or consommé.

PASTA, RICE & GRAINS

Barley Pilaf Supreme

½ cup margarine
½ pound fresh mushrooms
½ cup chopped onions
1⅓ cups pearl barley

½ cup chopped carrots
1½ cups chopped celery
5 cups chicken broth, divided

Preheat oven to 350°. Sauté mushrooms and onions with margarine until lightly browned. Add barley and slightly brown. Remove from heat and turn into 2 quart casserole. Add carrots and celery. Pour into mixture 2 cups chicken broth. Bake, covered, for 30 minutes. Stir in additional 2 cups chicken broth. Bake additional 30 minutes. Stir in 1 more cup chicken broth. Bake remaining 20 minutes, uncovered.

NOTE: This freezes well. Can be thawed and warmed in microwave. This works well as a company dish or as an accompaniment to chicken or meat.

Yield: Serves 10.

Carol P. Fogel

Lemon-Dill Rice

3 tablespoons olive or
   vegetable oil
1 cup long-grain white rice,
   uncooked
1 cup finely diced celery
1 cup finely diced onion
1 large garlic clove, minced
1¾ cups chicken stock
2 tablespoons fresh lemon juice

2 tablespoons margarine or
   butter
¼ cup minced fresh dill
1 tablespoon sugar
½ teaspoon salt
¼ teaspoon pepper
Lemon slices and fresh dill for
   garnish

In flame-proof casserole, combine oil and uncooked rice. Cook over medium heat, stirring often, until grains are light golden brown, about 5 minutes. Add celery and onion and cook, stirring, until slightly softened, about 3 minutes. Add garlic and cook 1 minute. Add chicken stock, lemon juice, margarine or butter, dill, sugar, salt, and pepper. Bring to a boil, reduce to low, and arrange lemon slices on top. Cover tightly and cook at low simmer until rice is tender and liquid is absorbed, about 18 to 22 minutes. Let stand, covered, 10 minutes. Serve garnished with dill.

NOTE: Great with fish or poultry.

Yield: Serves 6-8.

Amy Freedland

Baked Couscous with Chick Peas

3¾ cups chicken stock
2½ cups couscous, about 1
    pound
¾ teaspoon coriander seeds
2 tablespoons fennel seeds
¾ teaspoon cumin seeds
¼ teaspoon ground turmeric
5 tablespoons olive oil
2 medium red bell peppers, cut
    into 1 inch pieces

1 onion, cut into ½ inch pieces
1 cup drained chick peas
⅓ cup raisins
⅓ cup pine nuts, toasted
1 clove garlic, minced
Salt and pepper
Fennel and parsley optional for
    garnish

In a large saucepan, bring stock to a boil. Remove from heat. Stir in couscous. Cover and let stand 5 minutes. Transfer to a large bowl. Fluff couscous with fork and set aside. Preheat oven to 350°. Cook coriander, fennel, and cumin in heavy small skillet over medium heat until aromatic, stirring frequently, about 3 minutes. Cool spices. Finely grind in coffee grinder or mini food processor. Mix into couscous with turmeric.

Heat 2 tablespoons oil in skillet over high heat. Stir fry peppers 5 minutes. Transfer to couscous with slotted spoon. Add onion to skillet and stir fry, about 3 minutes. Transfer to couscous with slotted spoon. Add chick peas, raisins, pine nuts and garlic; cook 1 minute. Combine with couscous. Add remaining oil to mixture. Season with salt and pepper.

Spoon couscous mixture into a 9 x 13 x 2 inch pan. Cover with foil and bake until heated through — about 30 minutes. Mound couscous on platter. Garnish with fennel and parsley, if desired.

NOTE: This can be prepared 2 days ahead. Refrigerate couscous; bring to room temperature before reheating.

Yield: Serves 6.   Carol P. Fogel

Gina's Noodle-Rice Side Dish

1 (8-ounce) package fine
  noodles
1 cup butter or corn oil
  margarine
2 (10-ounce) cans chicken broth
2 (10-ounce) cans onion soup

1 cup water
2 cups converted rice
1 teaspoon soy sauce
1 (8-ounce) can sliced water
  chestnuts, drained

Preheat oven to 350°. In a large frying pan, melt butter or margarine and sauté the uncooked noodles until lightly browned. Combine all other ingredients in large bowl. Add the contents of the frying pan and mix gently. Pour into a 9 x 13 casserole and bake at 350° for 45 minutes-1 hour.

NOTE: This can be made in advance.

Yield: Serves 8-10.

Bobbie Blitz

Easy Vegetable Lasagna

1 quart any flavor Italian sauce
1 pound lasagna noodles,
  uncooked
2 (10-ounce) boxes frozen
  spinach, thawed

1 pound Ricotta cheese
1 pound Mozzarella cheese,
  shredded
1 pound cottage cheese

Wet lasagna noodles under cold running water as you layer them with other ingredients. Start with a small amount of Italian sauce in the bottom of a 9 x 13 microwave-safe pan. Place one layer of lasagna noodles in pan. Place half of undrained spinach over the layer. Place half of Ricotta cheese over spinach, then layer half of cottage cheese, more sauce, and half of Mozzarella cheese. Repeat, beginning with sauce, noodles, spinach, then cheeses, ending with mozzarella cheese. Microwave on high, covered, for 30 minutes. Uncover and microwave for 5 more minutes.

NOTE: Favorite nuts may be added, if desired.

Yield: 6 servings.

Evalyn Heavenrich

Colorful Vegetarian Lasagna

2 tablespoons olive oil, divided
10 uncooked lasagna noodles
1 large onion, minced
1-2 cloves garlic, minced
1 pound mushrooms, sliced
1 pound carrots, peeled and
    shredded
¾ cup pitted ripe olives, sliced
1 (15-ounce) can tomato sauce
1 (6-ounce) can tomato paste
1½ teaspoons oregano

⅛ teaspoon freshly ground
    pepper
2 cups cottage cheese, well-
    drained
2 pounds spinach, cooked and
    drained dry
1½-2 pounds Mozzarella
    cheese, grated
3 tablespoons grated Parmesan
    cheese

Preheat oven to 375°. Spray a 9 x 13 inch glass dish with a non-stick vegetable spray. Boil 6 quarts of water in a 2 gallon pot. Add 1 tablespoon oil and 2-3 lasagna noodles at a time. Cook 8-10 minutes and drain. Cover with warm water to prevent sticking. In a fry pan, heat 1 tablespoon oil. Add onion and garlic. Sauté about 2 minutes over medium heat. Add mushrooms, stirring often, until liquid evaporates, about 10-12 minutes. Add carrots and cook about 3 minutes. Stir in olives, tomato sauce, tomato paste, and seasonings. Remove from heat.

Line bottom of casserole with 5 drained noodles to cover. Spread half of cottage cheese, half the spinach, and one-third of the Mozzarella cheese. Cover with half of the tomato mixture. Repeat process. Top with remainder of the Mozzarella cheese. Sprinkle with Parmesan cheese. Bake 45 minutes or until it bubbles.

NOTE: This can be frozen and reheated.

Yield: 8 large servings.   Barbara Lebus

Rice Noodle Casserole

1 cup rice, uncooked
1 (8-ounce) package ¼ inch
    noodles, uncooked
1 package onion soup mix

1 small can sliced mushrooms
¼ cup margarine
4 cups boiling water

Preheat oven to 350°. Combine all ingredients in a large deep casserole. Cover and bake one hour.

Yield: 4 servings.   Ruth Rosenthal

Healthy Spinach Lasagna

1 (10-ounce) package frozen
   spinach
Non-stick vegetable spray
1 large onion, finely chopped
3 cloves garlic, minced
1 tablespoon dried oregano
1 teaspoon marjoram
½ teaspoon thyme
1 teaspoon basil
½ teaspoon rosemary
1 (15-ounce) can low sodium
   tomato purée
¼ cup tomato paste

½ cup dry red wine
12 lasagna noodles, white,
   green, or whole wheat—not
   egg noodles
1 egg white
2 cups Ricotta cheese, part
   skim milk
½ teaspoon freshly ground
   black pepper
1 cup shredded part skim
   Mozzarella cheese
½ cup grated Parmesan cheese

Cook spinach according to directions. Drain well and let cool; set aside. Spray a large skillet with non-stick spray. Cook onions, garlic, and all spices over a medium heat until the onions are soft, about 10 minutes. Add tomato purée, tomato paste, and wine. Cover and simmer for about 10 minutes. Uncover and cook until sauce thickens and is reduced to about 2½ cups; about 10 minutes. Meanwhile, cook noodles according to package directions. Preheat oven to 350°. Spoon ¼ of the sauce into a 9 x 13 x 2 inch baking dish. Arrange four noodles lengthwise on the bottom of pan. Spread half the spinach over the noodles on the bottom.

In a small bowl, lightly beat egg white. Blend in Ricotta cheese and pepper. Spread half of this mixture over the spinach. Sprinkle with ⅓ of the Mozzarella cheese and ⅓ of the Parmesan cheese. Add another ¼ of the tomato sauce. Top with 4 more noodles, remaining spinach, remaining Ricotta mixture and another ⅓ of Mozzarella and Parmesan cheese. Then layer, in order, remaining 4 noodles, tomato sauce, and Mozzarella and Parmesan cheese.

Bake, uncovered, for 30-35 minutes or until hot and bubbly. Let cool about 10 minutes before cutting.

Yield: Serves 8.

Mary Schwartz

Fresh Vegetable Pasta with Olives and Cheese

¼ cup olive oil
4 teaspoons minced fresh garlic
1 pound ripe plum tomatoes, seeded and chopped
1 medium zucchini, cut in thin strips
1 medium green pepper, cut in thin strips
1 medium red pepper, cut in thin strips
1 pound fusilli or rotelle pasta
4 medium scallions, whites and 2 inches of green, sliced thin

¾ cup coarsely chopped fresh basil or 3-4 teaspoons dry basil
12-14 Greek olives, black and green, pitted and coarsely chopped
4 tablespoons chopped fresh parsley
1 cup freshly grated Parmesan cheese; or ¼ pound Asiago cheese; or chunks of feta cheese
Salt and pepper, to taste

Preheat oven to 375°. In a 3 quart casserole, combine olive oil and minced garlic. Bake for 5-10 minutes until slightly golden. Add tomatoes, zucchini, and red and green peppers. Toss well and return to oven to bake 10 minutes, or until vegetables are slightly softened.

Meanwhile, in a large pot, cook pasta until tender but still firm, about 6-8 minutes. Drain pasta and add to vegetables in casserole.

Add scallions, basil, olives, parsley, and half of the cheese. Toss well and season with salt and pepper, if needed. Serve warm or at room temperature. Pass remaining cheese at the table or sprinkle over the top of the casserole.

NOTE: This dish reheats well in the microwave. Cover with plastic wrap and reheat at medium-high setting for 5 minutes.

Yield: Serves 6-8.   Sally Mayer

 To keep noodles from sticking, add 1 tablespoon oil to the cooking water.

Skillet Green Bean and Noodle Toss

1 clove garlic, crushed
¼ teaspoon rosemary, crushed
½ teaspoon herb and spice mix
  seasoning
1 tablespoon olive oil
1 (16-ounce) can stewed
  tomatoes

½ cup uncooked penne or other
  tube pasta
1 (16-ounce) can cut green
  beans, drained (reserve
  liquid)

In 8 inch skillet, cook garlic, rosemary, and herb and spice seasoning in oil for 1 minute. Pour liquid from beans into skillet. Add tomatoes and bring to boil. Cook, uncovered, over medium heat for 10 minutes. Stir in uncooked pasta. Reduce heat; cover and cook about 18 minutes. Add beans during last 5 minutes.

Yield: 4 to 6 servings.

Ruth Savage

Cousins Spinach Noodle Casserole

2 (10-ounce) packages frozen
  spinach
6 eggs
1 cup melted margarine
2 packages dry onion soup mix

16 ounces liquid non-dairy
  creamer
2 (10-ounce) packages wide
  noodles
Sesame seeds to taste

Preheat oven 350°. Grease 9 x 13 inch casserole pan. Cook spinach and drain well. Beat eggs well and add margarine, soup mix, and non-dairy creamer. Cook noodles and drain without rinsing. Combine spinach, egg mixture, and noodles. Place in casserole and sprinkle sesame seeds on top. Bake 45 minutes, uncovered. Let stand before serving.

Yield: 12 servings.

Carolyn Schreiber

Mushroom Noodle Casserole

3 tablespoons margarine or
   butter, divided
1 onion, sliced
½ cup sliced mushrooms plus
   8 whole mushrooms
3 tablespoons sherry plus ½
   cup sherry
1 pint cream

1 cup milk
1 (8-ounce) package egg
   noodles, cooked al dente
1 cup grated Parmesan cheese
¼ cup grated Gruyère or Swiss
   cheese
Paprika

Preheat oven to 350°. Butter 9 x 13 x 2 inch baking dish. In saucepan, melt 2 tablespoons margarine or butter. Add onion and ½ cup sliced mushrooms. Sauté 3-5 minutes. Blend in 3 tablespoons sherry. Remove from heat and transfer to large bowl. Melt remaining margarine in saucepan. Add whole mushrooms and sauté 3 minutes. Set aside separately.

Add cream, milk, ½ cup sherry, and noodles to mushroom and onion mixture. Blend well. Pour into greased baking dish. Arrange whole mushrooms over top. Sprinkle with cheese and paprika. Bake about 30 minutes until brown.

NOTE: This can be assembled ahead and baked before serving according to directions.

Yield: Serves 8.   Ann Zousmer

Tortellini With Sun-Dried Tomato Sauce

1 pound cheese-filled tortellini
½ pint heavy whipping cream
8 sun-dried tomatoes
6 garlic cloves

6 fresh basil leaves
½ cup grated Parmesan cheese
2 tablespoons olive oil

In a saucepan, boil tortellini until it is tender-firm or al dente. Drain and keep warm. In the blender, combine cream, tomatoes, garlic, and basil. Purée 1-2 minutes. Place in a saucepan and heat over medium heat until very hot. Add Parmesan cheese and oil. Toss with warm tortellini. Serve immediately.

NOTE: This sauce can be frozen.

Yield: Serves 4.   Jody Astrein

Baked Spaghetti Casserole

12 ounce box vermicelli or thin
    spaghetti
6 (8-ounce) cans meatless
    seasoned tomato sauce
2 tablespoons oregano
Several pinches fennel seed
Salt and pepper to taste
3 tablespoons cooking wine

1 medium onion, diced
4 tablespoons margarine or
    butter, divided
Garlic powder to taste
Parmesan cheese to taste
Parsley flakes to taste
1 package Swiss cheese slices
Bread crumbs for dusting

Pour tomato sauce into a large saucepan and add oregano, fennel seed, salt, pepper, wine, and onion. Stir together and simmer, approximately 15-20 minutes. Cook spaghetti according to package directions. Place back in pot and add 2 tablespoons margarine or butter, garlic powder, Parmesan cheese, and parsley flakes. Toss to coat. Put noodles in a 9 x 13 x 2 inch baking dish and pour in sauce, thoroughly covering noodles. Cut Swiss cheese slices in half and cover top of spaghetti with cheese. Dot remaining margarine or butter over cheese and cover completely with a thin layer of bread crumbs. Bake at 400° for 30 minutes and broil for 3-5 minutes until crust is slightly golden.

Yield: Serves 8-10.

Tina Pinter

Eggplant Sauce for Pasta

2 cloves garlic, crushed
¼ cup olive oil or vegetable oil
1 medium eggplant, peeled and
    cubed
1 (28-ounce) can whole
    tomatoes
1 (8-ounce) jar spaghetti sauce

¼ cup water
1 teaspoon salt (optional)
⅛ teaspoon pepper
⅛ teaspoon basil
8 ounces whole wheat shells or
    any pasta
Grated Parmesan cheese

In a large skillet, cook garlic in the oil a few minutes. Add the eggplant and sauté until lightly browned. Stir in tomatoes, spaghetti sauce, water, salt, pepper and basil. Cover and simmer about 45 minutes or until eggplant is tender. Cook pasta according to directions. Drain. Combine pasta with sauce. Sprinkle Parmesan cheese on top.

NOTE: The sauce can be prepared 1 day in advance.

Yield: 6-8 servings.

Sandra Leshman

Cold Spinach Pasta

1 pound spinach noodles
1 (2-ounce) jar pimentos,
   drained
¾ cup chopped scallions
¼ cup Italian dressing

½ cup mayonnaise-type salad
   dressing
½ cup sour cream
1 teaspoon salt
½ cup salted sunflower seeds

Cook noodles in rapidly boiling water. Drain and rinse in cold water. Add pimentos, scallions, Italian dressing, mayonnaise-type dressing, sour cream, and salt to noodles and toss in large bowl. Just before serving, add sunflower seeds.

Yield: Serves 6.

Ann Baruch

Pasta Parmesan

¼ cup oil
2 cups diced broccoli
¼ cup sliced shallots or green
   onions
1 clove garlic, chopped
¼ cup pine nuts (optional)

½ teaspoon basil
½ teaspoon salt
½ pound cooked pasta (rotini or
   other)
½ cup grated Parmesan cheese
1 cup cherry tomatoes, halved

Heat oil in a large skillet over medium-high heat. Add broccoli, onions, garlic, pine nuts, and basil. Stir until broccoli is soft (about 4 minutes). Remove from heat. Toss with salt, pasta, Parmesan cheese, and tomatoes. May be served chilled or warmed.

Sally Green

Mushroom Risotto with White Wine

4 tablespoons margarine or
  butter
1 tablespoon olive oil
1 cup finely chopped onion,
  divided
1 garlic clove, minced
8 ounces fresh mushrooms,
  thinly sliced
1 teaspoon dried thyme
¼ teaspoon dried rosemary

1 tablespoon fresh parsley,
  minced
1 cup dry white wine
2 cups Arborio rice
1 teaspoon salt, divided
½ teaspoon pepper, divided
6-8 cups clear broth
¾ cup freshly grated Parmesan
  cheese

In a large frying pan, melt 2 tablespoons margarine or butter with olive oil over medium heat. Add ½ cup onions and garlic, cook until onions are soft, 2-3 minutes. Stir in mushrooms and cook for 3-4 minutes. Stir in thyme, rosemary, and parsley. Season with ¼ teaspoon salt and ⅛ teaspoon pepper. Remove from heat and cover to keep warm.

Melt remaining margarine or butter in large heavy saucepan over medium heat. Cook remaining ½ cup onions until soft. Add wine and cook over high heat until reduced to ½ cup, about 4-5 minutes. Add rice, remaining salt and pepper, and stir to coat evenly, allowing wine to be absorbed. Add 2 cups broth, reduce heat to medium, and stir until stock is absorbed, 5-6 minutes. Continue to add as much broth as needed, one cup at a time, stirring until rice is creamy and tender, but firm. Process should take 15 to 18 minutes. Stir in reserved mushroom mixture. Remove from heat and stir in ½ cup Parmesan cheese. Pass remaining Parmesan cheese.

Yield: Serves 4-6 as a main dish, 6-8 as a side dish.   Ruth Mayer

 Mushrooms keep better if they are unwrapped and refrigerated in a loose brown paper bag.

Wild Rice with Dried Cranberries and Scallions

4 cups de-fatted chicken stock
1 tablespoon low-fat margarine
   or walnut oil
2 cups wild rice
½ teaspoon ground cloves or
   cardamom

1 teaspoon ground ginger
2 tablespoons chopped fresh
   parsley
1 scallion, thinly sliced
¾ cup dried cranberries

Bring stock and margarine or oil to a boil in a saucepan. Add wild rice and bring to a second boil. Cover, reduce heat, and simmer for about 30 minutes or until wild rice looks "expanded" but not mushy. Season with the cloves or cardamom, ginger, and parsley and fluff using two forks. When ready to serve, add the scallion slices and cranberries and fluff again.

Yield: Serves 6-8.

Elwin Greenwald

Wild Rice with Pecans and Raisins

½ pound wild rice
5½ cups chicken stock
1 cup pecan halves
1 cup yellow raisins
⅓ cup fresh orange juice
Grated rind of 1 orange

¼ cup chopped cooked meat
4 green onions, thinly sliced
¼ cup olive oil
1½ teaspoons salt
Ground pepper to taste

Wash rice well. Bring the stock to a rapid boil. Pour rice in stock and simmer 45 minutes, uncovered. Check after 30 minutes to be sure rice isn't too soft. Drain rice and add all other ingredients. Stir well. Serve at room temperature.

NOTE: This can be made ahead.

Yield: 6 servings.

Sally Schottenfels

MEAT

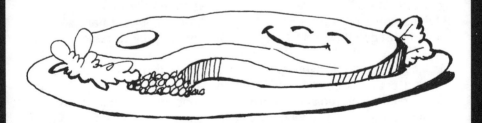

Beef with Snow Peas and Mushrooms

1½ pounds sirloin, sliced thin
3 tablespoons oil
1 pound mushrooms, sliced
1 pound fresh snow peas

½ cup chicken bouillon
5 green onions, cut into 1 inch
   pieces

MARINADE:
2 cloves garlic, crushed
1 tablespoon cornstarch
½ teaspoon salt

Ground pepper
3 tablespoons soy sauce
2 teaspoons sherry

Marinate beef slices for ½ hour. Heat oil in large skillet. Add beef and sauté for three minutes. Remove beef from pan. Sauté mushrooms. Add snow peas and cook for five minutes. Add a small amount of bouillon, if necessary, to keep from sticking. Add green onions, beef, and remaining bouillon and stir well. Heat thoroughly and serve with rice.

Yield: 4 servings.

Barbara Kuhlik

Beef Oriental

1½ pounds flank steak, cut into
   strips
½ cup plus 2 tablespoons soy
   sauce
1 tablespoon honey mustard
½ teaspoon garlic powder
2 tablespoons oil
1 head broccoli flowerets

½ red pepper, sliced
½ green pepper, sliced
2 garlic cloves, chopped
½ cup dry sherry
1 tablespoon sugar
2 teaspoons cornstarch
Dash of red pepper flakes
Salt and pepper to taste

Marinate flank steak overnight in mixture of ½ cup soy sauce, honey mustard, and garlic powder. Heat oil in wok. Add steak and stir-fry. Remove meat. Add broccoli, red and green peppers, chopped garlic and stir-fry. Mix together sherry, 2 tablespoons soy sauce, sugar, and cornstarch. Add to wok and stir. Add meat and red pepper flakes. Heat through and season to taste with salt and pepper. Serve with rice.

Yield: Serves 6.

Sandra Leshman

 When sautéeing fresh mushrooms, sprinkle with a little lemon juice to prevent discoloration.

Brisket - Sweet and Sour

4 pound brisket
Salt, pepper, garlic powder - to
    taste
1 envelope onion soup mix

1 (12 ounce) can or bottle beer
½ cup ketchup
1 (8 ounce) can whole cranberry
    sauce

Place seasoned brisket in 9 x 13 inch pan. Mix remaining ingredients and pour over brisket. Cover and bake at 350° for about 2 hours or until tender. Remove from oven and cool. Slice the meat. Remove the fat from the gravy and return sliced meat to pan. Reheat until heated through. This can be made ahead and reheated. Potatoes, carrots, and mushrooms can be added to pan for the last half of the cooking time.

NOTE: Freezes well.

Yield: Serves 6.   Jean Gavern & Barbara Mayer

Best Brisket

4-5 pound brisket
¼ cup water
1 cup ketchup
2 tablespoons yellow mustard

2 tablespoons grape or
    seedless black raspberry
    jam

Preheat oven to 325°. Mix together water, ketchup, mustard, and jam. Pour over brisket. Cover pan and roast slowly for 3-4 hours. Cool before slicing against the grain.

Yield: Serves 10.   Roberta Grosinger

 If you want browner gravy, add a little coffee. Gravy will be a richer color, but will not take on a coffee flavor.

Braised Short Ribs of Beef

4 pounds short ribs
3½ teaspoons flour
Salt and pepper, to taste
2 tablespoons oil
1 cup boiling water
1 cup cooked or canned
    tomatoes

1 garlic clove
6 medium potatoes
12 small onions
6 carrots

Season short ribs with salt and pepper. Dredge in 2 teaspoons of the flour. Heat oil in large pot and brown the meat on all sides. Add water, tomatoes, and garlic. Cover and simmer over low heat for 1½ hours. Add pared vegetables and cook until vegetables and meat are tender, ½ to 1 hour. Arrange meat and vegetables on platter. Thicken gravy with the remaining 1½ teaspoons of flour mixed with 2 tablespoons water. Serve with meat and vegetables.

Yield: Serves 6.

Sadie Pesick

Pot Roast Burgundy

ONE-POT-MEAL:

3-3½ pounds chuck roast
Flour
2 tablespoons oil
2 medium onions, cut in rings
4-6 carrots, cut in chunks
2 sweet potatoes, cut in chunks

2 yams, cut in chunks
½ cup burgundy wine
½ cup beef-flavored liquid
    bouillon
2 garlic cloves, finely chopped
2 bay leaves

Preheat oven to 350°. Dredge beef in flour. Heat oil in Dutch oven and brown beef on each side, 3-4 minutes per side. Put onions, carrots, sweet potatoes, yams, burgundy, bouillon, garlic, and bay leaves on beef. Bring to a boil on top of stove. Cover and place in oven for 2½ hours, basting every ½ hour. Drain off liquid and remove fat. Serve juices on the side.

NOTE: If made the day before, the fat is more easily removed, and the meat and vegetables reheat well.

Yield: Serves 6.

Janice Goldstein Wanetick

Bulgur Meatloaf with Pine Nuts

¾ cup bulgur
1¾ pounds ground veal or lean lamb
¾ cup pine nuts, lightly toasted
¾ teaspoon salt
½ teaspoon sugar
Pepper to taste
2 cups finely chopped onion

¼ pound ground chuck
2½ tablespoons unsalted margarine
1 cup finely chopped fresh parsley
1 cup finely chopped fresh basil leaves or 1 tablespoon dried basil

Soak bulgur in cold water to cover by 2 inches for one hour. Drain well. In a large bowl, mix bulgur, veal, pine nuts, ½ teaspoon of the salt, sugar, and pepper. Press half of the mixture into a greased 9 inch square baking pan. In a large skillet, cook onion and ground chuck in 1 tablespoon margarine over moderate heat until the onion is softened. Stir in parsley, basil, and the remaining ¼ teaspoon salt. Spread the onion mixture over the veal mixture. Cover with the remaining veal mixture. With a knife, cut the meat into 8 triangles. Dot with remaining margarine. Bake at 375° for 45 minutes.

Yield: Serves 5-6.

Sheila Guyer

Marinated Flank Steak

1 flank steak, 2-3 pounds

MARINADE:
1 cup chili sauce
¼ cup soy sauce
2 tablespoons Worcestershire sauce
2 tablespoons molasses

½ teaspoon chili powder
½ teaspoon dried minced onion
½ teaspoon liquid smoke
¼ teaspoon garlic powder
Freshly ground pepper to taste

Combine all ingredients in marinade. In glass, oblong baking pan, or plastic bag, cover flank steak and marinate at least 2 hours, or overnight, in refrigerator. Pour off marinade and broil or barbeque 5 minutes on each side.

NOTE: If flank steak is 1-2 pounds, marinade ingredients may be cut in half.

Yield: 8 servings.

Marsha Zucker

Dutch Meat Loaf

PART I:

1½ pounds lean, ground beef
1 cup fresh bread crumbs
1 medium onion, chopped
4 ounces canned tomato sauce

1 egg, beaten
Salt to taste
¼ teaspoon pepper

Lightly mix Part I ingredients and form into loaf. Place in shallow pan. Put in preheated 350° oven. Bake for 15 minutes.

PART II:

4 ounces canned tomato sauce
2 tablespoons prepared
　mustard

2 tablespoons vinegar
2 tablespoons brown sugar or
　molasses

Combine Part II ingredients and pour over meat loaf in oven. Continue baking for 1 hour longer, basting a few times. Serve on a bed of noodles.

NOTE: Oatmeal or cornflake crumbs may be substituted for bread crumbs. Recipe may be divided in half for 2 small loaves, which become crusty outside and moist inside; reduce cooking time accordingly.

Yield: 4-6 servings.

Lillian Chinitz

Horty's Meat Balls

1 pound ground beef
½ cup cracker or bread crumbs
1 egg, beaten
1 teaspoon dried minced onion
¼ teaspoon dry mustard
Pinch of salt

Freshly ground pepper to taste
Oil to cover bottom of skillet
1 (16-ounce) can whole
　cranberry sauce
1 (8-ounce) can tomato sauce

Combine ground beef, crumbs, egg, onion, mustard, salt, and pepper and mix well. Shape in bite-size meatballs. In large skillet, over medium-high heat, brown meatballs on all sides. Drain pan of any excess oil. Mix cranberry sauce and tomato sauce in small bowl. Pour over meatballs and simmer, covered, for 30 minutes.

Yield: 6-8 servings.

Horty Falk

Skewered Steak and Mushrooms

MARINADE:

½ cup Burgundy wine
1 teaspoon Worcestershire
   sauce
1 clove garlic, crushed
½ cup oil
½ teaspoon salt

2 tablespoons ketchup
1 teaspoon sugar
1 tablespoon white vinegar
½ teaspoon marjoram
½ teaspoon rosemary

Mix together all marinade ingredients. Pour over cubed steak and marinate in covered bowl (or plastic bag) for at least 2 hours in the refrigerator.

2 pounds beef tenderloin, cut
   into ½ inch cubes

12 large mushroom caps

Alternate steak and mushrooms on skewers. Cook on hot grill, turning and basting frequently with the remaining marinade.

NOTE: Onions and peppers may be added to skewers for beef shish kabob.

Yield: 6-8 servings.   Joyce Rubenstein

Pickled Tongue in Raisin Sauce

1 pound pickled tongue, sliced
½ cup light brown sugar
1 teaspoon dry mustard
2 tablespoons cornstarch
2 tablespoons red wine vinegar

2 tablespoons lemon juice
1 cup water
¾ cup raisins
2 tablespoons margarine
¾ cup tomato sauce

Mix brown sugar, dry mustard and cornstarch. Slowly stir in vinegar. Add lemon juice, water, raisins, margarine, and tomato sauce. Stir over low heat until thickened.

Place sliced tongue in a baking dish. Pour sauce over tongue. Preheat oven to 350°. Bake for 45 minutes.

NOTE: This can be prepared several days in advance. Serve with rice pilaf and green salad. Freezes well.

Carol Fogel

Osso Buco

2½-3 pounds veal shanks or
veal stew meat
1 can condensed tomato soup

2 tablespoons soy sauce
1 pound fresh baby carrots
2 medium onions, chopped

In a large skillet, stir soup and soy sauce together. Add veal. Heat to boiling, reduce heat to simmer, cover pan, and cook 1 hour, stirring occasionally. Add carrots and onions. Cook another hour or until meat is tender.

NOTE: If desired, small potatoes may be added with carrots and onions.

Yield: 3-5 servings, depending on kind of meat used.   Dorothy Haber

Veal Italian with Pasta

2 tablespoons margarine
1 small onion, chopped
½ garlic clove, minced
2 pounds thin veal steak
2 cups tomato sauce
2 cups canned tomatoes

1 teaspoon salt
¼ teaspoon pepper
¾ teaspoon dried oregano
1 (8-ounce) package pasta, any
kind
2 tablespoons snipped parsley

In hot skillet, melt margarine. Sauté onion and garlic until lightly browned; remove and reserve. Cut veal into eight pieces and sauté on both sides until golden brown. Add the tomato sauce, tomatoes, salt, pepper, oregano, and the reserved onion mixture. Simmer, uncovered, for thirty minutes or until the meat is fork tender, stirring occasionally. Meanwhile, cook the pasta al dente in boiling water. Drain.

To serve, turn pasta onto heated platter; top with meat and sauce. Sprinkle with parsley.

Yield: Serves 6.   Phyllis Schwartz

Osso Buco Alla Milanese

GREMOLATA:

Grated rind of 2 large lemons
½ teaspoon Kosher salt
3 garlic cloves, minced

⅓-½ cup chopped parsley
½ can (1-ounce) flat anchovies, mashed

Mix together all gremolata ingredients and set aside (can use food processor).

2 medium onions, minced
¼ pound celery, minced
¼ pound carrots, minced
4 tablespoons margarine, divided
4-4½ pounds shanks of veal, cut to 1-1½ inch thick
Flour for dredging
2 tablespoons olive oil
⅔ cup dry white wine
1½ pounds fresh tomatoes, peeled, seeded, chopped OR 1 can (28-ounce) Italian plum tomatoes, seeded and drained

1½-2 cups beef broth
¾ teaspoon crushed rosemary leaves
1 teaspoon crushed sage leaves
1 teaspoon salt
Freshly ground pepper

Melt 2 tablespoons margarine in large oven-proof skillet. Add onions, celery, and carrots and cook over low heat, stirring frequently until vegetables are softened. Remove from pan and set aside. Place flour on waxed paper. Dip both sides of veal in flour, shake off excess and set aside. Sauté veal in skillet, using rest of margarine and olive oil. Do not crowd. Do in two or three batches until brown. Remove veal from pan. Add wine to pan and loosen brown bits with wooden spoon. Add vegetables to pan in an even layer. Place veal over vegetables. Sprinkle chopped tomatoes over contents and add broth. Heat liquid to rapid simmer. Cover loosely with foil. Simmer 1-1½ hours until veal is tender. Remove veal with slotted spoon to a warm serving platter. In pan, add rosemary and sage. Rapidly simmer until mixture measure 3-3½ cups. Stir in gremolata, salt, and freshly ground pepper. Spoon sauce over veal.

Carrie Mayer

123

Veal Brisket #1

3-3½ pounds brisket of veal
¼ cup sherry
⅓ cup brown sugar
1 package onion soup mix

2 tablespoons tomato paste
1 (16-ounce) can whole
   cranberry sauce

Place brisket in covered roaster. Pour sherry over meat. Make a paste of brown sugar, onion soup mix, and tomato paste. Rub over brisket. Pour cranberry sauce over it. Roast in oven for about 2½-3 hours at 350°. Slice and let meat warm in juices.

NOTE: Ketchup may be substituted for tomato paste. Meat can be prepared in advance and reheated. Veal brisket freezes well.

Yield: 6-8 servings.

Joyce Siegel

Veal Brisket #2

1 veal brisket
4-6 potatoes, peeled and
   quartered
12 ounces chili sauce (or
   barbeque sauce)

12 ounces ginger ale
¾ cup white wine
¼ package onion soup mix

Preheat oven to 350°. Put veal in roasting pan. Surround with potatoes. Mix together the remaining ingredients and pour over veal and potatoes. Cover pan and roast for 2 hours. Cool and slice.

NOTE: If desired, a can of butter beans may be added after 1½ hours of roasting.

Yield: 3-5 servings.

Sheila Guyer

 Always let roasted meats rest for 15 to 20 minutes for easier carving.

Veal Roast

2-3 pounds veal roast (brisket)
Salt and freshly ground pepper
**   to taste**
1 teaspoon rosemary

1 tablespoon olive oil
1 carrot, chopped
1 large onion, chopped
1 cup white wine

Season meat on all sides with salt, pepper, and rosemary. In hot skillet, brown meat in olive oil quickly on all sides. Place in covered roasting pan. In same skillet, sauté carrot and onion until soft. Add wine to deglaze pan and cook for a few minutes. Pour over veal. Place in preheated 375° oven and cook, covered, for 1½ hours. Remove from oven and let sit for 15 minutes before slicing. Serve with sauce on the side.

Yield: Serves 4-6 .   Helen Shevin

Veal Stew Accini

3 pounds stewing veal
1¼ cups flour, for dredging
⅛ teaspoon seasoned salt
⅛ teaspoon salt
2 teaspoons freshly ground
**   pepper**
3 teaspoons olive oil
2 medium onions, cut in half
**   and sliced**

1 bunch green onions, sliced
**   diagonally**
1 teaspoon thyme
½ cup fresh parsley
2 cups chicken broth
½ cup cold water

Combine flour, salts, and pepper in paper bag. Add veal and shake to coat, reserving flour. Brown veal in olive oil on all sides. Transfer meat and drippings to oven-safe casserole. Add sliced onions, green onions, thyme, parsley, and chicken broth. Cover and bake at 350° for 1 hour 20 minutes. Make a roux with cold water and reserved flour and add to casserole to thicken. Stir and heat through. Serve with noodles or any pasta.

Yield: 6 - 8 servings.   Claudia Gold

Veal Scallop Super Supper

1-2 pounds veal shoulder
   cutlets
2 tablespoons olive oil
2-3 tablespoons flour
2 teaspoons oregano
1 teaspoon basil

2 teaspoons onion powder
1 teaspoon pepper
1 (6-ounce) can tomato paste
⅓ cup red wine
½ cup chicken broth
½ pound mushrooms, sliced

Sauté veal in oil and remove from pan. Lower heat and add flour, oregano, basil, onion powder, and pepper. Blend with tomato paste until smooth. Add wine and chicken broth. Stir until blended. Return meat to pan and add mushrooms. Cover and cook for 10-15 minutes, until tender.

NOTE: Serve with wild rice pilaf and green salad.

Yield: 4 to 6 servings.

Carol Fogel

Easy Grilled Lamb with Mustard and Rosemary

3- 3½ pounds boneless leg of
   lamb, trimmed of fat

MARINADE:
3 large garlic cloves, minced
1 small onion, minced
⅔ cup light olive oil
¼ cup fresh lemon juice
2 tablespoons Dijon mustard
2 teaspoons mustard seed
   (optional)

Freshly ground pepper to taste
Salt to taste
1 tablespoon dried rosemary
Lemon, garnish

Combine marinade ingredients and pour into jumbo plastic bag. Add the lamb. Seal tightly. Marinate the meat for at least 12 hours and up to 2 days, turning the bag several times. Grill or broil for 15 minutes on each side.

NOTE: Shoulder of lamb can be substituted for leg.

Yield: Serves 6- 8.

Sally Mayer

Lamb with Plum Sauce

7-9 pounds leg of lamb (either
    lamb shanks or shoulder
    type cut can be substituted)
Salt and pepper
2 garlic cloves, minced
¾ teaspoon crumbled basil
1 (29-ounce) can purple plums
    in heavy syrup, drained,
    reserving syrup

3 tablespoons lemon juice
1½ tablespoons soy sauce
1½ tablespoons Worcestershire
    sauce

Place lamb, fat side up, on rack in shallow roasting pan. Season with salt, pepper, garlic, and basil. Roast in 325° oven for 3 to 3½ hours or until meat thermometer reads 175-180°. While meat is roasting, drain plums, reserving all of the syrup. Pit plums and put through a sieve. In saucepan, combine the reserved syrup, sieved plums, lemon juice, soy sauce, and Worcestershire sauce. Cook over low heat and simmer sauce until slightly thickened. After meat has roasted 1 hour, start basting with above sauce every ½ hour until lamb is glazed. Reserve half of the sauce to be passed separately.

Yield: Serves 8 - 10.

Miriam Tepper

Lamb Kabobs

2 pounds boneless lamb, cut
    into 1 inch cubes
Juice of 1 lime
Juice of 1 lemon
½ cup olive oil
1 garlic clove

3 tablespoons margarine
½ cup dry white wine
1 cup beef broth
A few mint leaves, chopped
A few tarragon leaves, chopped
Salt and pepper to taste

Thread lamb on 6 skewers. Combine juices, olive oil, and garlic in shallow pan. Turn to coat well. Cover and marinate 2-3 hours, turning often.

Melt 2 tablespoons margarine in a large skillet. Add brochettes, a few at a time, and cook until brown. Set aside and keep warm. Add white wine to pan and reduce it to a glaze. Add stock, mint, and tarragon. Reduce liquid to half. Add remaining tablespoon of margarine. Salt and pepper to taste and heat until margarine melts. Pour into blender and blend until smooth. Pour sauce on platter and arrange skewers over sauce.

Yield: Serves 6.

Rona Freedland

POULTRY

Charlotte's Apricot Chicken

2 fryers, cut up
Salt
Pepper
Paprika, enough to cover
  chicken

6 tablespoons margarine
3 tablespoons chives
3 tablespoons rosemary
Juice of 1 lemon
8 ounce jar apricot preserves

Line 11 x 17 inch shallow baking pan with foil. Arrange chicken in pan, skin side up. Sprinkle with salt, pepper, and paprika. In saucepan, heat margarine and blend in chives, rosemary, and lemon juice. Brush about 3 tablespoons onto chicken. Bake approximately 1 hour at 350°. Heat remainder of herb mixture and apricot preserves and brush all on chicken; cook for ½ hour longer or until done.

NOTE: Rice pilaf is a nice accompaniment.

Gayle Hirsch

Chicken and Oranges

1 clove garlic, crushed
3 tablespoons margarine,
  softened
3 whole chicken breasts, halved
1½ cups orange juice
½ cup chutney
½ cup raisins

1 tablespoon curry powder
½ teaspoon cinnamon
Pinch of nutmeg
1 (11-ounce) can mandarin
  oranges with juice
Salt and pepper to taste
1 banana, sliced

Combine garlic and margarine. Rub chicken breasts with mixture. Place in baking dish, skin side up. Bake in preheated 475° oven for 15 minutes.

While chicken is baking, combine orange juice, chutney, raisins, curry, cinnamon, nutmeg, and juice from mandarin oranges. Pour over baking chicken. Season with salt and pepper. Reduce heat to 325°. Bake chicken 1 hour, basting frequently. Before serving, add oranges and bananas. Return to oven until fruit is heated thoroughly. Serve immediately.

Edie Klein

Cranberry-Apricot Chicken

4 whole chicken breasts, split,
    skinned, and boned

MARINADE:

2 tablespoons Dijon mustard
1 teaspoon firmly packed brown
    sugar

2 tablespoons sliced green
    onions

Heat oven to 350°. Put chicken in 11 x 9 inch pan. Combine ingredients for the marinade and spread on the chicken. Bake, uncovered, for 20 minutes, turning occasionally.

SAUCE:

1 tablespoon cornstarch
1 tablespoon firmly packed
    brown sugar
1 (16-ounce) can whole berry
    cranberry sauce

1 (16-ounce) can apricot halves
    in extra light syrup, drained
    and reserve
½ cup apricot liquid

In a saucepan, combine the sauce ingredients including reserved ½ cup apricot liquid, and cook over medium heat, until thickened and bubbly. Spoon ½ cup of the sauce over the chicken in the oven. Bake for 20 minutes. Add the apricot halves and bake 10 minutes or until chicken is done. Arrange on a plate and spoon remaining sauce over the chicken.

Yield: Serves 4-6.   Rhoda Horton

Honey Mustard Chicken

¼ cup margarine, melted
6 tablespoons honey
3 tablespoons Dijon mustard

2 teaspoons curry powder
4 chicken breast halves

Preheat oven to 375°. Mix all ingredients except chicken. Pour mixture into a 9 x 13 inch pan and add chicken, coating with marinade. Bake for 1 hour, turning every 20 minutes. Serve on a bed of shredded lettuce.

Yield: Serves 4.   Helen Shevin & Frieda Langnas

Black Raspberry Glazed Chicken Breasts with Wild Rice and Almond Stuffing

CHICKEN:

8 halved chicken breasts
 (6-8 ounces), boned,
 skinned, and gently flattened

½ cup lemon juice
Salt and pepper to season
All-purpose flour for dusting

RICE STUFFING:

1 (7-ounce) box long grain and
 wild rice mix

2 cups chicken broth
½ cup toasted slivered almonds

Season chicken with lemon juice, salt, and pepper; set aside. Prepare the rice according to package directions, except substitute 2 cups chicken broth for the 2 cups water. When rice is tender and all the liquid is absorbed, stir in the almonds. Place one part stuffing in center of each half breast. Roll and secure with a wooden toothpick. Dust stuffed breasts lightly with flour. Place in a 9 x 13 inch baking pan. Bake at 325° for 40 minutes.

GLAZE:

½ cup seedless black raspberry
 jam
½ cup honey
2 tablespoons frozen orange
 juice concentrate, undiluted

1 teaspoon finely grated orange
 peel
2 tablespoons white wine

In a saucepan, heat all ingredients together and stir until blended.

After chicken has baked 40 minutes, baste with the glaze and continue baking and glazing until chicken is tender and highly glazed, about 30 minutes. (Baste 2 or 3 times during the final baking period). Remove toothpicks and serve.

NOTE: Recipe can be prepared earlier in the day, but shorten baking time by 10 minutes. Continue baking and glazing until just before ready to serve.

Yield: Serves 6-8.   Laurel Portner

Orange Honey Chicken

1 chicken, cut up
½ cup orange juice
¼ cup soy sauce
¼ cup ketchup
½ cup honey

1 teaspoon salt
1 teaspoon basil
½ teaspoon pepper
1 orange, sliced for garnish
Parsley for garnish

Preheat oven to 350°. Place chicken pieces in 9 x 12 inch baking pan. Mix remaining ingredients together and pour over chicken. Bake, uncovered, for 1 hour. To serve, place on platter and place slices of orange on the chicken and surround with sprigs of parsley.

Sarah Kier

Grilled Chicken with Tomato Topping

6 chicken breast halves,
    skinned and boned

MARINADE:

2 garlic cloves, minced
Juice of 1 lemon
2 tablespoons olive oil

2 teaspoons fresh rosemary
    leaves

In a glass or ceramic dish, combine garlic, lemon juice, 2 tablespoons oil, and rosemary. Place breasts in mixture side by side (do not overlap) creating a single layer. Place in refrigerator and marinate chicken for 2-3 hours. Broil or grill chicken on high heat until done. Serve chicken breasts with tomato mixture.

TOMATO TOPPING:

2 medium sized ripe tomatoes,
    chopped
4 tablespoons minced fresh
    basil
1 tablespoon capers

1 tablespoon Balsamic vinegar
2 tablespoons olive oil
Salt and freshly ground pepper
    to taste

Combine in separate bowl: tomatoes, basil, capers, vinegar, and remaining oil. Season to taste.

Yield: 4-6 servings.

Sherry Haffner

Pecan Chicken Breasts in Raspberry Sauce

Vegetable spray
1 cup bread crumbs
¼ cup chopped pecans

½ cup Dijon mustard
4 whole chicken breasts, split,
  skinned, and boned

Spray cookie sheet with vegetable oil. Combine bread crumbs and pecans. Brush breasts with mustard and dip in crumb mixture. Bake at 350° for 30-45 minutes.

SAUCE:

½ cup raspberry preserves

¼ cup raspberry vinegar

While chicken is baking, combine and warm sauce ingredients. Arrange chicken breasts on dinner plates and spoon sauce over.

Edie Klein & Marsha Zucker

Spiced Peaches and Chicken

1 cup flour seasoned with salt
  and pepper to taste
1-2 tablespoons oil for
  sautéeing
2-2½ pounds chicken, cut up
1 cup orange juice

2 cups sliced frozen peaches
2 tablespoons brown sugar
2 tablespoons white vinegar
1 teaspoon nutmeg
1 teaspoon basil
1 garlic clove, minced

Coat chicken with seasoned flour and brown in heated oil, browning both sides.

In a saucepan, combine orange juice, peaches, brown sugar, vinegar, nutmeg, basil, and garlic. Cook slowly for 10 minutes. Transfer chicken to casserole, pour sauce over and place in refrigerator. This may be done the night before. Prior to cooking, bring to room temperature. Place in 325° oven for about 40 minutes or until heated through.

NOTE: Boneless chicken breasts work as well.

Edie Klein

Grilled Chicken Dijonnais

MARINADE:

¼ cup oil
⅛ cup lemon juice
¼ teaspoon freshly ground
   pepper

3 whole chicken breasts, split,
   boned, and skinned

Combine oil, lemon juice, and pepper in a shallow dish. Swirl chicken in mixture to coat. Cover with plastic wrap and refrigerate for at least 30 minutes.

SAUCE:

3 tablespoons tarragon vinegar
2 tablespoons dry white wine
1 teaspoon tarragon
½ teaspoon freshly ground
   white pepper

4 tablespoons margarine
2 tablespoons Dijon mustard

Combine vinegar and wine in heavy small saucepan and boil over medium-high heat until liquid is reduced to about 2 tablespoons. Remove from heat and add tarragon and pepper. Whisk in margarine, one tablespoon at a time, blending well after each addition. Place over low heat and continue whisking until sauce has thickened slightly. Whisk in mustard. Set sauce aside and keep warm, but be careful that it doesn't separate.

Drain chicken well and grill over hot coals or under broiler, 3-4 minutes per side. Serve with sauce.

NOTE: Marinating the chicken this way tenderizes the meat. The chicken, without the sauce, is a wonderful addition to a salad.

Yield: 3-4 servings.   Wendy Wagenheim

Barbequed Chicken

2 to 3 frying chickens, cut into
  eighths
3 large onions, sliced

4 tablespoons margarine
2 cloves garlic, crushed

Sauté onions in margarine. Add garlic, and sauté until onions are golden brown.

SAUCE:

1 cup ketchup
½ cup water
¼ cup steak sauce
½ cup Worcestershire sauce

¼ cup white vinegar
¼ cup sugar or 3 tablespoons
  brown sugar
1 tablespoon salt (optional)

In a saucepan, combine ketchup, water, steak sauce, Worcestershire sauce, vinegar, and sugar. Add sautéed onions and garlic, and bring mixture to a boil. It will be quite tart. Place chicken parts in shallow pan. Pour sauce evenly over chicken, cover, and marinate 24 hours.

Next day, remove chicken to shallow baking pan, add small amount of marinade and bake uncovered at 350° for about 1 hour. Add more sauce if necessary, as it bakes, so chicken does not dry out.

Variation: Put chicken on hot grill and baste until done; or cook in oven for about ½ hour, then finish on the grill.

Yield: 10-12 servings.   Babette and Joyce Rubenstein

Baked Chicken Breasts with Wine and Mushrooms

3 whole chicken breasts, split,
  skinned, and boned
1 egg, beaten
1 cup seasoned bread crumbs
½ pound fresh mushrooms,
  sliced

1 cup chicken consommé
½ cup white wine
Slivered almonds for topping

Soak chicken in beaten egg and dip in bread crumbs. Put in baking dish and bake at 325° for ½ hour. Pour on mushrooms, consommé, and white wine. Bake, uncovered, another 40 minutes. Top with slivered almonds.

Yield: 3-4 servings.   Marilyn Levine

Dilled Lemon Chicken

4 small chicken breast halves,
  skinned and boned, about
  4 ounces each
½ cup flour
3 tablespoons margarine
½ cup chicken broth

1 tablespoon lemon juice
Salt and pepper to taste
2 lemon slices
1 tablespoon chopped fresh dill
2 tablespoons sliced scallions

Dredge chicken lightly in flour, shaking off excess. Heat margarine in a medium skillet until bubbling. Add chicken and sauté over medium heat until nicely browned, about 4 minutes per side. Pour excess margarine from pan and add broth, lemon juice, salt, and pepper. Arrange lemon, dill, and scallions on chicken, cover and simmer 8-10 minutes, or until chicken is cooked through. Remove chicken to a plate and keep warm under aluminum foil. Cook sauce, uncovered, just until slightly thickened. Return chicken to skillet, sprinkle with scallions, and serve immediately.

Yield: 2-3 servings.   Lauren Cohen

Lemon Barbequed Chicken

1 teaspoon grated lemon rind
1½ teaspoons salt
½ teaspoon dry mustard
½ teaspoon oregano
1 teaspoon Worcestershire
  sauce

½ cup lemon juice
½ cup salad oil
1 tablespoon chopped scallions
2 broiler-fryer chickens, halved
  or quartered

Mix together lemon rind, salt, dry mustard, oregano, and Worcestershire sauce in a small bowl. Gradually stir in lemon juice. Add oil and scallions. Pour over chicken in large bowl and marinate in refrigerator 2 hours. Remove chicken from marinade and place skin side down on hot grill. Grill 20 minutes or until lightly browned, brushing occasionally with marinade. Turn and grill another 15-20 minutes or until done.

Yield: 4-6 servings.   Rona Freedland

Chicken Piccata

4 whole chicken breasts, split
  and boned
¾ cup corn oil
1½ cups flour
3 eggs, beaten

Juice of 2 lemons
4 tablespoons margarine,
  melted
Dash of garlic powder
White pepper to taste

Flatten chicken breasts with mallet between waxed paper. Heat oil in skillet. Dredge chicken in flour and dip into beaten eggs. Brown quickly on both sides in hot oil. Remove and drain on paper towel. Place in one layer in baking dish. Pour lemon juice and melted margarine over chicken. Sprinkle with seasonings. Bake at 350° for 5 minutes.

NOTE: Serve with rice pilaf.

Yield: 6-8 servings.

Barbara Kuhlik

Chicken Breasts with Wine and Capers

4 whole chicken breasts, split,
  skinned, and boned (or with
  skin)
2 eggs, beaten
¾ cup Italian bread crumbs
1 garlic clove, chopped
  (optional)

½ cup olive oil
Juice of 1 lemon, divided
1 cup white wine, divided
½ cup capers
1 lemon, sliced thinly

Dip dry chicken breasts into eggs, then bread crumbs. Sauté garlic in 3 tablespoons olive oil, then put in chicken and brown, about 5 minutes per side, until done. While breasts are browning, add ½ of the lemon juice and ½ cup of the wine. Remove chicken and place into a baking dish. Add remaining wine and lemon to remaining olive oil. Use a wire whisk and beat the liquid until well blended. Pour over chicken. Cover and bake at 350° for 35 minutes. Uncover, and bake an additional 10 minutes. Sprinkle top of chicken with capers and garnish with thinly sliced lemon.

Yield: 6-8 servings.

Marsha Gordon

Mushroom Sherry Chicken

6 whole chicken breasts,
   skinless, boneless, and cut
   into bite-size pieces

1 cup flour, seasoned with
   garlic, pepper, and salt
2-3 tablespoons margarine

Coat chicken pieces in flour mixture. Brown in margarine and drain on paper towels. Put into a 9 x 13 inch glass baking dish.

SAUCE:

6 tablespoons unsalted
   margarine
¾ cup cooking sherry

2-3 tablespoons soy sauce
2 tablespoons lemon juice
½ teaspoon ginger

Bring ingredients for sauce to boil and pour over chicken. Cover and refrigerate until next day or until dinner.

TOPPING:

1 pound fresh mushrooms,
   sliced

When you are ready to bake, put mushrooms over top. Bake at 325° for 45 minutes or until tender. After about ½ hour, stir a little so everything will have sauce on it. Continue baking until done.

NOTE: Serve over rice pilaf.

Debbie Silber

Chicken Marsala

2 (8-ounce) chicken breasts,
   skinned and boned
Flour for dredging
2 tablespoons margarine
4 fresh mushrooms, sliced

2 small shallots or onions,
   chopped
½ cup marsala wine
½ cup chicken broth

Dredge chicken in flour lightly. Melt margarine in frying pan, add chicken, and brown on both sides. Add mushrooms and shallots and sauté with chicken. Add wine and chicken stock. Reduce liquid to ⅓. Remove chicken to platter and pour sauce on top.

Sandra Leshman

Grilled Lime Chicken and Salsa

4 chicken breasts with or
   without bones

MARINADE:

½ cup lime juice

¼ cup frozen apple juice
   concentrate

Marinate chicken in lime and apple juice for 1 hour.

SALSA:

6 plum tomatoes, chopped
½ cup spicy vegetable juice
4 scallions, diced

½ teaspoon hot sauce
1 teaspoon lime juice
½ cup chopped cilantro

Combine all salsa ingredients and allow to sit for 30 minutes. Grill chicken until done and serve with salsa on the side.

Penny Blumenstein

Mediterranean Chicken

½ cup olive oil
Juice of 1 lemon
1 tablespoon oregano
1 teaspoon paprika

1 teaspoon salt
¼ teaspoon pepper
1 chicken cut into eighths or
   4 whole chicken breasts

In a shallow baking dish, stir together olive oil, lemon juice, oregano, paprika, salt, and pepper. Place chicken in marinade, turning to coat. Let marinate one hour or can be marinated overnight. Place chicken in 350° oven, skin side up, for 1 hour. Baste occasionally with remaining marinade.

Variation: 1½ crushed garlic cloves can be added to the marinade. Potatoes can be added to pan and roasted with chicken.

Yield: 3-4 servings.

Susan Alterman & Coleen Tishlias

Chicken Fajitas

MARINADE:

1 clove garlic, minced
1 tablespoon vegetable oil
1½ tablespoons fresh lemon or
   lime juice

3 tablespoons Worcestershire
   sauce
⅛ teaspoon freshly ground
   black pepper

Combine garlic, oil, lemon or lime juice, Worcestershire sauce, and pepper in a bowl.

2 pounds chicken breasts,
   skinned and boned
2 teaspoons vegetable oil
1 large onion, sliced into ⅛ inch
   strips

1 large green pepper, sliced
   into ⅛ inch strips
8 corn or flour tortillas

Preheat broiler.

Cut chicken lengthwise into thin ⅜ inch strips. Add to marinade, toss to coat evenly, and let chicken marinate in refrigerate 10-20 minutes. Turn at least once.

Heat 2 tablespoons oil in a non-stick skillet. Add onions and peppers, sauté, stirring constantly, about 5 minutes or until onion is slightly brown.

Wrap tortillas in foil and heat in 300° oven.

Place chicken on broiling pan and broil about 3 inches from heat for 4 minutes.

To serve, place cooked chicken strips on each tortilla, top with onions, peppers, and assorted garnishes as desired.

NOTE: Salsa and guacamole make nice additions.

Lillian Chinitz

 Garlic Hint...Freeze whole garlic cloves in a closed container. When you need a clove, the skin will slip off intact.

Moroccan Chicken

12 chicken breast halves,
   skinned and boned
3 cloves of garlic, minced
½ cup olive oil
¾ cup raisins

1 cup Greek olives
1 lemon, thinly sliced
Juice of 1 lemon
Salt, pepper, paprika

Place chicken in roasting pan with garlic. Pour olive oil over chicken. Sprinkle with raisins and olives. Cover with sliced lemon and lemon juice. Sprinkle with salt, pepper, and paprika. Bake 45 minutes at 350°. Baste often.

Yield: Serves 6.

Sally Schottenfels

Filipino Chicken Adoba

1 frying chicken, cut into parts
½ cup soy sauce
¾ cup white vinegar
5-6 garlic cloves, crushed

3 bay leaves
½ tablespoon peppercorns
Salt to taste

Combine chicken parts together with soy sauce, vinegar, garlic, bay leaves, and peppercorns. Cover and bring to a boil. Simmer for 30 minutes. Skim fat. Remove chicken pieces from the pot and broil them in a pan until brown on both sides. Let the sauce boil in a pot until it is reduced by half and has thickened. Cover chicken with sauce and serve hot with rice.

Yield: Serves 6-8.

Nena Dillick

 To peel garlic...put clove(s) on a board and whack with the flat side of a heavy knife or bottom of a saucepan. Papery skin will lift off.

Shiny Chicken

2 packages chicken wings
    (approximately 24) or
    small drumsticks

SAUCE:

⅓-½ cup brown sugar or honey
4 garlic cloves, sliced
5 slices ¼ inch fresh ginger or
    1 teaspoon dried ginger

¾ cup soy sauce
⅓ cup sherry

Heat all sauce ingredients in skillet, to blend. Add cleaned, dried chicken pieces, turn to coat with sauce. Cook over low flame about 45 minutes until well glazed and tender.

NOTE: Amounts in sauce can vary with whim of the cook. This makes a good appetizer or an entrée with rice.

Yield: Serves 4-6.

Harriet Kanter

Szechuan Chicken Stir Fry

2 tablespoons soy sauce
1½ tablespoons white wine
    vinegar
1½ teaspoons sugar
4 chicken breast halves,
    skinned and cut into ½ inch
    pieces

3 tablespoons cornstarch
2 tablespoons vegetable oil
3 garlic cloves, minced
3 green onions, cut on diagonal
Freshly cooked rice

Combine first 3 ingredients in small bowl and set aside. Dredge chicken in cornstarch. Heat oil in wok or heavy skillet over medium-high heat. Add chicken and garlic and stir fry until chicken is opaque, about 5 minutes. Add soy sauce mixture and stir fry 30 seconds. Mix in green onions, stir another 30 seconds. Serve immediately with rice.

NOTE: An assortment of vegetables may also be added and should be stir-fried separately and added to the chicken before serving.

Sherry Haffner

Chicken Satay with Spicy Peanut Sauce

1¼ pounds chicken breasts,
    skinless and boneless
2 tablespoons sesame oil
2 tablespoons corn oil
¼ cup dry sherry
¼ cup soy sauce

2 tablespoons lemon juice
1½ teaspoons minced ginger
¼ teaspoon salt
¼ teaspoon pepper
Dash of hot sauce

Cut chicken into ½ x 3 inch strips. Combine with remaining ingredients and marinate in the refrigerator for 1-12 hours.

SATAY SAUCE:

4 teaspoons corn oil
2 teaspoons sesame oil
½ cup minced red onion
2 tablespoons minced garlic
1 teaspoon minced fresh ginger
1 tablespoon red wine vinegar
1 tablespoon brown sugar
⅓ cup peanut butter (chunky or
    smooth)

½ teaspoon ground coriander
3 tablespoons ketchup
3 tablespoons soy sauce
1 tablespoon lime or lemon
    juice
½ teaspoon pepper
Dash of hot sauce
⅓-½ cup hot water

Heat corn and sesame oils in a small saucepan. Add onion, garlic, and ginger and sauté over medium heat until softened. Add vinegar and sugar and continue to cook, stirring until sugar dissolves. Remove from heat and stir in remaining ingredients (or combine in a food processor for a completely smooth sauce).

Preheat oven to 375°. Thread each piece of chicken on a wooden tooth pick or small skewer. Arrange on baking sheet. Bake 5-10 minutes or until cooked. Serve hot with a bowl of room temperature sauce for dipping.

NOTE: Beef or lamb may substituted for the chicken. Sauce can be made in advance. If it thickens or separates, whisk in a little hot water until the sauce is the desired consistency.

Adrienne Gavern-Tomlinson

 To make fresh ginger root last longer and grate easily...wrap it, unpeeled, and freeze. Peel, if you wish, then grate while still frozen. Or thaw briefly and cut off a piece. Return unused portion to freezer.

Chinese Chicken

2 large chicken breasts, split,
    boned, and skinned
1 tablespoon naturally brewed
    soy sauce
1 tablespoon dry sherry
4 scallions, cut in 1 inch pieces
1 teaspoon fresh minced ginger
    or ½ teaspoon ground
    ginger

½ cup orange juice
2½ teaspoons cornstarch
¼ cup peanut oil
½ cup fresh snow peas
1 red pepper, cut into thin strips
½ cup chopped peanuts

Cut chicken into 1½ x ½ inch strips. In a medium size bowl, mix soy sauce, sherry, scallions, and ginger. Add chicken and toss well. Set aside. In a small bowl, combine orange juice and cornstarch; set aside. Heat oil in a large skillet or wok. Stir fry chicken with marinade until chicken loses its color, about 2 minutes. Add pea pods, red pepper, and peanuts and stir fry for 2 additional minutes. Stir orange juice mixture and add to chicken. Stir fry until slightly thickened. Serve immediately.

NOTE: Excellent over hot rice. Freezes well.

Yield: Serves 4.   Edith Zaffren

Indonesian Chicken

1-2 tablespoons sesame oil
1 medium onion, diced
1 small piece ginger root, diced
2 cloves fresh garlic, minced

1 fryer chicken, cut up, or 4
    chicken breasts, split
1 (13-ounce) can coconut milk
    or coconut flavoring

Heat sesame oil in a large frying pan. Sauté onion, ginger, and garlic. Add chicken, cooking until tender. Turn frequently while cooking. Last 5 minutes, add coconut milk to blend all flavors before serving.

Yield: Serves 4.   Harriet Abramowitz

145

Red Rice Jambalaya with Chicken

Vegetable cooking spray
4 chicken breast halves,
   skinned
1 cup diced onion
4 large garlic cloves, sliced
1 cup diced sweet pepper,
   divided
1 cup sliced green onions
2 (10½-ounce) cans ready-to-
   serve chicken broth

1 (8-ounce) can "no salt added"
   tomato sauce
½ teaspoon salt
¼ teaspoon red pepper
¾ teaspoon liquid smoke
1 bay leaf
1¾ cups long grain rice,
   uncooked

Coat a Dutch oven with cooking spray; place over medium heat until hot. Add chicken, meat side down; cover and cook 15 minutes. Turn chicken over and cook additional 15 minutes. Remove chicken from Dutch oven; let cool. Add onion, garlic, and half each of sweet red pepper and green onions; sauté until crisp-tender. Stir in chicken broth and remaining ingredients. Bring to a boil, cover, reduce heat, and simmer 20 minutes. Remove chicken from bone; shred. Add chicken and reserved sweet red pepper and green onions; toss gently and cook until thoroughly heated. Remove bay leaf. Serve with green salad.

Yield: 8 cups.

Carol Fogel

Chicken Kabobs

1 pound chicken breasts,
   skinned, boned, and cut into
   1 inch cubes
½ cup oil
Juice of 1 lemon

6 cloves of garlic, crushed
1 teaspoon salt
¼ teaspoon nutmeg
¼ teaspoon pepper
1 pound fresh mushrooms

In a bowl, mix together the oil, lemon juice, garlic, salt, nutmeg, and pepper. Add chicken and marinate for 1 hour. Remove chicken from marinade; reserve marinade. On each of 4 skewers, arrange chicken and mushrooms. Place skewers on grill over hot coals, about 8 inches from heat. Cook, turning and basting, about 30 minutes - or until fork can be inserted in chicken.

NOTE: Serve over rice pilaf.

Yield: Serves 4.

Joyce Rubenstein

Chicken Tabasco

12 small chicken breasts
Hot sauce, to spread on
chicken
¼ cup oil
1 large onion, chopped
¾ cup chopped celery
1½ tablespoons chopped
parsley
1½ tablespoons scallion tops,
chopped

1 clove garlic, minced
1 green pepper, finely chopped
1 teaspoon salt
½ teaspoon pepper
½ pound mushrooms
1 (6-ounce) can tomato paste
1½ cups water
½ teaspoon hot sauce
4 cups cooked rice

Rub each piece of chicken with hot sauce, using at least a drop on each side. Use additional hot sauce if desired. Brown in oil in heavy skillet. Remove chicken, then add onion, celery, parsley, scallion tops, garlic, green pepper, salt, and pepper to skillet. Mix well; cook 5 minutes, add mushrooms. Cook an additional 5 minutes, add tomato paste, water, and ½ teaspoon hot sauce. Mix well. Return the browned chicken to the skillet, cover, and cook until tender; about 40 minutes. Place chicken on platter, bordered with mounds of rice.

Yield: Serves 8.   Phyllis Schwartz

Crunchy Baked Chicken

2 cups fat-free French dressing
¼ cup finely chopped green
pepper (optional)
1 teaspoon chili powder,
divided

½ teaspoon onion powder
1½ cups cornflake crumbs
8 chicken breast halves,
skinned and boned

Preheat oven to 375°. Combine dressing, green pepper, ½ teaspoon chili powder, and onion powder in flat dish. Reserve ⅓ cup. Combine cornflake crumbs with ½ teaspoon chili powder in another flat dish. Dip chicken breast halves, first in dressing mixture, then in crumbs to coat evenly. Spray pan with non-stick vegetable coating. Arrange chicken in a single layer in the prepared pan. Bake for 15 minutes. Top the chicken with the ⅓ cup reserved dressing. Continue baking until done; approximately 15 more minutes.

NOTE: To reduce the number of servings, reduce amount of chicken only.

Yield: Serves 8.   Lorrie Isenberg

Crispy Potato Chicken

1 large potato, peeled
3-4 tablespoons Dijon mustard
1 large garlic clove, minced
2 whole chicken breasts,
  skinned and split

½-1 teaspoon olive oil or Italian
  dressing
Ground black pepper
Fresh parsley, rosemary or
  chives for garnish

Shred potato with grater or food processor. Transfer potato to bowl of ice water, let stand for 5 minutes.

Meanwhile in a small bowl, combine mustard and garlic, mix well. Rinse chicken and pat dry. Brush mustard mixture evenly on meaty side of chicken. Place chicken, bone side down, on foil lined baking sheet. Drain potatoes and dry thoroughly with paper towel. Place in a medium bowl and toss with oil or dressing to coat. Top each piece of chicken with ⅓ cup potato mixture in even layer to form skin. Sprinkle lightly with pepper. Bake in a 425° oven for 30-40 minutes or until chicken is no longer pink and potato shreds are golden. If potatoes are not browning, transfer pan to broiler and watch carefully. Garnish with fresh herbs. Serve immediately.

Yield: Serves 4.

Karol Moxley

Herbed Roast Chicken

1 (3½-5 pound) roasting
  chicken
Seasoned salt and pepper
1 lemon, cut in half

2 cloves garlic
1 large onion
2-3 tablespoons dried tarragon

Rub outside of chicken with cut lemon. Season chicken, inside and out. Fill cavity with cut lemon, garlic, onion, and tarragon. Heat oven to 450°. Place chicken in heavy Dutch oven and cover. Roast, covered, for 1 hour at 450°. Remove cover for the last 5 minutes. Skin should be crisp and brown.

Yield: Serves 3-4.

Sue Kaine

40 Clove Garlic Chicken

1-2 tablespoons olive oil
4 pounds chicken pieces with
   the bone, skinned
Salt and pepper, to season
40 large cloves of garlic,
   unpeeled
2 cups dry white wine

¼ teaspoon thyme
½ teaspoon rosemary
2-3 tablespoons cognac
½ cup chopped fresh parsley
12 (½ inch thick) slices coarsely
   grained bread, toasted

Preheat oven to 350°. Heat oil over medium heat in a heavy-bottomed skillet, season the chicken with salt and pepper and sauté on both sides for about 5 minutes each. Remove chicken.

To the skillet, add garlic, reserving several cloves, and sauté stirring for 3-5 minutes, until beginning to brown. Spread the cloves in a single layer in a heavy-bottomed, flameproof casserole and put the chicken pieces on top. Add the wine, thyme, and rosemary, and cover tightly. Place the casserole in oven and bake 45-60 minutes, or until chicken is very tender and fragrant.

Toast the bread slices in a 350° oven for about 10 minutes, or until lightly browned. Rub both sides of the bread with the cut side of the reserved garlic cloves. Set aside.

Remove casserole from oven. Pour cognac over chicken and light with a match. Shake the casserole until the flames die down. Taste the sauce, adjust the seasonings, and sprinkle with fresh parsley.

To serve, place 2 toasted garlic bread slices on each plate and top with one or two pieces of chicken, some of the sauce in the pan, and several garlic cloves, which your guests should squeeze out onto the bread.

Yield: Serves 6.   Laurel Portner & Wendy Wagenheim

Chicken Chili

1 pound chicken breasts, skinned, boned, and cut into 1 inch cubes
2 tablespoons corn oil
4 medium onions, coarsely chopped
2 large green peppers, coarsely chopped
3 large garlic cloves, minced
1 teaspoon ground cumin
1 teaspoon oregano
½ teaspoon ground coriander
½ teaspoon dried thyme

½ pound lean ground round (optional)
2 bay leaves
3 tablespoons chili powder
3 (one pound) cans tomatoes, undrained
2 tablespoons tomato paste
Salt and freshly ground pepper
Fresh lemon juice
1 cup plain lowfat yogurt
1 small avocado, diced
½ cup minced fresh cilantro or Italian parsley

Wrap chicken and freeze until firm, but not solid. Grind coarsely in food processor, using on/off turns. Heat oil in large heavy pot or Dutch oven over medium-high heat. Add onions, pepper, and garlic. Cook until golden, stirring frequently, about 15 minutes. Mix in cumin, oregano, coriander, and thyme. Stir 2 minutes. Add chicken, ground beef, and bay leaves. Cook until meat and chicken are not pink, about 5 minutes. Add chili powder. Reduce heat to medium, cook 5 minutes, stirring frequently. Add tomatoes, breaking up with spoon. Mix in tomato paste, salt, and pepper. Reduce heat, cover, and simmer 45 minutes. Stir occasionally. Uncover, reduce heat to lowest setting. Cook 1½ hours. Stir frequently near end. Add water if necessary. Adjust seasoning.

To serve, ladle chili into large soup bowls. Sprinkle with lemon juice. Spoon 2 tablespoons yogurt in center of each; top with avocado and minced cilantro.

Yield: Serves 8.

Penny Blumenstein

 Freeze leftover tomato paste…in ready-to-use amounts by dropping tablespoonsful on waxed paper, freezing until firm, peeling off paper and popping into a freezer container.

Tex-Mex Chicken Stew

3 whole chicken breasts, split, skinned, and boned
1 cup chopped onion
1 medium green pepper, chopped
2 cloves garlic, minced
2 tablespoons vegetable oil
2 (14½-ounce) cans stewed tomatoes
1 (15½-ounce) can pinto beans
⅔-¾ cup picante sauce, as desired
1 teaspoon chili powder
1 teaspoon ground cumin
½ teaspoon salt
Optional toppings: green onion slices, diced avocado

Cut chicken into 1 inch pieces. Cook chicken, onion, green pepper, and garlic in oil in Dutch oven until chicken loses its pink color. Add remaining ingredients. Simmer 20 minutes. Ladle into bowls. Add toppings.

NOTE: Serve over rice or pasta. Freezes well.

Yield: Serves 6-8.   Joyce LaBan

Edie's Turkey Meatballs with Sauce

1½ pounds fresh ground turkey
⅓ cup seasoned bread crumbs
½ cup finely chopped onions
½ teaspoon garlic salt or powder
1 tablespoon cooking oil
1 tablespoon margarine
2 cups prepared spaghetti sauce

Mix turkey, bread crumbs, onion, and garlic salt or powder. Shape into 1 inch meatballs. Heat oil and margarine in large skillet over medium-high heat until hot. Cook meatballs until brown, drain. Add spaghetti sauce. Bring to a boil; reduce heat. Cover and simmer until meatballs are no longer pink; 10-12 minutes. Serve over cooked pasta.

Yield: Serves 5.   Joyce Sherman

Tacchino Tonnato

TURKEY WITH TUNA SAUCE:

1 (3-4 pound) turkey breast with skin and bone
2 (7-ounce) cans white meat tuna, packed in oil, undrained
1 large onion, sliced
10 anchovy filets
½ large dill pickle, sliced
2 cloves garlic, sliced
4 stalks celery with leaves, sliced
1 medium carrot, sliced
Pinch of thyme
Few sprigs parsley
2 cups dry white wine
1 cup olive oil
Chicken stock to cover
2-3 cups mayonnaise
Juice of one lemon
Salt and pepper to taste
2-3 tablespoons capers, well drained
Cooked rice with parsley

In a heavy saucepan, place turkey breast, tuna, oil from tuna cans, onions, anchovies, pickle, garlic, celery, carrot, thyme, and parsley. Add wine, olive oil, and stock. Bring to a boil. Cover pan and lower heat to simmer gently until turkey is tender; 1½ to 2 hours.

Let turkey cool and refrigerate in juices overnight. The following day remove breast and skim off fat from pan. Place the sauce in a blender and blend until smooth. Add mayonnaise until the sauce is the consistency of coffee cream. Add lemon juice, salt, and pepper, if necessary.

Discard skin and carve turkey breast. To serve, mound parsleyed rice on a large platter. Arrange turkey slices overlapping. Spoon sauce over meat. Sprinkle with capers. Pass remaining sauce separately.

Yield: Serves 8-10.

Rona Freedland

Indonesian Grilled Turkey

1 turkey breast half, boned
  (2½-3 pounds)
½ cup chunky peanut butter
½ cup teriyaki sauce
¼ cup lemon juice
¼ cup vegetable oil

2 teaspoons ground ginger
2 teaspoons sweet basil
2 teaspoons onion powder
2 teaspoons garlic powder
¼-½ teaspoon crushed red
  pepper

Place turkey in plastic bag. Combine remaining ingredients in food processor or blender. Process until smooth. Reserve ½ cup sauce. Pour remaining sauce over turkey, turning to coat evenly. Marinate in refrigerator 30 minutes. Place turkey on grill, set over drip pan with 2 inches of water. Arrange coals around drip pan. Grill, covered, over medium-high coals, or bake, uncovered, at 400° for 1 to 1½ hours. Baste with marinade occasionally. Carve and serve with sauce.

Yield: Serves 8.

Stuart Freedland

Wine Basted Turkey

10-12 pound turkey

BASTING SAUCE:

1½ cups dry red wine
½ cup margarine, melted
1 tablespoon lemon juice
1 tablespoon chopped fresh
  chives

1 tablespoon chopped fresh
  parsley
¼ teaspoon marjoram
¼ teaspoon thyme

Prepare turkey as usual for roasting. Mix together ingredients for basting sauce. Baste every ½ hour until done. Drain excess fat from basting sauce and serve hot with turkey.

NOTE: ½ cup of chicken broth can be substituted for margarine.

Joyce Rubenstein

Cider-Glazed Escallopes of Turkey Breast

1 small or ½ large fresh turkey
   breast, skinned
½ cup smooth Dijon mustard
¼ cup canola oil
Coarsely ground black pepper
1 bay leaf

½ cup apple cider
¾ cup de-fatted chicken stock
8 Delicious apples (4 red & 4
   yellow), cored, and cut into
   rings or wedges

Preheat oven to 475°. Combine mustard and canola oil and smear all over the turkey breast. Shake the pepper evenly all over (amount of pepper, your choice). Place the turkey on a rack on a baking sheet. On the bottom of the baking sheet place the bay leaf, cider, and de-fatted chicken stock. Place in the oven and roast for about 20 minutes. Reduce heat to 325° and cook for approximately another 45 minutes (check for doneness), basting periodically with pan liquids. Ten minutes before it is completely cooked, add the apple pieces to the bottom of the pan to cook. When done, remove turkey and cut into an equal number of scallops with a serrated knife. Place on a warmed platter. Remove the cooked apple juices and garnish turkey with them. Remove bay leaf from the pan juices, place juices in gravy boat, and serve with Escallopes of Turkey.

NOTE: Make chicken stock using chicken pieces that have been skinned and have had all fat removed.

Yield: 6-8 servings.

Elwin Greenwald

 To clarify broths, consommé or used oils or fats...let them drip through a coffee filter fitted into a funnel.

FISH

Baked Fish with Vegetables

3 pounds whitefish or trout,
   boned and cut into 6 pieces
3 carrots, sliced
Salt, pepper, and paprika to
   taste

1 tablespoon butter or
   margarine

Preheat oven to 350°. Arrange carrot slices on greased, large baking pan. Rinse fish and dry with paper towels. Place fish on carrots. Season with salt, pepper, and paprika. Dot with butter or margarine. Bake in oven while preparing sauce.

SAUCE:

1 large rib of celery, chopped
2 medium onions, chopped fine
½ green pepper, chopped
2 tablespoons butter or
   margarine

1 (10¾-ounce) can tomato soup,
   diluted with one can of water

Sauté celery, onions, and green pepper in butter or margarine until soft. Add diluted tomato soup; bring to a boil. Pour sauce over fish and continue baking for a total cooking time of 1 hour, until fish is cooked through.

NOTE: Small whole potatoes and/or fresh green beans may be placed around fish before adding sauce.

Yield: Serves 6.

Rebecca Fineman

Marinated Cold White Fish

1 whitefish, 2⅓ to 3 pounds
1 (8-ounce) bottle French
   dressing

Parsley for garnish

Fillet whitefish. Place the pieces in a 9 x 13 inch glass oven-safe dish. Cover with bottle of French dressing. Wrap in foil or plastic wrap and marinate overnight. The following day, pour off the dressing from the fish. Wash and dry the dish, then spray the dish with vegetable spray. Place fish in a dish. Bake 45 minutes at 350°. Refrigerate fish until cold. Before serving, remove skin. Garnish with parsley.

Yield: Serves 4.

Hermine Silver

Broiled Soy Halibut Steaks

2 pounds halibut steaks
3 tablespoons soy sauce
1 teaspoon ground ginger
½ teaspoon garlic powder
1 teaspoon grated lemon peel

¼ cup lemon juice
¼ cup water
Lemon slices
Parsley

Place fish in ungreased rectangular baking dish, 13 x 9 x 2 inch. Mix remaining ingredients, except lemon slices and parsley; pour onto fish. Cover and refrigerate at least 8 hours. Drain fish, reserve marinade. Place fish on greased, or vegetable sprayed, broiler rack. Broil fish with tops 4 inches from heat, brushing occasionally with reserved marinade; 5-7 minutes on each side. Garnish with lemon slices and parsley.

NOTE: Salmon steaks may be substituted for halibut.

Yield: 6 servings. Fran Cook

Fillet of Sole a la Erdle

6 fillets of sole (2 pounds)
1 teaspoon salt
⅛ teaspoon fresh ground
   pepper
⅛ teaspoon mace
⅛ teaspoon thyme
½ cup dry Vermouth

2 tablespoons lemon juice
2 tablespoons melted butter
1 tablespoon minced chives
2 tablespoons minced onions
24 mushroom caps
Chopped parsley for garnish
Lemon quarters for garnish

Preheat oven to 325°. Combine salt, pepper, mace, thyme, and sprinkle on both sides of fillets. Place fish in buttered, oven-proof skillet. Combine Vermouth, lemon juice, butter, and pour over fish. Sprinkle with chives and onions. Place mushrooms on and around the fish. Cover pan and bring to a boil very slowly over heat. Immediately uncover pan and place in oven. Bake 15 minutes, basting often. Garnish with parsley and lemon quarters.

Yield: Serves 6. Terran Leemis

Sole Goujonettes with Tartar Sauce

MAYONNAISE:

1 whole egg
1 tablespoon freshly squeezed
    lemon juice
1 tablespoon tarragon vinegar

⅛-¼ teaspoon cayenne pepper
¼ teaspoon dry mustard
¼ teaspoon salt
1 cup vegetable oil

Put everything, except oil, in a food processor. Turn on machine and add oil a few drops at a time until mixture thickens. Continue adding rest of oil in a slow, steady stream, until combined. Store in refrigerator.

TARTAR SAUCE:

1 cup mayonnaise
1½ teaspoons Dijon mustard
1 tablespoon finely chopped
    scallions, white part only
1 teaspoon finely chopped
    capers
⅓ cup finely chopped
    cornichons (sour gherkins)

1 tablespoon finely chopped dill
1 tablespoon finely chopped
    parsley
½ teaspoon salt
¼ teaspoon freshly ground
    white pepper

Mix all ingredients together and store in refrigerator until needed (up to 2-3 days).

SOLE GOUJONETTES:

Dash of cinnamon
1 cup flour
1 teaspoon salt
¼ teaspoon freshly ground
    white pepper
1½ pounds fillet of Sole cut into
    ½ inch slices

3 egg whites, slightly beaten
1 cup Japanese bread crumbs
    (available in Oriental food
    markets)
Vegetable oil for frying
1 bunch of fresh dill

Mix cinnamon, flour, salt, and pepper together and sift into a plastic bag. Toss fish slices in a bag with flour mixture. Remove from the bag and dip fish in egg whites. Roll in bread crumbs. Place 3 inches of oil in an iron skillet or wok and heat to 360°. Fry fish in small batches until golden and drain on paper toweling. Place fish on a bed of washed, dried dill and serve hot or warm with tartar sauce.

Kari Izu

Fish in the Style of Tangiers

2 tablespoons olive oil
2 tablespoons peanut oil
1 tablespoon sweet paprika
½ teaspoon fresh ground black
 pepper
¼ teaspoon cayenne, optional
1 teaspoon ground cumin
3 garlic cloves, crushed
¼ cup chopped fresh parsley
¼ cup chopped fresh cilantro

Salt to taste
1 whole fish (3½ pounds) or
 2 pounds of steaks
1½ pounds potatoes, pared and
 sliced thick
1 medium onion, sliced thin
1 medium ripe tomato, peeled,
 seeded, and sliced
1 lemon, sliced thin
½ cup water

Preheat oven to 375°. Blend oils and seasonings together. Coat surface and cavity of fish with this paste and let sit for 1 hour. Oil a baking dish big enough to hold fish in a single layer. Layer potatoes and onion in dish. Add water, cover with foil, and bake 30 minutes. Remove from oven, place fish on top of vegetables. Put lemon and tomato slices on and around fish. Add more water if necessary. Bake, uncovered, 35-45 minutes, basting 3-4 times.

NOTE: Any firm-fleshed fish can be used; swordfish is good if using steaks.

Yield: Serves 4-6.   Harriet Kanter

Grilled Fish

2 pounds firm-fleshed fish, for
 grilling
½ cup oil
½ cup toasted sesame seeds
Juice of 2-3 lemons

3 tablespoons soy sauce
1 garlic clove, crushed
1 teaspoon salt
¼ cup sherry or brandy,
 optional

Mix all ingredients together in a glass baking dish large enough to hold fish. Place fish in dish with sauce and marinate for one hour, turning once. Grill until done (about 8 minutes), basting generously. Remaining sauce can be used with fish.

Yield: Serves 6-8.   Elizabeth Cohen

Italian No-Dish Delicious Fish

4 fillets of whitefish
1 Bermuda onion, sliced thin
1 large tomato, sliced
1 (6-ounce) can tomato paste
1 (6-ounce) can tomato-
    vegetable juice

No-salt seasoning
Oregano to taste
Black pepper to taste

Preheat oven to 350°. Place each fillet on large square of foil. Layer with slices of tomato and onion. Cover with tomato paste thinned with juice. Season well. Fold foil into packet and seal edges tightly. Bake for 30 minutes, or cook over grill for 10-15 minutes per side.

Yield: Serves 4.

Andrea Asarch

Ann Schuman's Salmon Loaf Soufflé

¼ cup margarine or butter
3 carrots, peeled and sliced
3 eggs, or 6 egg whites, divided
1 white or yellow onion, cut into
    pieces
1 (16-ounce) can salmon,
    drained and boned

½ cup milk (2% or regular)
½ cup bread crumbs
½ teaspoon summer savory
Salt and pepper to taste

Preheat oven to 350°. Melt margarine or butter in loaf pan and coat sides. Put cut carrots and 2 eggs (or 4 egg whites) in blender and grate. After 20 seconds, add another egg (or egg whites) and onion and finish grating. Add this mixture to the other ingredients which have been stirred together in a large bowl. Mix well and pour into loaf pan. Bake 45 to 60 minutes until golden on top.

NOTE: Non-stick vegetable spray can be used instead of butter to coat the pan.

Yield: Serves 6-8.

Lorelei Cohen

Chilled Poached Salmon with Dill Yogurt Sauce

6 salmon steaks
4 cups white wine
4 cups water
2 bay leaves
1 teaspoon thyme
¼ cup fresh parsley, chopped
    with stems

1 cup finely chopped celery
1 cup finely chopped carrots
½ cup finely chopped onions
¼ teaspoon black pepper

Combine white wine, water, bay leaves, thyme, parsley, celery, carrots, onions, and pepper in a fish poacher or covered casserole. Bring to a full boil, cover, and boil for 15 minutes, then reduce to a low simmer. Place salmon steaks on poaching rack. Insert the poacher and cover. Poach for 10-12 minutes, depending on thickness. Remove salmon from poacher and chill.

DILL YOGURT SAUCE:

1 cup low-fat yogurt
1 tablespoon finely chopped
    fresh dill

¼ teaspoon finely chopped
    fresh thyme
¼ teaspoon white pepper

Drain off excess water from yogurt, fold in spices, and chill.

NOTE: This recipe can be used to poach a whole butterflied salmon or trout.

Yield: Serves 6.   Amy Freedland

Baked Salmon

4 salmon steaks
¼ cup non-fat yogurt
4 tablespoons margarine,
    melted

2 tablespoons stoneground or
    Dijon mustard
2 tablespoons capers

Preheat oven to 425°. Coat salmon steaks with yogurt. Blend margarine with mustard and capers. Brush on salmon steaks, both sides. Place salmon in baking pan and bake 10 minutes. Place under the broiler and brown.

Yield: Serves 4.   Audrey Saperstein

Grilled Salmon with Almond Baste

2 pounds fresh salmon fillets
1 cup slivered almonds
5 tablespoons butter or
    margarine

⅓ cup grated onion
2 tablespoons soy sauce
1 lemon

Preheat grill. Toast slivered almonds. Chop almonds and set aside. Melt, but do not brown, butter or margarine in skillet and sauté grated onion. Remove from heat and stir in almonds and soy sauce until well mixed. Place basting sauce into small bowl and set aside. Rinse salmon, with skin on, and pat dry. Cut fish into serving size pieces and place on platter. Squeeze lemon juice over salmon and let sit ½ hour. Place salmon on preheated grill, skin side up for approximately 5 minutes. When fish is firm, turn and spread almond baste over entire meat side of salmon. When skin side is cooked, remove and serve.

Yield: Serves 4.

Mel Goldstein

Grilled Salmon with Vegetables

4 salmon fillets
Salt and pepper to taste
1 medium zucchini, sliced thin
2 medium tomatoes, chopped

Juice of 1 lemon
4 tablespoons Parmesan
    cheese

Place each salmon fillet on an individual sheet of aluminum foil. Sprinkle with salt and pepper. Top each fillet with sliced zucchini and chopped tomatoes. Sprinkle each piece with lemon juice and Parmesan cheese. Seal salmon in foil. Grill for 8-12 minutes or bake at 450° for 15-20 minutes.

NOTE: This can be prepared early in the day and kept in the refrigerator until ready to grill. After grilling, remove fish from foil by placing spatula between flesh and skin.

Yield: 4 servings.

Wendy Wagenheim

 To test fish for doneness, probe gently into the thickest part of the fish to see if the flesh separates and falls easily into its natural divisions.

Karen's Brown Sugar Baked Salmon

6 salmon steaks, 1 inch thick,
or a 2 pound salmon fillet

MARINADE:

¼ cup brown sugar
2 tablespoons melted butter
3 tablespoons soy sauce

2 tablespoons fresh lemon juice
2 tablespoons dry white wine or
water

In a small bowl, combine all marinade ingredients. Place salmon steaks or fillet on foil-covered baking pan that holds fish snugly in one layer. Pour marinade over fish. Cover and marinate in refrigerator for 30 minutes to 6 hours. Uncover pan. Place on middle rack of preheated 400° oven. Bake 15-20 minutes or until fish is done, basting every 5 minutes. Serve immediately.

Yield: Serves 6.   Rosie Schlussel

Stuffed Baked Salmon

3-4 pounds whole salmon,
butterflied and boned

STUFFING:

3 tablespoons oil
1 apple, peeled, cored and
sliced
¼ cup minced onions
½ cup cooked rice
¼ cup raisins

¼ cup unsweetened shredded
coconut
1 clove garlic, crushed
Dash of hot pepper sauce
¼-½ teaspoon curry powder

Heat oil in heavy saucepan. Sauté onion and apple until soft. Combine rest of ingredients, except fish. Stuff fish by laying filling on one side of fish. Cover with the other side and sew both sides together. Bake 10 minutes per inch thickness (stuffed).

Yield: Serves 4-6.   Rona Freedland

Salmon En Papillote

1½ pounds skinless, boneless salmon fillets, preferably the tail end, cut into 4 pieces of equal size
4 carrots (¾ pound)
½ pound fresh mushrooms
2 tablespoons butter
Juice of ½ lemon
½ cup scallions, cut into 2 inch lengths

Salt to taste
1 tablespoon fresh tarragon, finely chopped
8 teaspoons shallots, finely chopped
4 teaspoons dry white wine
Freshly ground pepper to taste
6 tablespoons melted butter or oil, for greasing foil

Preheat oven to 525° or as high as possible, and heat baking sheet for 5 minutes. Holding knife at an angle, cut salmon into very thin slices (as if you were slicing smoked salmon). Lay out a length of heavy-duty foil or parchment paper and cut 4 rounds, using a 12-inch round baking dish as outline.

Scrape and trim carrots and cut crosswise into 1 inch lengths. Cut each length into thin slices. Stack the slices and cut into match-like sticks, yielding approximately 3 cups. Remove mushroom stems. Cut caps crosswise into thin slices. Heat 2 tablespoons butter in saucepan. Add mushrooms, sprinkle with lemon juice. Cook, shaking and stirring, for 1 minute. Add carrots, scallions, and salt. Cover and cook 7-8 minutes. Add tarragon and stir. Cover and set aside.

Brush each round of foil or paper with butter or oil. Spoon equal portion of vegetable mixture slightly off center, leaving ample margin for folding over. Cover vegetable mixture with slices of raw salmon, leaving them slightly overlapping, but making a compact roll that just covers the vegetables. Sprinkle each serving with 2 teaspoons shallots and 1 teaspoon wine. Sprinkle with salt and pepper.

Fold over each round of foil or paper to completely enclose filling. Fold and pleat the margins over and over to seal filling as tightly as possible. Arrange packages on preheated baking sheet. Place in oven and bake 7 minutes.

NOTE: This may be prepared early in the day. Even though the directions are long, this is a very simple recipe. Salmon will slice easier if slightly frozen.

Yield: Serves 4.   Penny Blumenstein

Steamed Salmon with Yogurt Dill Sauce

3 tablespoons prepared yellow
   mustard
1 tablespoon Dijon mustard
½ cup plain lowfat yogurt
2 tablespoons olive oil
1 tablespoon chopped fresh dill
¼ cup chopped scallions

Freshly ground black pepper
1 tablespoon white wine
   vinegar
16 springs fresh dill
4 salmon steaks (6 ounces
   each)

Put the mustards, yogurt, olive oil, chopped dill, scallions, pepper, and vinegar in a small saucepan. Blend well with a whisk. Press 2 sprigs of dill onto the bottom of each salmon steak. Place the salmon in a steamer and press 2 more sprigs of dill on top of each steak. Cover, bring the water in the bottom of the steamer to a boil, and steam for about 6 minutes. The fish is done when the bone in the center loosens. Turn the heat off and let the fish rest in a covered steamer for 3 minutes.

Gently heat the sauce until it is warmed through. Transfer the fish to serving plates. Remove the bone and peel away the skin. Serve the fish with the sauce.

NOTE: Presentation: Spoon the sauce all around the fish, but not over it. Place a small boiled potato at the closed end of the fish. Alongside the fish, place 2-3 pieces of cucumber, shaped and cut into 1½ inch lengths.

Yield: 4 servings.   Penny Blumenstein

Steamed Fish with Black Bean Sauce

2-3 fish fillets (sole, snapper,
   orange roughy)
5 slices fresh ginger root,
   peeled and chopped
2 green onions, chopped

2 cloves garlic, chopped
2 tablespoons fermented black
   beans, chopped
2 tablespoons vegetable oil
5 tablespoons sherry

Place fish on a pie plate and top with remaining ingredients. Bring 12 ounces water to a boil in wok. Place steaming rack in wok or place a saucer upside down in wok and place pie plate with fish on top of it. Cover and steam 10 minutes or until ready. Place in serving dish and pour sauce over it. Serve with rice.

NOTE: The more you chop the soft black beans, the richer the sauce.

Yield: Serves 2.   Beth Hirsch

Braised Sea Bass with Ginger and Scallions

1½ pounds sea bass, cleaned
and slashed diagonally at ¼
inch intervals on both sides
1 teaspoon salt
2 tablespoons flour or
cornstarch
4 tablespoons vegetable oil
2 tablespoons light soy sauce
2 tablespoons medium-dry
sherry

¾ cup chicken broth
1 teaspoon cornstarch
Freshly ground black pepper
6 scallions, cut into 1 inch
pieces
3 slices peeled ginger, finely
julienned
1 tablespoon hot Oriental chili
sauce or more (optional)
Coriander leaves for garnish

Rub salt inside and outside of fish. Coat outside with flour. Heat wok over high heat and add oil until very hot. Add fish and lower heat, frying both sides until golden brown, about 2-3 minutes. Remove fish from wok. Mix soy, sherry, stock, cornstarch, and freshly ground pepper (to taste) together. Increase wok temperature and add ginger and scallions. Stir for a few seconds, add sauce mixture, and stir. Add chili sauce, if desired, and return fish to wok for a few minutes until fish is cooked. Place fish on a platter and pour sauce over it. Garnish with coriander.

Kari Izu

Grilled Tuna, Thai Style

¼ cup peanut oil
4 garlic cloves, finely chopped
3 tablespoons finely minced
fresh peeled ginger root
3 tablespoons light soy sauce
2 tablespoons Thai fish sauce
1 tablespoon Szechuan chili
paste

2 tablespoons sugar
16 (1-inch square) pieces fresh
tuna (or other firm fish)
⅔ cup coarsely chopped,
roasted peanuts (unsalted
preferred)

Combine first seven ingredients in a glass or stainless steel bowl. Add the tuna pieces and gently mix so all the pieces are covered. Cover and refrigerate mixture for about 1 hour, stirring once or twice during this period.

Thread tuna on small wooden or metal skewers. Grill on a preheated grill just until the tuna is medium-rare. Immediately take off the grill, roll in nuts, and serve.

Yield: Serves 4.

Beth Hirsch

SAUCES & MARINADES

Herbs for No Salt Diet

#1-ALL-PURPOSE MIX:

½ teaspoon cayenne pepper
1 tablespoon garlic powder

1 teaspoon each: basil, thyme, mace, onion powder, black pepper, sage, parsley, and savory

#2-FOR VEGETABLES AND MEAT:

1 teaspoon thyme
1 teaspoon marjoram

¾ teaspoon rosemary
½ teaspoon sage

#3-FOR VEGETABLES, MEAT & POULTRY:

¾ teaspoon marjoram
½ teaspoon thyme
½ teaspoon oregano

½ teaspoon sage
½ teaspoon rosemary

#4-FOR MEAT, POTATOES & VEGETABLES:

1 teaspoon dry mustard
½ teaspoon sage

½ teaspoon thyme
¼ teaspoon marjoram

#5-FOR FISH:

¾ teaspoon parsley flakes
½ teaspoon onion powder
½ teaspoon sage (dill may be substituted)

¼ teaspoon marjoram
¼ teaspoon paprika

Use a spice grinder or blender to process each mix.

Fanya Green

Spicy Mustard Sauce

⅓-½ cup dry mustard
½ cup white vinegar

½ cup sugar
1 egg yolk

Combine mustard and vinegar in small bowl. Cover and let stand at room temperature overnight. In small saucepan, combine mustard-vinegar mixture, sugar, and egg yolk. Simmer over low heat until slightly thickened. Cover and store in refrigerator for up to one month. Serve at room temperature.

NOTE: Good with egg rolls, spinach balls, and cocktail franks.

Yield: 1⅓ cups.

Edie Klein

Vic's Barbeque Sauce

¼ cup oil
1 medium onion, finely chopped
½ cup water
¼ cup wine vinegar
¼ cup Worcestershire sauce
¼ cup honey
⅛ cup liquid smoke
⅛-¼ teaspoon chili powder
1 teaspoon salt

¼-1 teaspoon black pepper
1 tablespoon dry mustard
1 cup brown sugar
½ teaspoon hot sauce
2 tablespoons prepared
    mustard
25 ounces ketchup
24 ounces tomato juice

In a 3-quart saucepan, heat oil and add onion. Sauté until onions are clear. Add all ingredients, except ketchup and tomato juice, and simmer for at least 30 minutes. Add ketchup and juice and continue simmering for at least one more hour. Take your time—your reward will come.

NOTE: You can play with the amounts of chili powder, black pepper, dry mustard, and brown sugar, according to taste.

Vic Hirsch

Melon Salsa for Grilled Fish or Chicken

2 tablespoons water
¼ cup peanut oil
6 dried apricots, diced ¼ inch
½ large red onion, diced ¼ inch
2 dried hot red chili pods
    (discard seeds), crumbled
    (or ½ teaspoon dried red
    pepper flakes)
½ cup red pepper, diced ¼ inch

½ cup honeydew, diced ¼ inch
½ cup cantaloupe, diced ¼ inch
1 mango, diced ¼ inch
    (optional)
⅔ cup additional cantaloupe if
    omitting the mango
juice of 2 limes
2 tablespoons chopped fresh
    cilantro (optional)

Combine first five ingredients in small saucepan; cover and cook over medium heat for five minutes. Add diced red pepper; cover and cook for another 5 minutes. Everything should remain crisp. Let this mixture cool in a bowl while preparing the fruit. When cool, mix all ingredients together. Serve cold as a side salsa with grilled or poached fish or chicken.

NOTE: Best when eaten on the day it is made, or refrigerate for up to three days.

Yield: 2 cups.

Anita Sudakin

Currant-Mustard Marinade

½ cup currant jelly

4 tablespoons Dijon mustard

Whisk until blended or put in blender. Particles will separate within 10-15 minutes. Keeps well in refrigerator.

NOTE: This is especially good with chicken.

Laurel Portner

Chili Sauce for the Tomato Gardener

50 tomatoes
10 large yellow onions, chopped
1 bunch of celery, chopped
5 hot red peppers, chopped
5 medium green peppers, chopped
3 garlic cloves, chopped
1 tablespoon powdered cumin
1 teaspoon nutmeg

1 tablespoon powdered allspice
1 tablespoon powdered cloves
2 tablespoons powdered mustard
4 cups white sugar
½ cup salt
4 cups cider vinegar
2 small cans or 1 large can of tomato paste

Peel, seed, and squeeze excess liquid from tomatoes. Put the spices in a cheese cloth bag. Put all ingredients in a large pot. Add salt, sugar, and vinegar. Bring to a boil. Boil for several hours until thick. Add tomato paste and cook 15 minutes longer. Pour into sterilized pint jars.

Yield: 14 pints.

Louise Newman

Rose Petal Jam

Several quarts of rose petals
1 cup honey

1 cup water
1 teaspoon lemon juice

In the morning, when still dewy, gather several quarts of rose petals. Stack and cut off white tips. Chop fine. Simmer together honey and water for 10 minutes. Add 2 cups chopped rose petals. Add lemon juice. Simmer 30 minutes and pour into sterilized jars.

NOTE: Not only is the taste delicious, but so is the aroma.

Dorothy Kaufman

Cranberry Walnut Conserve

4 cups cranberries
1½ cups water
1 stick cinnamon
2½ cups sugar
1 cup golden seedless raisins
1 large tart apple, peeled, cored, chopped

⅓ to ½ cup chopped candied ginger
Grated rind and juice of 1 lemon and 1 orange
½ teaspoon salt
6 tablespoons port wine
1 cup chopped walnuts

In a large heavy saucepan, combine cranberries, water, and cinnamon stick. Bring to a boil, reduce heat, and simmer until the skins pop — about 10 minutes. Add sugar, raisins, apple, ginger, lemon rind and juice, orange rind and juice, and salt. Continue simmering, uncovered, over medium heat for 15-20 minutes, stirring occasionally. Remove from heat and set aside to cool to room temperature. Stir in port wine and walnuts. Store in tightly covered containers. Will keep refrigerated for several months.

Yield: 4 cups.   Roslyn Goldstick

Teriyaki Marinade

FOR CHICKEN OR BEEF:
2 cloves garlic, finely chopped
¼ cup light soy sauce
¼ cup pineapple juice; or 1 can unsweetened pineapple chunks (juice and fruit)
2 tablespoons oil

1 tablespoon lemon juice or vinegar
2-3 tablespoons brown sugar
½ teaspoon ginger
¼ teaspoon paprika

Mix all ingredients together. Marinate 1-2 hours. Broil or barbeque.

Dorothy Kaufman

Fresh Lemon Barbeque Sauce

½ cup ketchup
1 teaspoon fresh grated lemon peel
2 teaspoons fresh lemon juice

2 teaspoons Worcestershire sauce
2 teaspoons prepared mustard
Dash of onion powder

Combine all ingredients in a small bowl. Use to baste broiled or grilled fish.

Yield: ½ cup.   Irene Lawson

Versatile Tomato-Vegetable Sauce

FOR PASTA:

3 large garlic cloves
1 large onion
1 leek, white part only
2 carrots, peeled
1 rib celery
1 red pepper, seeded
¼ cup olive oil
½ cup dried mushrooms,
    soaked in 18 ounces boiling
    water; reserve liquid
1 cup vermouth
6 large tomatoes, peeled and
    seeded or 1 (28-ounce) can
    tomatoes

Handful of parsley
1 teaspoon salt
½-¾ teaspoon red pepper flakes
1½ teaspoons basil
¾ teaspoons oregano
½ teaspoons tarragon
½ teaspoon thyme
16 ounces tomato paste
2 tablespoons olive oil
Mushroom liquid to fill 2-3 cans
    from tomato paste
Fresh grated Parmesan,
    optional
Burgundy wine, optional

In food processor mince garlic, onion, leek, carrots, celery, and red pepper. Heat olive oil in Dutch oven and sauté vegetables over medium heat — approximately 5 minutes. Drain mushrooms and reserve liquid. Cut soaked mushrooms and add vermouth; simmer, uncovered, until most of the liquid has disappeared—approximately 15 minutes. Chop tomatoes in processor and add to the sauce with all of the spices. Cook, uncovered, until thickened—approximately 45 minutes. Add tomato paste and reserved mushroom liquid; adjust seasonings if necessary. Use extra 2 tablespoons of oil to pour over cooked pasta, before adding sauce to keep the pasta from sticking together.

NOTE: Burgundy wine may be added at end of cooking sauce if too thick; gives a full-bodied flavor. Sauce will keep 3 days in refrigerator, or freeze. Best if made in advance.

Sue Kaine

TRADITIONAL & HOLIDAY

Traditional

The observance of Jewish holidays and festivals is based on historic events, geared to seasonal festivals and fast days. During each holiday, traditional food which have symbolic and spiritual significance are served.

Rosh Hashanah, the New Year, a round challah symbolizes life without end. Apple dipped into honey symbolizes our hopes for a sweet year. Dishes abound with honey, raisins, carrots, and apples — all seasonal reminders of hope for the coming year.

Succoth and Simchat Torah, which occur during the fall harvest are full of joy in the Torah. We eat filled foods, such as stuffed cabbage, knishes, strudel, and kreplach.

Chanukah, is the miracle of the oil burning for eight days in the rededicated Temple, therefore we eat latkes, pancakes, and donuts fried in oil.

Purim, we eat three-cornered filled pastries called Hamantashen, to remember the victory over the tyrant Haman, who wore a three-cornered hat.

Passover, the festival of freedom, requires that we have fresh greens and lamb on our menu, matzo (unleavened bread) and matzo products. Wine, gefilte fish, eggs, fresh fruits, and vegetables are typically served. The Hagaddah tells in detail the symbolic foods that are traditionally eaten and the reasons for eating them.

Shavuot, the festival of the Torah which is compared to milk and honey, we eat foods made with milk and dairy products, such as blintzes, cheesecake, and cheeses.

Sabbath is a day blessed for refreshing body and spirit and for that reason it is time for feasting and drinking wine. In addition, bread, chicken soup, tsimmes, kugel, gefilte fish, chopped liver, roast chicken or meat are some dishes traditionally served.

Gefilte Fish Mold

4 pounds whitefish, ground
2 pounds pickerel, ground
½ cup matzo meal
3 tablespoons sugar
½ teaspoon pepper
1 tablespoon salt
3 carrots

3 large onions
2 tablespoons oil
4 eggs
¼ cup water
Green pepper and carrots to
    decorate mold

Place fish in large mixing bowl. Put all other ingredients in blender; medium speed for about 3 minutes. Add to fish and mix at rapid speed for 4 minutes. (Increase speed gradually to keep from spattering.) Spoon into a 12 cup mold, sprayed with no-stick spray. Place mold in 1½ inches water in broiler pan in 325° oven for 1½ hours. It browns and comes away from the mold.

NOTE: Keeps well in the refrigerator for 10 days and also freezes well. Each slice equals 145 calories.

Yield: 20 slices.   Tillie Brandwine

Kasha

"THE OLD-FASHIONED WAY":
1 cup kasha (buckwheat
    kernels)
1 egg, beaten

¼ teaspoon salt
1 tablespoon chicken schmaltz
1 cup chicken or beef stock

Mix kasha with beaten egg in a hot skillet (ungreased) until each grain is separate. Add salt, chicken schmaltz, and stock. Cover with aluminum foil and keep cooking over low heat for 10 minutes. Put kasha in a "schmaltzed" casserole. Cook in low oven until ready to serve.

CRUST:
1 egg, beaten   1 tablespoon cold water

Beat egg with 1 tablespoon of cold water. Pour over cooked kasha. Increase heat until crust forms.

NOTE: Serve kasha by spooning in bottom of an individual soup bowl and pouring soup on top. Kasha will keep for several days in refrigerator.

Yield: 4-6 servings.   Josephine Weiner

Kreplach

FILLING:

½ pound chuck

2 small onions, peeled and
quartered

1 medium carrot, scraped and
cut in half

1-2 celery stalks with leaves

½ teaspoon salt

Cover chuck and 1 onion, carrot, and celery with water. Add salt. Bring to a boil and skim if necessary. Cover and simmer for 1½ hours. Drain meat and set aside to cool. Discard vegetables, strain broth, and use for soup base, if desired. When meat is cool, grind the meat with 1 small raw onion.

DOUGH:

1 egg, lightly beaten

½ cup flour

1 tablespoon soda water

Add soda water to beaten egg. Pour into flour and work lightly with fingers until dough is formed. If dough is too sticky, add a little flour. Leave dough to rest on board 1 hour, covered with a towel. Divide dough into 4 parts. Roll out ⅛ inch thick on floured board and cut into 2-2½ inch squares. Place ½ teaspoon filling in each square. Fold over square to form a triangle, pinching edges together. Edges may be moistened with water if needed to make them stick together. Set aside and repeat with rest of dough.

Cook kreplach for 20 minutes in gently boiling broth of your choice.

NOTE: Uncooked kreplach freezes well. Freeze on cookie sheet. When frozen, put in plastic bag. DO NOT DEFROST, just drop into soup broth.

Yield: Approximately 25 kreplach.   Velma Friedman & Sally Mayer

Kasha Varnishkas

(AUNT BEA TAUBER):

1 cup kasha (groats)
1 large egg, beaten
1 small onion, minced
4 cloves garlic, minced
3 tablespoons chicken fat

1 heaping teaspoon paprika
2½ cups chicken broth
8 ounces bowtie noodles,
  cooked
Salt and pepper to taste

In a large, heavy fry pan, cook kasha which has been mixed with beaten egg. Place over low flame and, stirring constantly, cook until toasted and dry. Mince onion and garlic. Add onion, garlic, and chicken fat to pan. Cook for 3-4 minutes. Add paprika and chicken broth, bring to a boil, cover, and reduce heat to a simmer. Simmer for 15 minutes or until most of the liquid has been absorbed. Combine kasha, cooked bowties, salt, and pepper to taste. Bake in a 350° oven for 20 minutes.

NOTE: More chicken fat or brisket gravy can be added if too dry. If needed, this may be prepared up to baking point, refrigerated, and then baked 20 minutes.

Yield: 4-6 servings.

Berta Myerson Molasky

Pareve Noodle Pudding

1 (16-ounce) package broad
  noodles
4 eggs
½ cup margarine
4 apples, grated

1 cup orange marmalade
½ cup raisins
½ cup sugar
¾ teaspoon cinnamon

Cook noodles and drain. Beat eggs and add noodles, melted margarine, apples, marmalade, and raisins. Pour into a 9 x 13 greased pan and sprinkle with sugar and cinnamon mixture. Bake in 375° oven for 45 minutes.

Yield: 8 servings.

Rose Bobry

177

Tzimmes

2 tablespoons vegetable oil
1 pound, peeled and coarsely
  grated carrots (5 cups)
1 medium onion, peeled and
  coarsely grated (⅓ cup)
3½ pounds lean beef (chuck,
  flank, brisket)
¼ teaspoon salt
⅛ teaspoon pepper
2½-3 pounds sweet potatoes,
  peeled and cut in 2 inch
  chunks (about 6 cups)

½ pound pitted prunes
  (1½ cups)
4½ ounces dried apricot halves
  (¾ cup)
1¾ cups water
1 tablespoon Kosher salt
¼ cup honey
¼ cup fresh lemon juice
1 tablespoon brown sugar

Heat oven to 375°. In large Dutch oven or oven-proof pot, heat oil over moderate heat. Add carrots and onions and cook 3-5 minutes, stirring frequently. Cut meat into 3 inch chunks; sprinkle meat with salt and pepper. Place meat on top of carrots and onions, then add sweet potatoes; then prunes and apricots. Combine water, Kosher salt, and honey and pour over ingredients in the pot. Cover pot and bake 1½ hours. Mix lemon juice with brown sugar and sprinkle over the fruit and sweet potatoes. Cover pot and bake another 30 minutes. Uncover and bake 30 minutes longer, basting potatoes and fruit 2 or 3 times with pan juices.

Yield: 6 servings.   Frieda S. Leemon

Fried Noodle Kugel

½ pound fine egg noodles
2 tablespoons margarine or
  chicken fat
1 large onion, diced
6 tablespoons vegetable oil,
  divided

2 eggs, lightly beaten
1 teaspoon salt
½ teaspoon pepper

Cook noodles according to directions on package; drain. Add margarine or fat, mix well. In small skillet, sauté onion in 2 tablespoons oil until golden. Add onions to noodles. Add eggs, salt, and pepper, mix well. In large skillet, heat 4 tablespoons of oil. When hot, pour in noodle mixture and smooth into large pancake. Reduce heat and cook until brown on bottom, then turn over and brown on other side, adding more oil if necessary.

Hilda Erman

Low Fat Noodle Kugel

½ pound no-yolk noodles
3 tablespoons melted
   margarine
⅓ cup sugar
¼ cup white raisins
1 cup orange juice

¼ cup low-fat small curd
   cottage cheese (optional)
¼ teaspoon cinnamon
   (optional)
1 whole egg and 3 egg whites
2 apples, peeled and grated

Cook noodles and drain. Mix noodles, margarine, sugar, and raisins in a bowl. Pour orange juice over noodle mixture and let stand in bowl for 1 hour in refrigerator. Remove from refrigerator and if using cottage cheese and cinnamon, add at this point. Beat egg and egg whites together; fold into noodle mixture with grated apples. Pour noodle mixture into a sprayed 11 x 7 x 2 inch pan. Bake, uncovered, at 350° for 45 minutes to 1 hour.

Yield: 6 servings.

Lillian Finkelstein Falick

Mama's Company Kugel

½ cup margarine (1 stick)
8 ounces cream cheese,
   softened
2 cups sour cream
4 eggs
6 tablespoons sugar

2 teaspoons vanilla
¼ teaspoon salt
Lemon juice to taste
1 cup raisins
8 ounces wide noodles
Cinnamon and sugar

Cream margarine and cream cheese together, then add remaining ingredients, one at a time, in order listed, blending well. Pour into an 11 x 13 inch greased pan. Sprinkle top with sugar and cinnamon and bake at 350° for 1 hour.

NOTE: Tube pan or bundt pan can be used.

Yield: 10-12 servings.

Gertrude Braun

Upside Down Noodle Kugel

¼ cup margarine
8 pineapple slices
8 maraschino cherries
½ cup brown sugar
2 eggs
¼ cup oil or margarine
¼ cup sugar
½ teaspoon salt

½ teaspoon cinnamon
½ teaspoon grated lemon rind
1 tablespoon lemon juice
8 ounces wide noodles, cooked
  and drained
½ cup finely cut dried fruit
½ cup raisins
½ cup chopped nuts (optional)

Melt margarine in a 9 inch square pan. Arrange drained slices of pineapple with cherry in middle of pineapple on bottom of pan. Sprinkle with brown sugar. In a large bowl, beat eggs and add all remaining ingredients. Bake at 350° for 40-50 minutes. Let stand for 5 minutes. Loosen sides with spatula and invert over serving dish.

NOTE: 1 (8-ounce) can drained crushed pineapple can be substituted for pineapple slices; omit cherries, and use an 8-cup ring mold. Freezes well.

Yield: 8 servings.   Shulamith Benstein & Jewel Kretchmer

Potato Kugel Krispies

½ cup flour
½ teaspoon baking powder
1½ teaspoons salt
Pinch of pepper

6 medium potatoes, peeled
2 eggs
1 large onion, chopped
¼ cup oil

Preheat oven to 350°. Stir together flour, baking powder, salt, and pepper; set aside. Grate potatoes so they will not discolor. Squeeze out excess liquid. Add eggs and mix well. Add dry ingredients. Sauté onion in oil until lightly browned, and then add onion and oil to batter. Stir well. Pour into greased 15 x 10 x 1 inch jelly roll pan. Bake for ½ hour. Remove from oven and cut into squares. Bake again for another ½ hour.

NOTE: Serve hot with applesauce. Freezes well. Cut into squares, freeze on cookie sheet, then store in plastic bag in freezer.

Yield: 6-8 servings.   Debbie Iwrey

Potato Latkes

5 pounds potatoes
6 eggs
3 tablespoons flour
3 teaspoons salt

Pepper to taste
3 medium onions, grated
¾ teaspoon baking powder
Oil

Finely grate the potatoes in a food processor. If desired, use the steel blade in addition to the grater. Drain well to remove as much of the liquid as possible. Add the remaining ingredients and mix well. Drop by tablespoons into hot oil. Brown on both sides. Drain on paper towel or brown paper bags to remove excess oil.

NOTE: Freezes well.

Yield: About 50.   Wendy Wagenheim

Hamantashen Cookie Dough

¾ cup egg substitute or 3 eggs
1 cup sugar
½ cup canola oil
½ cup orange juice

4½ cups flour
¼ teaspoon baking soda
3 teaspoons baking powder
½ teaspoon salt

In large mixing bowl, beat the egg substitute or eggs, adding the sugar gradually while beating. Continue beating, adding the oil and orange juice. In another bowl, combine the dry ingredients, mixing well. Add to beaten egg mixture. The dough will be a little sticky.

On a lightly floured pastry board, roll part of the dough to a thickness of ⅛ inch (don't add too much flour in rolling out or the cookies will come out hard). Cut rolled dough with a 3 inch round cutter. Place about 1 teaspoon prune filling (See Prune Filling recipe below) in the center of each dough round. Shape each dough round into Haman's hat by folding its three edges toward the center, pinching lightly to seal and leaving center slightly open so filling is exposed and steam can vent. Repeat, incorporating the scraps into the batch of fresh dough. Bake on lightly greased cookie sheet at 350° for about 20 minutes.

Jean Hollander, Mary Schwartz & Roberta Grosinger

Prune Filling for Hamantashen

1 (12-ounce) box pitted prunes
    (1¼ cups)
½ cup seedless raisins
Water or sweet wine to cover

½ cup chopped almonds
Juice and grated peel of
    1 lemon
½ cup sugar

Soak prunes and raisins in water or wine for 2-3 hours or overnight. Drain well and discard liquid. Place all ingredients in food processor fitted with metal blade. Process thoroughly.

Yield: Fills 48 hamantashen.

Mary Schwartz

Heating lemons and oranges before extracting juices will provide more juice.

Sephardic Seven Fruit Haroset

4 ounces unsweetened coconut
4 ounces chopped or whole
   unsalted cashews
¼ cup sugar
1 tablespoon cinnamon
4 ounces raisins

8 ounces dried apples
8 ounces dried prunes
8 ounces dried pears
8 ounces dried apricots
4 ounces strawberry jam
Sweet red wine

Combine all ingredients (except the jam and red wine) in a large heavy pot which has been sprayed with a non-stick spray. Add enough water to cover ingredients; cover pot and simmer over low fire, stirring occasionally with a wooden spoon. Add a small amount of water periodically so mixture does not stick to the pot, and continue stirring. Cook for at least 1½ hours. When mixture is cohesive, stir in jam. Let stand until cool. Add enough sweet wine to be absorbed by the haroset mixture and refrigerate.

Yield: 5 cups.

Ina Lutz

Passover Matzo Soufflé

6 eggs
½ cup sugar
½ teaspoon salt
¼ teaspoon cinnamon
½ cup raisins
¼ teaspoon lemon rind

¼ teaspoon orange rind
3 matzos, soaked in water and
   drained
4 tart apples, grated
¼ cup melted margarine
Cinnamon and sugar

Beat eggs with sugar, salt, and cinnamon. Add raisins, lemon and orange rinds, matzos, and apples. Put into a greased 1½ quart casserole. Pour melted margarine on top and sprinkle with cinnamon and sugar. Bake at 350° for 45 minutes.

NOTE: This can be partially baked and frozen, or can be prepared and refrigerated a day ahead.

Yield: Serves 10.

Stephanie Bernstein

Passover Rolls or Bagels

1 cup water
1 teaspoon salt
½ cup oil or margarine

1½ cups matzo meal
4 eggs

Preheat oven to 400°. Bring water to a boil, add salt, and oil. Remove saucepan from heat and add matzo meal, all at once. Stir well and return to heat for three minutes, stirring continuously. Remove from heat and let stand 10 minutes. Add eggs, one at a time, and mix vigorously. Oil your hands and shape two tablespoons of dough into a little ball, then into a 5 inch rope. Pinch ends together to get a bagel shape, or leave as a ball. Put on a greased cookie sheet. Bake 40 minutes or until browned.

Yield: 12-14 bagels.

Nana Goodfriend

Traditional Charoset

4 apples, pared, cored and
   chopped
2 cups chopped walnuts

2 teaspoons cinnamon
4 tablespoons honey
6 tablespoons red wine

Combine apples and walnuts. Add remaining ingredients and mash together. Correct seasonings to taste.

Yield: About 3 cups.

Gail Nemer

Mock Carrot Kishka

2 cups grated carrots, well
   packed
½ cup melted margarine

1 cup matzo meal
Salt to taste

Preheat oven to 375°. Combine all the ingredients on a cookie sheet covered with aluminum foil. Form kishka in the shape of a loaf. Bake for 1 hour or until brown.

Yield: 6-8 servings.

Celia Lubetsky

~~~~~~

Passover Vegetable Fruit Kugel

1 cup grated apple
1 cup grated sweet potato
1 cup grated carrot
1 cup cake meal
½ cup margarine

1 teaspoon baking soda
1 teaspoon cinnamon
⅓ cup sugar
1 teaspoon salt

Preheat oven to 325°. Combine all ingredients and mix well. Spread into a greased 10 inch baking dish. Cover with aluminum foil and bake for 45 minutes. Raise oven temperature to 350°, remove cover, and bake for another 10 minutes.

Yield: 8 to 10 servings.

Sharon Fishman

Passover Vegetable Kugel

¼ cup chopped green pepper
1 cup chopped onion
½ cup chopped celery
1½ cups chopped carrots
2 tablespoons oil
1 (10-ounce) package frozen
    chopped spinach

3 eggs, beaten
1½ teaspoons salt
⅛ teaspoon pepper
6 tablespoons melted
    margarine
¾ cup matzo meal
Sour cream, optional

Sauté green pepper, onion, celery, and carrots in the oil for about 10 minutes, stirring occasionally. Cook spinach and drain. Combine all the vegetables, eggs, salt, pepper, melted margarine, and matzo meal. Spoon into 12 well-greased large muffin tins. Bake in 350° oven for 45 minutes or until firm. Cool 10 minutes before removing from pan. Serve plain or with sour cream.

NOTE: This may also be put in a 8 x 8 x 2 inch greased pan; double recipe and use a 9 x 13 x 2 inch pan.

Yield: 8-12 servings.

Lillian Chinitz

Dairy Apricot Farfel Kugel

2 cups farfel	⅓ cup melted margarine
3 eggs	½ cup white raisins
¼ cup sugar	½ cup apricot preserves
2 cups creamed style cottage cheese	½ cup finely chopped walnuts
1 cup sour cream	2 tablespoons sugar
	1 teaspoon cinnamon

Soak farfel in cold water. In mixing bowl, beat eggs until light, gradually adding sugar until fluffy. Squeeze out excess water from farfel and combine with cottage cheese, sour cream, margarine, raisins, and apricot preserves. Add to egg mixture and blend well. Pour into a 2 quart baking dish. Mix nuts, sugar, and cinnamon and sprinkle on top of farfel mixture. Bake in 350° oven for 40-45 minutes.

Variation: Use non-dairy sour cream and 1 cup quartered apricots in kugel plus remaining sliced apricots on top. Also add ¼ teaspoon nutmeg and ¼ teaspoon cinnamon to kugel. Omit cottage cheese.

Variation: Add 1 Granny Smith apple, peeled and chopped, to kugel. Topping could be dry farfel, brown sugar, and cinnamon.

Yield: 10-12 servings.   DarrAnn Rosenberg, Ricki Herling,
                                          Bessie Erlichman, & Carol Sue Coden

Individual Farfel Kugel

6 cups farfel	½ cup margarine
6 cups hot water	6 eggs
2 onions, chopped	Salt and pepper to taste

Combine farfel and hot water in a large mixing bowl and let stand for 1 hour. Sauté onions in melted margarine. Mix eggs and add to farfel; add onions, margarine, salt and pepper to taste. Spoon into greased muffin tins (¾ full). Bake in 350° oven for 1 hour and 20 minutes.

Variation: Mushrooms and green peppers can be added.

NOTE: This can be prepared early in the day and let stand at room temperature. Reheat at 325° until warm.

Yield: 30 servings.   Carol Sue Coden

Best Potato Kugel

3 eggs
5 medium potatoes, peeled
   and quartered
1 onion, quartered

½ cup oil
⅓ cup matzo meal
1 teaspoon salt
¼ teaspoon pepper

Beat eggs in an electric blender; add potatoes a few at a time to the blended eggs. Add onion pieces to the potato mixture and blend again. Pour mixture into a large bowl and add oil, matzo meal, salt, and pepper. Mix well. Pour into a lightly greased 8 x 8 inch pan. Bake, uncovered, at 400° for 45 minutes to 1 hour or until slightly brown.

Yield: 6 to 8 servings.

Pearlena Bodzin

Passover Sponge Cake

8 eggs
1¼ cups sugar
Rind of 1 lemon, grated
Juice of 1 orange

½ cup cake meal
½ cup potato starch
Dash of salt

Beat eggs at high speed for 10 minutes. Add sugar and beat for 5 minutes at medium speed. Combine rind of 1 lemon and juice of orange in a small bowl. Mix together ½ cup cake meal, potato starch, and salt. Alternately add liquid and cake meal mixture to sugar and eggs until well blended. Pour into ungreased tube pan and bake at 325° for 1 hour. Invert pan until cool.

Yield: 10 servings.

Mary Steffin & Josephine Colton

 For grated orange or lemon peel ... use a potato peeler to pare the peel in thin strips. Drop these into a whirling blender. Presto — grated peel!

Marble Chiffon Cake

10 eggs, separated
1¾ cups sugar, divided
¼ teaspoon salt
2 tablespoons cocoa

½ cup oil
½ cup orange juice
¾ cup cake meal
¼ cup potato starch

Beat egg whites with ½ cup sugar and ¼ teaspoon salt until stiff. Mix cocoa with ¼ cup sugar and enough boiling water to make a paste. Set aside. Beat yolks with oil and orange juice. Add remaining sugar and cake meal and potato starch, which have been sifted together. Fold in beaten egg whites and pour half into ungreased tube pan. Add chocolate mixture to remaining batter. Pour chocolate batter over and swirl with a knife. Bake in 350° oven for 1 hour. Invert to cool.

NOTE: Freezes well.

Yield: 10-12 servings.

Lillian Chinitz

Big Apple Torte

6 large eggs, separated (room
   temperature)
2 cups sugar plus 1 tablespoon
   sugar
¾ cup cake meal
¾ cup potato starch
1 cup apple juice

1 tablespoon finely grated
   lemon rind
½ teaspoon vanilla
3 large Golden Delicious
   apples, peeled, cored, and
   sliced thin
1 teaspoon cinnamon

In a large bowl, beat yolks until thick and pale. Gradually add 1¾ cups of sugar and beat until very thick. In a small bowl, sift together cake meal and potato starch; add to yolks, alternating with apple juice. Add rind and vanilla and beat until well combined. Clean beaters and in a small bowl beat egg whites until they hold soft peaks. Add ¼ cup sugar, a little at a time, and beat until stiff. Stir ½ cup whites into above mixture and fold rest in gently. Pour into a greased 9 x 13 x 2 inch pan and arrange apples slices on top, overlapping slightly. Mix together remaining 1 tablespoon sugar and 1 teaspoon cinnamon and sprinkle on apples. Bake at 325° for 50-55 minutes.

Yield: 12 servings.

Ricki Herling

Passover Banana Cake

7 eggs, separated
1 cup sugar
½ teaspoon salt
1 cup mashed ripe bananas
   (about 3)

¾ cup matzo cake meal
¼ cup potato flour (starch)
2 tablespoons orange juice
1 teaspoon lemon rind

Beat egg whites until stiff and set aside. Beat yolks, sugar, and salt until consistency of cake batter (about 5 minutes on high speed). Add 1 cup mashed bananas. Blend in cake meal, potato flour, orange juice, and lemon rind. Fold in ¼ of stiffly beaten egg whites, then fold in remaining whites. Pour into ungreased 9 inch tube pan. Cut through batter several times with spatula or knife blade to work out any large air bubbles. Bake at 325° for 45 to 50 minutes or until top springs back. Invert pan until cool.

NOTE: Chocolate chips or ½-1 cup coarsely chopped nuts may be added.

Yield: 12 servings.   Reta Fishman & M. Lindenbaum

Passover Dessert Elegant

1 (8-inch or 9-inch) sponge
   cake, baked
1 pound semisweet chocolate
6 tablespoons sugar

6 tablespoons cold water
8 eggs, separated
Whipped cream

Melt chocolate in double boiler. Add sugar and water and remove from heat. Blend in well-beaten egg yolks. Cool. Beat egg whites until stiff. Fold into chocolate mixture. Line sides and bottom of a 10-inch springform pan with slices of sponge cake. Pour half of chocolate mixture into pan. Add a layer of sponge cake slices, then remaining chocolate mixture. Refrigerate overnight. Top with whipped cream.

Yield: 10 servings.   Fiddler Favorite

 Beaten egg whites are stiff enough if they do not slide when the bowl is turned upside down.

Fruit and Nut Torte

TORTE:

2 cups walnuts	1 (16-ounce) can sliced peaches
2 tablespoons matzo meal	in heavy syrup, drained
4 eggs, separated, room	1 pint strawberries
temperature	1 cup seedless grapes
⅔ cup sugar	1 tablespoon honey

Preheat oven to 350°. In food processor with chopping blade attached, finely grind walnuts with matzo meal. In large bowl with mixer at high speed, beat egg whites until soft peaks form. In small bowl, with same beaters and with mixer at high speed, beat egg yolks and sugar until very thick and lemon-colored. Fold nut mixture, then yolk mixture into egg whites. Pour batter into a greased 4 cup bundt pan. Bake 25 to 30 minutes until top of cake springs back when touched with finger. Cool the cake in pan on wire rack 5 minutes. Remove from pan; cool on wire rack.

LEMON CURD FILLING:

1 lemon	3 whole eggs
½ cup margarine, cut up	3 egg yolks
⅓ cup sugar	

Grate 1 tablespoon rind from lemon and squeeze ⅓ cup juice. In double boiler over hot, not boiling, water, cook lemon peel and juice, margarine, sugar, eggs and egg yolks, stirring until mixture is very thick and coats back of a spoon well, about 15 minutes (do not boil or mixture will curdle). Pour filling into bowl; cover with plastic wrap.

Assemble torte: place cake, indented side up, on plate. Spoon lemon curd filling onto top of cake. Arrange fruit in a pretty design on filling. Heat honey to thin slightly. Brush fruit with honey.

NOTE: Lemon curd filling can be made earlier in the day or a few days ahead. Torte can be made ahead and frozen.

Yield: 10 servings.   Phyllis Schwartz

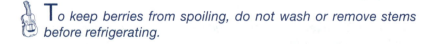

To keep berries from spoiling, do not wash or remove stems before refrigerating.

Passover Apricot Pastry

PASTRY:

½ pound softened margarine
2 egg yolks
Pinch of salt
1 cup sugar

2 cups sifted cake meal
2 teaspoons grated lemon rind
1 teaspoon vanilla

Preheat oven to 325°. Combine ingredients for pastry. Spread ¾ of dough on bottom of greased 9 x 13 inch pan, and up the sides 1 inch. Bake 20 minutes.

FILLING:

1 (1 pound) jar apricot
   preserves

½ cup lemon juice
½ cup chopped nuts

Combine filling ingredients; reserve nuts. Remove crust from oven. While hot, spread filling on top and sprinkle with nuts and crumble remaining dough on top. Bake for another 30-35 minutes. Cut when cool.

Geta Richman

Matzo Drop Cookies

3 cups cake meal
3 cups coarsely crumbled
   matzo
2¼ cups sugar
1½ cups raisins (optional)
1 cup coarsely chopped nuts

2 teaspoons cinnamon
¾ teaspoon salt
½-¾ package chocolate chips
6 eggs
1 cup vegetable oil

Blend all ingredients, except eggs and oil, with a fork. Beat in the eggs and oil. Form balls with wet hands and place balls on baking sheet. Bake at 350° for 15-17 minutes. Remove from baking sheet while warm.

NOTE: These cookies freeze well.

Carol Maltzman

Date and Chocolate Bit Squares

1 cup diced pitted dates
1½ cups boiling water
1½ teaspoons baking soda
2 eggs
1 cup sugar
¾ cup oil
¾ teaspoon baking soda
½ teaspoon salt
1½ cups cake meal

⅛ cup potato starch
Grease and cake meal for the
   pan
2 bars (1½ ounces each)
   semisweet chocolate
¼ cup sugar for topping
1 cup finely chopped nuts for
   topping

Combine the dates, boiling water, and baking soda in a small saucepan. Bring to a slow boil. Remove from heat. Set aside to cool. In processor, cream the eggs with the sugar and oil until well blended; add the cooled date mixture. Sift together the soda, salt, cake meal, and starch into a small bowl. Combine the dry ingredients with the date mixture and process until smooth. Grease and dust with cake meal 9 x 13 inch pan. Pour the batter into the pan. Chop the chocolate into bits and sprinkle over the batter. Sprinkle the ¼ cup sugar and 1 cup finely chopped nuts over the chocolate bits. Bake at 350° for 40 to 45 minutes. Cool and cut into bars or squares.

Margie Kurzmann

Kyra's Passover Mandelbrot

3 eggs
¾ cup sugar
¾ cup oil
¾ cup matzo cake meal
¾ cup chopped almonds
   (4 ounces)

¼ cup matzo meal
½ teaspoon salt
2 tablespoons potato starch
1 teaspoon cinnamon

Beat eggs and sugar in a mixer until well blended. Very slowly add oil. Stir dry ingredients together and mix into batter. Refrigerate overnight. Shape dough into 3 or 4 long rolls on an oiled cookie sheet. Bake at 350° for about 30 minutes or until lightly browned. Slice, turn on sides, and return to oven to dry out, about 5 to 10 minutes per side.

NOTE: Freezes nicely.

Karen Kurzmann

Passover Rocky Road Bars

CRUST:

¼ cup matzo cake meal
1 teaspoon baking powder
⅛ teaspoon salt
⅓ cup brown sugar

½ cup chopped walnuts
1 egg
1 tablespoon soft unsalted
  margarine

Sift cake meal with baking powder and salt. Add all of the remaining ingredients except the nuts and beat until smooth. Stir in nuts. Press this mixture into a 9 x 9 x 2 inch square pan. Preheat oven to 350° and bake for 15 minutes, just until the top is lightly browned and springs back when touched. Remove from oven.

TOPPING:

1 cup toasted coconut
  marshmallows (quartered)
½ cup chopped walnuts

6 ounces Passover chocolate,
  broken into small pieces

Place the marshmallows on top of the crust, cover with the nuts, and spread with chocolate pieces evenly on top of the nuts. Return the pan to the oven for 2 to 6 minutes until the chocolate is softened. Remove from oven and swirl chocolate over the nuts and marshmallows with a knife. Cool and cut into squares.

NOTE: This freezes well.

Lisa Winer

Passover Meringue Cookies

2 egg whites (¼ cup)
¾ cup sugar
2 tablespoons cocoa

¼ teaspoon salt
1 tablespoon orange juice
2 cups chopped pecans

Beat whites until stiff, but not dry. Fold in sugar, cocoa, and salt. Stir over medium heat for 5 minutes. Cool at room temperature. Add orange juice and nuts. Drop on foil covered cookie sheet allowing ⅔ teaspoon for each cookie. Bake in 300° oven for about 30 minutes or until firm. Do not remove from foil until cookies are cold.

Margie Kurzmann

Passover Mandel Bread

1¼ cups cake meal
1 cup potato starch
1 teaspoon salt
3 eggs
1 cup sugar

1 cup oil
1 cup semisweet chocolate,
  chopped, or chopped nuts
Cinnamon and sugar mixed
  together

Preheat oven to 350°. Combine cake meal, potato starch, and salt. Set aside. Beat eggs, sugar, and oil together until well mixed. Sift dry ingredients into oil mixture. Add chopped chocolate or nuts. Stir together until combined. Let stand 20 minutes. Grease large cookie sheet. Dough should be stiff enough to hold its shape when mounded, or add additional cake meal. With rubber spatula or oiled hands, shape dough on cookie sheet into 2 strips 1½ inches wide and the length of sheet. Bake for 25-30 minutes, or until lightly brown on edges. Cut in ½-inch slices while warm. Lower oven temperature to 325°. Place cut side down on cookie sheet. Sprinkle lightly with cinnamon and sugar mixture. Bake 5 minutes; turn over; sprinkle with more cinnamon and sugar and bake 5 minutes longer. Cool on racks. Store uncovered.

NOTE: Dough will spread in oven.

Yield: 3 dozen cookies.   Fiddler Favorite

Sugar Cookies

½ pound sweet butter or
  margarine
1 cup sugar
1 egg

1½ cups cake meal
2 heaping tablespoons potato
  starch

Cream butter, sugar, and egg. Add cake meal and potato starch. Mix well. Divide into 3 rolls (about 2 inches in diameter). Roll in 3 pieces of waxed paper and refrigerate overnight. Cut each roll into ¼ inch slices. Make impression with finger in center of each cookie and place a walnut piece or jam of choice. Bake on ungreased cookie sheet at 400° for 15-20 minutes or until edges are slightly brown. Allow to cool before removing.

NOTE: ½ teaspoon lemon rind and/or 1 teaspoon lemon juice may be added to the dough.

Yield: 48 cookies.   Helen Kessel

Ingberlach

CANDY-LIKE COOKIE:

4 cups farfel
2 eggs
1 cup honey
1 cup sugar

1 teaspoon ginger
1 cup chopped nuts
Pinch of salt

Beat eggs in a small bowl. Pour farfel onto an ungreased cookie sheet. Pour eggs over farfel and rub with hands until all of the egg is absorbed. Let it dry in warm oven (225 to 250°), for 30 to 45 minutes. Occasionally stir and break up pieces with hands. Bring honey and sugar to a boil. Add farfel, nuts, ginger, and salt. Stir over low heat 15 to 20 minutes, until golden in color. Pour onto board covered with water or wine, or onto any surface covered with parchment paper. Dip hands in cold water and pat down until ¼ inch thick. Let cool until slightly warm and cut into small pieces.

Margie Kurzmann

Passover Fruit Pudding

2 cups orange juice
4 tablespoons lemon juice
1 (10-ounce) package mixed
    dried fruit, cut in pieces
2 large apples, peeled, cored
    and grated
4 eggs
½ teaspoon salt

6 tablespoons oil
4 tablespoons honey
⅔ cup sugar
2 tablespoons grated lemon
    rind
½ teaspoon cinnamon
1½ cups matzo farfel

Combine orange juice, lemon juice, and dried fruit in a bowl. Cook, covered, in microwave for 4 minutes. Add apple to fruit mixture. In large bowl, beat eggs and salt. Stir in oil, honey, sugar, lemon rind, cinnamon, and dry fruit mixture. In a sieve, pour hot water through matzo farfel to moisten; fold into fruit mixture and let stand for 15 minutes. Spoon into a 2 quart casserole; sprinkle extra cinnamon on top. Bake at 350° for 1-1¼ hours or until firm on top and beginning to pull away from sides.

Yield: 8 servings.

Gloria Siegel

Passover Lemon Meringue Pie

CRUST:

1 cup matzo meal
¼ teaspoon salt
½ teaspoon cinnamon
2 teaspoons sugar

¼ cup shortening
1 egg yolk
4 tablespoons chopped nuts

Blend dry ingredients, except nuts. Combine with shortening. Mix in egg yolk and then nuts. Pat evenly over the bottom and sides of a 9 inch pie pan. Bake at 375° for 10 minutes.

FILLING:

2 lemons
1 cup sugar
3 tablespoons flour
3 tablespoons potato starch
Dash of salt

1½ cups boiling water
2 egg yolks
1 tablespoon butter or
    margarine

Using a potato peeler, peel the yellow portion of lemon rind, being careful not to include any of the bitter white pitch. Squeeze juice from lemons and measure ⅓ cup juice. Process lemon rind with 1 cup sugar until finely minced, beginning with 4 quick on/off turns, then letting machine run about 30 seconds. Add flour, potato starch, and salt. While machine is running, add boiling water through feed tube. Process about 5 seconds. Transfer to a heavy saucepan and cook over medium heat, stirring constantly, until mixture thickens and boils. Boil 1 minute. Process egg yolks with lemon juice for a few seconds. Add about half of the hot mixture and process about 8 to 10 seconds. Return mixture to saucepan and boil 1 minute longer, stirring constantly. Remove from heat and stir in butter.

MERINGUE:

3 egg whites

6 tablespoons sugar

Assembly: Pour hot filling into pie shell. Using electric mixer, beat egg whites until foamy. Beat in sugar a tablespoon at a time. Continue beating until stiff and glossy and the meringue does not feel grainy when rubbed between your fingers. Pile meringue onto hot pie filling, sealing meringue onto edge of crust to prevent shrinking and weeping. Bake at 350° for 8 to 10 minutes, until golden. Cool away from drafts.

NOTE: Do not freeze.

Yield: 6-8 servings.

Margie Kurzmann

Passover Hot Fruit Casserole

2 cans almond or coconut
  macaroons, divided
1 large can each of the
  following, drained:
  Sliced peaches
  Sliced pears
  Chunk pineapple
  Dark pitted cherries

½ cup slivered almonds,
  toasted
¼ cup brown sugar
½ cup sweet red wine or liqueur
  of choice

Preheat oven to 350°. Butter a 2-quart glass casserole. Cover bottom with one can of crumbled macaroons. Layer fruit. Top with one can crumbled macaroons. Sprinkle with almonds and wine or liqueur. Bake 30 minutes. Serve hot or cold.

Yield: 12 to 16 servings.   Fiddler Favorite Submitted by Erma Zeldes

Matzo Balls or Dumplings

We did not receive a single matzo ball recipe, but felt that one should be included. Our committee concluded that buying a mix consistently produced the best matzo balls. This is an excellent time-saver for an already busy holiday.

 Cut meringue pie easily by coating both sides of knife lightly with butter or margarine, or non-stick spray.

DESSERTS

Apple Crisp

FILLING:

6 cups peeled and thinly sliced
   apples
⅓ cup sugar
1 teaspoon cinnamon

½ teaspoon salt
2 tablespoons melted
   margarine

Mix together apples, ⅓ cup sugar, cinnamon, and salt. Add melted margarine. Place in a greased 8 inch square baking dish; set aside.

TOPPING:

¾ cup sugar
½ cup all-purpose flour

⅓ cup margarine

Combine ¾ cup sugar and flour; cut in margarine until crumbly. Sprinkle over apples. Bake at 375° about 45 minutes or until apples are tender. Serve warm.

NOTE: ½ cup chopped pecans may be added to topping or filling or both.

Yield: Serves 6-8.

Iris Zevin

Lou Ann's Pumpkin Shell Surprise

1 small pumpkin, about 7-10
   inches diameter
2 cups peeled, diced apples
1 cup raisins
1 cup chopped walnuts

⅓ cup sugar
1 teaspoon lemon juice
¼ teaspoon cinnamon
¼ teaspoon nutmeg

Preheat oven to 350°. Wash pumpkin. Slice off top for a lid. Remove seeds. Mix other ingredients. Fill pumpkin with mixture and replace lid. Bake until apples are tender, approximately 40-60 minutes. Serve hot or cold, scooping out some pumpkin with each serving.

NOTE: Wonderful over ice cream or frozen yogurt or use as a side dish for Thanksgiving.

Yield: 4-6 servings.

Laurel Portner

Lemon Fluff

CRUST:

2½ cups crumbled graham
    crackers (about 36 crackers)
6 tablespoons margarine,
    melted

1 teaspoon vanilla
3 teaspoons sugar

Mix together all ingredients and spread ¾ on bottom of a lightly buttered springform pan. Save rest for topping. DO NOT BAKE CRUST.

FILLING:

1 pint whipping cream
6 eggs, separated
1 cup sugar

½ cup lemon juice
Rind from lemon

Beat whipping cream. In separate bowl, beat egg whites until stiff. Add sugar slowly. Beat egg yolks in a separate bowl and slowly add to whites. Add lemon juice and rind to whipped cream and add that to egg mixture. Fold onto crust and sprinkle top with remainder of crumb crust. Freeze. Remove from freezer about 10-15 minutes before serving.

Yield: Serves 8-10.

Pam Opperer

Prune Whip

1½ cups pitted prunes
1½ cups water
3 egg whites
¼ teaspoon salt

⅓ cup sugar
2 tablespoons lemon juice
¼ cup chopped pecans

In saucepan, combine prunes and water; bring to a boil. Cover and simmer 10 minutes. Allow to cool in liquid. Drain. With kitchen shears, snip prunes into small pieces. Set aside. In large mixing bowl, beat egg whites with salt to form soft peaks. Gradually add sugar, beating to stiff peaks. In small mixing bowl, combine prunes and lemon juice. Beat until well blended. Fold into egg whites. Fold in nuts. Spoon into sherbet glasses or large serving bowl. Chill.

Yield: 6-8 servings.

Freddy Shiffman

Mango Mousse

3 medium-sized, very ripe
   mangoes
¼ cup shelled, unsalted
   pistachios
3 egg yolks
3 whole eggs

¾ cup sugar
2 cups heavy cream, whipped
   until stiff
2 packages unflavored gelatin,
   softened according to
   package instructions

Peel mangoes and purée in processor or blender. Add pistachios and blend for 10 seconds. In large bowl, beat together egg yolks and eggs. Add sugar and continue beating until mixture is thick and creamy. Fold mango purée into egg mixture. Add softened gelatin and chill for 10 minutes. Fold chilled mixture into the whipped cream and pour into lightly oiled (2-quart) mold. Chill thoroughly in refrigerator. Place in freezer 10 minutes before serving.

FOR DECORATION:

1 ripe mango, sliced
2 tablespoons finely chopped
   pistachios

½ cup heavy cream, whipped

Decorate with freshly sliced mango, chopped pistachios, and whipped cream.

Yield: Serves 8.

Marcie Freedland

Baked Pears in Custard Sauce

4 tablespoons unsalted butter
4 tablespoons sugar
4 Bosc or Bartlett pears, halved
   and cored

¼ teaspoon cinnamon
1½ cups heavy cream

Preheat oven to 375°. Butter a shallow baking dish with one tablespoon butter. Sprinkle one tablespoon sugar over the bottom. Put pears, cut side down, in dish. Sprinkle with cinnamon and rest of sugar. Dot with butter. Bake 10 minutes. Pour cream over pears and bake 25 minutes more. Serve warm.

Yield: Serves 8.

Joan Weil

Mixed Fruit Crisp

FOOD PROCESSOR:

3 ounces ginger cookies
12 dried apricots (more if you like)
⅓ cup sugar
1 cup plus 2 tablespoons unbleached flour
½ cup golden raisins
3 large Granny Smith apples (1½ pounds), cored and halved length-wise
3 firm Bosc pears (1½ pounds) cored and halved length-wise

½ cup firmly packed brown sugar
½ cup unsalted butter or margarine, chilled and cut into 8 pieces
2 teaspoons vanilla extract
Pinch of salt (optional)
Sour cream for garnish (optional)

Preheat oven to 350°. Spray 9 inch square baking pan with vegetable oil.

With metal blade, process two-thirds of the ginger cookies until finely crumbled. Add apricots, sugar and 2 tablespoons of the flour. Pulse (quick on and off) 8 times until apricots are finely chopped. Add raisins and process 2 seconds. Remove from bowl and set aside.

With all-purpose slicing disc (4MM), stand apples and pears in feed tube and use medium pressure to slice. Mix fruit and cookie mixture lightly in prepared pan.

With metal blade, process remaining ginger cookies until finely crumbled. Add remaining flour, brown sugar, butter or margarine, vanilla, salt, and process until blended and granular — about 15 seconds. Cover fruit with crumb topping. Bake 1 hour. Serve hot or room temperature. Serve with sour cream, if desired.

NOTE: Freezes well. Recipe can easily be doubled or tripled.

Yield: Serves 6-8.

Sally Mayer

 For quick fruit salad, toss cut up fruit with 1-2 tablespoons of undiluted orange juice, or a fruit liqueur.

"Light" Chocolate Mousse

1 cup semi-sweet chocolate bits
⅔ cup powdered skim milk
1 egg
2 tablespoons white or brown
   sugar

1 tablespoon rum, coffee, or
   orange flavored liqueur
Pinch of salt
¾ cup boiling water

Place all ingredients in electric blender and blend briefly until mixed. Remove cover and continue to blend while adding boiling water. Blend one minute. Pour into dessert glasses or pot de crème pots. Chill several hours and serve plain or garnished with shredded coconut, chopped nuts, or dabs of whipped cream.

Yield: Serves 5.

Gertrude E. Braun

Bread Pudding

PUDDING:

1 (1 pound) loaf French bread
¾ cup dried cherries
4 extra large eggs
1 quart milk

1 cup sugar
½ cup melted butter or
   margarine
1 tablespoon vanilla

Cube bread in little pieces in a large bowl. Plump cherries in colander by pouring boiling water over them. Let sit for 15 minutes. Beat eggs and milk and gradually add sugar. Beat until smooth. Add melted margarine and vanilla. Drain cherries and combine with bread cubes and egg mixture. Blend well. Turn into a greased 9 x 13 x 2 inch baking pan. Bake 45-60 minutes in 350° oven.

SAUCE:

6 tablespoons butter or
   margarine
⅓ cup confectioner's sugar

2 teaspoons vanilla
1½ tablespoons Bourbon
   whiskey

In double boiler, melt butter or margarine and stir with confectioner's sugar until dissolved, smooth and very hot. Remove from stove and add vanilla and whiskey and beat well. Spoon sauce over pudding and broil until brown. Watch carefully so it does not burn.

Yield: Serves 12.

Sue Kaine

Chocolate Mousse

12-ounce package semi-sweet
chocolate pieces
12 egg yolks
12 egg whites

⅛ teaspoon salt
5 tablespoons coffee flavored
liqueur
Whipped cream, optional

Melt chocolate pieces in microwave or in double boiler. Beat egg yolks until thick and lemon-colored, about 10 minutes. Beat egg whites, add salt and continue beating until stiff peaks form. Add chocolate to beaten egg yolks and blend well. Fold egg whites to chocolate mixture, blend well. Add the liqueur. Pour into an attractive bowl. Refrigerate several hours. Serve plain or with whipped cream.

Yield: Serves 6-10.

Shary Cohn

Chocolate Truffle Loaf

NO BAKE:
1 cup margarine
1 cup cocoa
2 tablespoons instant coffee
powder or granules
(optional)

1 cup sugar, divided into ¾ and
¼ measurements
4 extra-large eggs, separated
½ cup chopped almonds or
hazelnuts

Lightly grease 8 x 4 inch loaf pan. Line bottom and sides with foil. Melt margarine, stir in cocoa and coffee. Add ¾ cup sugar. Let cool in large bowl. Add egg yolks, one at a time. Beat well after each addition.

Beat egg whites with ¼ cup sugar. Beat chocolate mixture until smooth. Stir ¼ of the egg whites into the chocolate mixture. Fold remaining egg whites into chocolate mixture. Pour into prepared foil-lined pan. Chill overnight or freeze.

To serve, loosen sides of the pan. Invert to serving plate, remove foil and pat side and top with nuts.

NOTE: Very rich. Slice thin!

Yield: 12 servings.

Helene Cherrin

Hilda's Rice Pudding

½ cup regular rice
1 cup water, salted
1 quart whole milk
4 tablespoons butter
3 eggs

½ cup sugar
1 cup raisins
½ teaspoon vanilla
3 tablespoons sugar
1 tablespoon cinnamon

Pour rice slowly into rapidly boiling, lightly salted water in a 6-quart pot. DO NOT STIR. Cover tightly and cook on low for exactly 7 minutes at which time all the water will be absorbed and the rice will be slightly undone. Add the milk and butter; stir using a wooden spoon. Bring to a boil, cover, and cook slowly over low heat for 1 hour.

Meanwhile, in a mixing bowl, beat the eggs; add the sugar and raisins and vanilla. Pour this mixture into the rice, stirring slowly until the rice starts to thicken. Serve hot, warm or cold with a mixture of cinnamon and sugar sprinkled lightly and evenly over the top.

NOTE: You may substitute skim milk for the whole milk, margarine for butter, and dry sugar substitute for the sugar.

Yield: 4-6 servings.

Hilda Erman

Steven's Rice Pudding

½ gallon whole milk
1 cup long grain rice
1 cup sugar
4 eggs, well beaten
1 tablespoon pure vanilla
    extract

1 tablespoon cinnamon
6-8 ounces raisins, softened,
    drained and cooled

In a 6-quart pot on stove, mix milk, rice, and sugar together, bring to a boil and immediately turn down heat to low to allow for slow cooking—you must stir frequently and do not cover the pot. Cook mixture for 45-60 minutes until wooden spoon inserted in the middle will almost stand by itself. Remove from heat and slowly blend in the eggs. Add the vanilla and cinnamon; add raisins and mix. Transfer to a serving bowl, sprinkle completely with cinnamon. Allow to cool at room temperature. Refrigerate and serve cold.

NOTE: If pudding becomes too thick, add a little milk to restore creaminess.

Yield: Serves 10-12.

Dr. Steven Fischer

Zabaglione Trifle with Strawberries

2 cups fresh strawberries
2-3 tablespoons sugar
1 loaf frozen pound cake,
   defrosted
6 egg yolks

⅓ cup sugar
⅛ teaspoon salt
⅓ cup slightly sweet white wine
Whipped cream

Rinse strawberries and drain thoroughly on paper toweling. Remove caps and slice into a 2-quart bowl. Stir in 2-3 tablespoons sugar. Let stand about 5 minutes. Cut pound cake into ¾ inch cubes.

In the top of a double boiler, not heated, place egg yolks, sugar and salt. Beat with a rotary beater until thick and lemon colored. Gradually beat in the wine. Place over hot, not boiling water and beat until thick and fluffy, about 4-6 minutes. Remove from heat.

Arrange ⅓ of the cake cubes on bottom of a serving dish. Pour ⅓ of the wine custard over the cake. Add ⅓ of sliced strawberries in juice. Repeat layering twice. Chill in refrigerator several hours or overnight. Serve with slightly sweetened whipped cream or any whipped topping.

NOTE: Sponge cake or angel food cake can be substituted for pound cake.

Yield: 8-10 servings.   Sheila Brown

"The Best" Ice Cream Dessert

6 cream puffs, sliced
2-3 half gallons of ice cream,
   softened
1 package chocolate-covered
   toffee candy bars, crushed

1 large jar hot fudge sauce
Sliced bananas, strawberries,
   and nuts, for topping

Layer in a large glass bowl:
1st layer: 3 cream puffs, sliced
2nd layer: ½ of the ice cream
3rd layer: ½ package crushed candy
4th layer: ½ jar hot fudge

Repeat layers. Top with slice bananas, strawberries, and nuts. Freeze.

NOTE: Should be prepared at least one night before serving.

Yield: Serves a crowd.   Carole Maltzman

Chocolate Truffles

½ pound milk chocolate pellets
1½ tablespoons butter
½ cup whipping cream
1½ tablespoons liqueur of your
   choice

Have on hand: chocolate
   sprinkles, cocoa, and
   powdered sugar

Melt chocolate in either microwave or in double-boiler over hot water. Add butter and whipping cream. Mix well and add liqueur. Refrigerate until hard. Use a teaspoon to scoop up and roll into walnut-sized balls. Roll in either chocolate sprinkles, cocoa, or powdered sugar. Put into small candy paper cups.

Charlotte Edelheit

Mocha Crunch Ice Cream Pie

MOCHA SAUCE:

1½ cups water
½ cup sugar
2½ tablespoons instant
   espresso

12 ounces semi-sweet
   chocolate
6 tablespoons unsalted butter

Cook water, sugar, and espresso in heavy medium-sized saucepan over low heat, stirring until sugar dissolves. Add chocolate and butter. Stir until chocolate and butter are melted and sauce is smooth. Cool completely. (Note: sauce can be made 3 days ahead. Cover and refrigerate. Bring to room temperature before serving.)

CRUST:

2 cups coarsely chopped
   chocolate ice-box cookies

¼ cup melted butter

Oil a 9 inch springform pan. Crush cookies by hand. Blend crumbs and butter in medium bowl. Press firmly into bottom of prepared pan. Freeze until firm.

(Continued on next page)

(Mocha Crunch Ice Cream Pie, continued)

FILLING:

2 pints chocolate ice cream
2 pints coffee ice cream
¾ cup chopped chocolate-
    covered toffee candy bars

1 cup coarsely chopped
    chocolate ice-box cookies

Soften chocolate ice cream in refrigerator until spreadable, but not melted. Spread in pan and smooth top. Freeze until firm. Spoon ½ cup sauce over ice cream and sprinkle with 1 cup cookie crumbs. Freeze until firm. Soften coffee ice cream in refrigerator until spreadable, but not melted. Spread in pan. Smooth surface and freeze until firm. Spread ½ cup sauce over coffee ice cream. Sprinkle with chopped toffee bars and freeze until firm. Cover tightly.

Soften cake slightly in refrigerator, if necessary. Rewarm remaining sauce over low heat until lukewarm, stirring frequently. Remove pan sides from springform. Cut cake into wedges. Serve, passing warm mocha sauce separately.

Variation: Yogurt can be substituted for the ice cream.

NOTE: This can be prepared 3 days ahead.

Yield: 10-12 servings.   Iris Zevin

Frozen Fantasy

½ gallon pistachio ice cream or lime sherbet, slightly softened
1 pint lemon sherbet, slightly softened

1½ pints raspberry sherbet
½ cup semi-sweet chocolate chips

Line 3-quart bowl or decorative mold with plastic wrap, leaving overhang. Smooth out as many wrinkles from wrap as possible. Chill in freezer about 30 minutes. Spoon softened pistachio ice cream or sherbet into chilled bowl, pressing with back of spoon into an even 1-inch layer to line bowl completely. Freeze, covered with foil or plastic wrap, about 1½ hours, until firm.

Remove bowl from freezer. Spoon lemon sherbet into bowl over the first layer; press into an even layer about ½-inch thick to cover ice cream completely. Cover again with foil or plastic wrap. Freeze about 1 hour until sherbet layer is completely firm.

Stir raspberry sherbet in small bowl to soften slightly; stir in chocolate chips until evenly distributed. Spoon sherbet into center of ice cream lined bowl to fill completely; smooth top of all three layers. Freeze, covered, at least 3 hours or overnight until firm. Thirty minutes before serving, chill a large round serving platter in freezer. At serving time, remove bowl from freezer, insert end of metal spatula between plastic wrap and bowl to loosen bombe. Invert bombe onto chilled platter; peel off plastic wrap. If necessary, use warm spatula to smooth out wrinkles on outside of bombe.

NOTE: For easy serving, use sharp serrated knife to cut bombe in half and then into slices. Looks like a watermelon when sliced.

Yield: Serves 10-12.

Karen Marks

Frosted grapes make a lovely garnish for a fruit salad. Dip grape or clusters into slightly beaten egg whites or fresh lemon juice, then in granulated sugar.

Frozen Fudge Brownie Pie

FOOD PROCESSOR:

12 ounces semi-sweet
   chocolate chips, divided
½ cup sugar
¼ cup boiling hot coffee
4 large eggs

¾ cup unsalted margarine
1 tablespoon pure vanilla
   extract
1 cup chopped pecans
¼ cup flour

Preheat oven to 350°. In a food processor, mince 7 ounces of the chocolate chips with sugar, using a metal blade so that the chocolate is as fine as sugar. With the machine running, pour hot coffee through the feed tube and mix until chocolate is melted. Add eggs, margarine, and vanilla. Mix for 1 minute. Add, in this order: pecans, flour, and remaining chocolate chips. Pulse machine on and off three times. Scrape down sides of bowl with a spatula and pulse just to combine for one or two more times. Transfer to prepared 9 inch baking pan. Bake until pie is set around edges but slightly soft in center, about 30 minutes. Cool pie, then freeze for at least 4 hours or as long as 3 months before serving. Allow time to defrost. To serve, cut in wedges.

Carol Fogel

Chocolate-Dipped Fruit

1 pound dark chocolate discs
   (special for chocolate candy-
   making)
Dried whole apricots
Dried pineapple sliced,
   quartered, if possible

Fresh whole strawberries, with
   stems
Any dried fruit desired;
   peaches, pears, etc.

Place wax paper on a cookie sheet.

In double-boiler, with water hot—not boiling—place ¼ pound chocolate. Tilt top of boiler so chocolate is in front portion of pan. Dip rounded edges of pineapple, half of the apricot, and the bottom half of the strawberries, one at a time, in the chocolate and place on wax paper. Refrigerate fruit on cookie sheet until chocolate hardens, about 10 minutes.

NOTE: Dried fruit may be prepared in advance, but strawberries should be prepared no sooner than one day before serving.

Hope Silverman

Peanut Butter Balls

1 cup margarine
1 pound confectioner's sugar
2½ cups graham cracker
   crumbs
1 pound peanut butter, creamy
   or crunchy

1 teaspoon vanilla
12 ounce bag semi-sweet
   chocolate chips
2 tablespoons vegetable
   shortening

Melt margarine and stir in confectioner's sugar. Let cool. In a large bowl, combine graham cracker crumbs, peanut butter, and vanilla; mix well. Stir in margarine and sugar mixture; mix well again. Roll into walnut-sized balls and place on cookie sheets. Chill thoroughly.

Melt chocolate and vegetable shortening over hot (not boiling) water or in microwave carefully. Cool slightly and dip cool balls three-quarters down until just top shows. Place on waxed paper and chill again. Keep in refrigerator, covered.

NOTE: These can be frozen.

Yield: 60-70 pieces.

Stuart Freedland

Peanut Butter Soda Cracker Fudge

24 soda crackers, crushed fine
2 cups sugar
⅔ cup milk
6 tablespoons smooth peanut
   butter

12 ounce package peanut butter
   bits

Crush crackers fine. Measure peanut butter and peanut butter bits and have ready to add quickly. Put sugar and milk in a 3-quart pot. Bring mixture to a boil for EXACTLY 3 minutes (watch carefully). Remove pot from stove top immediately.

Into sugar/milk mixture, stir the crackers, peanut butter, and peanut butter bits. Mix until fairly smooth and thick. Spread in a buttered 9 x 9 inch dish.

NOTE: Chopped nuts can be sprinkled on top.

Yield: About 25 pieces.

Tina Pinter

Henry's Cheesecake

CRUST:

1⅔ cups graham cracker
   crumbs

¼ cup sugar
¼ cup butter, softened

Preheat oven to 300°. Make crust by mixing together graham cracker crumbs, ¼ cup sugar and softened butter. Lightly butter 10 inch round cake pan that is three inches high (not a springform pan). Press crumb mixture into bottom of pan and shake on sides to coat.

FILLING:

3 pounds cream cheese,
   softened to room
   temperature
1¾ cups sugar
9 eggs

1 teaspoon vanilla extract
¾ teaspoon almond extract
Juice of one lemon
1½ cups sour cream

With electric mixer, beat cream cheese with remaining sugar until smooth. Add eggs, one at a time, beating well after each addition. Add vanilla, almond extract, lemon juice, and sour cream, beating until mixture is smooth. Pour cream cheese mixture over crust. Place cake pan in another large, deep pan: pour water around cake pan to a depth of about 1½ inches. Bake in a 300° degree oven for two hours, or until center is set. When cake is cooked, chill several hours or overnight in refrigerator. To remove cake from pan, place cake on burner that has been heated and turned off for one minute. Carefully turn cake out onto 10 inch plate and then turn it right-side-up onto serving plate.

NOTE: This recipe can be cut in half and baked in a 6 inch deep pan. Best to cool overnight in refrigerator.

Henry Gordon

Autumn Spiced Mocha Cheesecake

Vegetable cooking spray
2 tablespoons graham cracker
   crumbs
1 teaspoon cinnamon
¼ teaspoon ground cloves
16 ounces low-fat sour cream
8 ounces Neufchâtel cheese,
   softened
Juice & zest of 1 orange or
   1 lemon

⅔ cup granulated sugar
1 tablespoon cornstarch
1 (8-ounce) carton frozen egg
   substitute, thawed
¼ cup unsweetened cocoa
1½ teaspoons instant espresso
   powder
2 tablespoons coffee-flavored
   liqueur

Preheat oven to 300°. Coat the bottom of a 9 inch springform pan with a thin film of cooking spray. In a small bowl, combine the crumbs with the cinnamon and cloves and blend. Dust the bottom of the pan with the spiced crumb mixture. In a large bowl, combine the sour cream, Neufchâtel cheese, juice, and zest. Beat on medium speed until smooth. Beat in the sugar and cornstarch until well blended. Add egg substitute (¼ cup at a time) beating at low speed until just blended. Place 1½ cups of the batter in a medium bowl. Add the cocoa, espresso powder, and liqueur and beat on low speed until blended. Spoon batters alternately into the pan. Rap the pan on the top of the counter so that any trapped air bubbles disperse. Using a knife, cut through the batters in marble pattern. Place pan on baking sheet and place in oven. Add about ¼ inch of water to the baking sheet and bake for about 35-40 minutes or until cake starts to pull away from sides of the pan and center is firm. Turn off oven and leave cake inside for about 1 hour. Remove baking sheet with cake on it from oven and let cool to room temperature. Remove pan from baking sheet, dry off bottom, and wrap entire pan in plastic wrap. Refrigerate for about 8 hours or overnight. When ready to serve, unwrap and carefully release the sides of the springform pan.

Elwin Greenwald

Fall Apple Torte

PART I:

¼ pound butter
1 cup sugar
2 eggs
1¾ cups flour

2 teaspoons baking powder
8-10 large Spy apples
Cinnamon

Preheat oven to 350°. Melt butter and add sugar gradually, beating well. Add eggs one at a time and mix well. Sift flour with baking powder, add to butter/sugar mixture and beat well. Spread mixture on bottom of 10 inch springform pan. Peel and core apples and cut into quarters. Stand on end in mixture in concentric circles until pan is covered. Sprinkle with cinnamon. Bake 1½ hours in 350° oven.

PART II:

¼ pound butter
1 cup sugar

2 eggs

Reduce oven temperature to 325°. Cream butter and sugar. Add eggs and pour over top of baked torte. Put back in 325° oven for 20-30 minutes. Bake until custard sets and is golden brown. Cut when completely cool.

NOTE: Do not freeze.

Sally Green

 To keep apples or peaches from turning brown, cover with water mixed with a little lemon juice. Drain and pat dry before using.

Great Apple Cake

4 large apples	1½ cups sugar
2 teaspoons cinnamon	4 eggs
½ teaspoon nutmeg	½ cup orange juice
1½ tablespoons sugar	2 teaspoons vanilla
1 cup oil, or 1 cup butter or margarine, melted and cooled	3 cups flour
	1 tablespoon baking powder
	½ teaspoon salt (optional)

Spray tube pan or 9 x 13 inch pan with vegetable spray. Preheat oven to 350°. Peel and slice apples. Combine cinnamon, nutmeg, and 1½ tablespoons of sugar and sprinkle over apples. Set aside. In processor, beat oil or margarine with sugar for 30 seconds. Add eggs. Process 30 seconds longer. Add orange juice. Pulse until blended. Mix flour, baking powder, and salt in a separate bowl and add to processor. Pulse only until flour disappears. Pour ¼ of the batter into the pan, layer ⅓ of the apples on top, then add batter, apples, batter, apples, ending with batter.

TOPPING:

¼ **cup sliced blanched almonds**

Sprinkle almonds on top. Bake 1 hour and 20-30 minutes. Cool. Do not invert.

ALTERNATE TOPPING:

½ **cup brown sugar**	2 **tablespoons softened butter**
½ **cup ground walnuts**	

Pour ½ of batter into 9 x 13 inch pan. Spoon all of the apples over batter. Pour remaining batter over the apples. Sprinkle alternate topping over cake. Bake at 350° for 60-70 minutes.

NOTE: Blueberries, peaches, or plums can be substituted for apples. Freezes well.

Geraldine Palmer, Rusty Rosman, Lois Shifman

Apricot Chocolate Torte

CRUST:

3 ounces unsweetened chocolate

2 cups whole walnuts

1½ cups all-purpose flour

¾ cup light brown sugar, firmly packed

½ teaspoon salt

½ cup butter, chilled, cut into pieces

2 tablespoons cold water

2 teaspoons vanilla

1 ounce shaved semisweet or milk chocolate, for garnish

Place chocolate in work bowl of processor and chop roughly. Add nuts and chop coarsely. Add flour, sugar, and salt and blend (bits of chocolate and walnut should be clearly visible). Add butter and process to blend. Add water and vanilla and mix using on/off turns until crumbly.

FILLING:

1 (11-ounce) box dried apricots or 2 (6-ounce) packages, finely chopped

1½ cups sugar

¾ cup water

3 tablespoons flour

Juice of ½ lemon

Combine all ingredients in heavy saucepan. Bring slowly to boil over low heat. Reduce heat and simmer, stirring frequently and mashing any large pieces of apricot, until mixture resembles thick jam, about 25 minutes. Remove from heat and let cool.

Preheat oven to 350°. Pat ⅔ of dough into bottom and 1 inch up sides of 8 or 9 inch springform pan. Add filling. Crumble additional dough over top to cover. Bake 40 minutes. Let cool. To serve, remove springform and decorate top with shaved chocolate.

NOTE: This cake freezes well. Cool thoroughly, leave cake on springform base and wrap well. Leftover dough can be frozen and used as a crumb topping for cakes or one-crust pies.

Carol Sue Coden

Almond Torte

CAKE:

8 eggs, separated
½ pound confectioner's sugar
½ pound blanched almonds,
    grated

⅛ teaspoon salt

Beat yolks and sugar until light lemon colored. Add grated nuts. Beat whites, add salt and add to nut mixture, folding in carefully. Pour into two buttered and floured cake pans. Bake at 325° for 20 minutes.

FILLING & ICING:

8 ounces sweet butter
2 cups confectioner's sugar

3 teaspoons strong coffee
Whole almonds, for garnish

Cream butter and sugar. Add coffee. Spread between layers and frost cake. Whole almonds may be used to decorate cake. Refrigerate for several hours before serving.

Joan Weil

Banana Pineapple Cake

3 cups all-purpose flour
2 cups sugar
1 teaspoon salt
1 teaspoon baking soda
3 slightly beaten eggs
2 cups mashed bananas
    (about 4)

1 cup cooking oil
1 (8¼-ounce) can crushed
    pineapple
1½ teaspoons vanilla
Powdered sugar for decoration

In mixing bowl, thoroughly stir flour, sugar, salt, and baking soda. Make a well in center. Combine eggs, bananas, oil, undrained pineapple, and vanilla. Add all at once to dry ingredients, stirring until well moistened. Pour batter into a greased and floured 10 inch fluted tube pan. Bake at 350° for 65-70 minutes or until cake tests done. Cool in pan for 15 minutes, remove, and cool on wire rack. Sprinkle with powdered sugar or drizzle with powdered sugar glaze.

Charlotte Edelheit

Chocolate Chip Cherry Cake

2 cups flour
¾ cup oil
¾ cup sugar
2 eggs
2 teaspoons vanilla
1 teaspoon baking soda
1 teaspoon cinnamon

Dash of salt
1 can (or 1 cup) cherry pie
    filling
16 ounces chocolate chips
1 cup nuts (optional)
Powdered sugar for decoration

Mix first 8 ingredients. Stir in the rest. Pour into greased tube or bundt pan. Bake at 350° for 1 hour. Cool for 10 minutes before removing. Sprinkle top with powdered sugar.

Charlotte Edelheit

Sour Cream Coffee Cake

½ cup butter or margarine
2 cups sugar
1 cup sour cream
1 teaspoon vanilla
2 eggs

2 cups flour
1 teaspoon baking powder
1 teaspoon baking soda
1 teaspoon salt

NUT MIXTURE:

2 teaspoons sugar
2 teaspoons cinnamon

¾ cup chopped walnuts

In mixer, beat butter and sugar until light and fluffy. Add sour cream and vanilla and remaining ingredients and beat at low speed until blended, constantly scraping the bowl. At medium speed, beat 3 minutes, occasionally scraping the bowl. Spoon half of mixture into a 10 inch greased tube pan. Sprinkle on nut mixture; then add rest of batter. Bake 60-65 minutes at 350° until cake pulls away from side of pan. Cool in pan on wire rack 10 minutes. Loosen inside edge. Invert from pan onto tray until cool.

Shelly Cooper

Pumpkin Snack Cake

4 eggs
1⅔ cups sugar
1 cup cooking oil
1 (16-ounce) can pumpkin
2 cups flour

2 teaspoons baking powder
1 teaspoon baking soda
2 teaspoons ground cinnamon
½ teaspoon salt

Beat together eggs, sugar, oil, and pumpkin until light and fluffy. Mix together flour, baking powder, baking soda, cinnamon, and salt. Add to pumpkin mixture and mix thoroughly. Spread batter in an ungreased 15 x 10 inch pan and bake in 350° oven for 25-30 minutes. Let cool and frost with cream cheese frosting.

FROSTING:

1 (3-ounce) package cream
    cheese
½ cup butter or margarine,
    softened

1 teaspoon vanilla
2 cups powdered sugar

Cream together cream cheese and butter or margarine. Stir in vanilla. Add powdered sugar, a little at a time, beating well until mixture is smooth. Frost cake and cut into bars.

Variation: Add 1 cup chopped nuts or raisins to batter. Add ¼ cup chopped nuts to icing and ice while bars are warm.

NOTE: Freezes well.

Trudy Weiss

 For more even cakes and bar cookies, spread batter evenly, make large X in pan with tip of rubber spatula pushing batter well into corners and leaving slight hollow in center.

Ada's Bobke Coffee Cake

5½ cups flour, divided
1 cup sugar
1 teaspoon salt
2 packages rapid-rise yeast
½ cup water

2¼ cups melted butter or
    margarine, divided
1 cup sour cream
3 eggs

TOPPING:

1 cup sugar
2 teaspoons cinnamon
1 cup chopped walnuts or
    pecans

2 cups raisins

Mix 4½ cups of the flour, sugar, salt, and yeast in mixer or processor. Heat water and 2 cups butter or margarine to 125-130°. Pour into flour mixture. Beat or process. Add sour cream and eggs. Beat or process. Add 1 cup flour. Beat or process. Dough will be sticky.

Grease a large bowl. Put in dough and grease top. Cover with plastic wrap and a damp towel. Refrigerate overnight.

Next day, punch dough down. Turn out onto well-floured pastry cloth. Knead for a few minutes, adding ¼ cup flour, if necessary. Combine sugar, cinnamon, and nuts. Set aside. Melt ¼ cup butter or margarine and set aside.

Divide dough into 4 parts. Roll each part into a 9 x 12 inch rectangle. Brush with melted margarine or butter. Sprinkle with ½ cup of topping mixture and ½ cup raisins. Roll up and cut into twelve 1 inch slices. Place, cut side down, into well-greased tube pan. Repeat with the rest of the dough.

Heat oven on warm for 2 minutes. Turn oven off. Put pan into oven and let rise for 50 minutes. Remove and heat oven to 350°. Bake for 1 hour. Turn out onto rack and cool.

Ada Feldman

 To test whether the dough has been kneaded enough, make an indentation in it with two fingers; dough should spring back.

Special Times Coffee Cake

1½ cups sugar
¾ cup butter, softened
3 eggs
1½ teaspoons vanilla
3 cups flour
1½ teaspoons baking powder

1½ teaspoons baking soda
¼ teaspoon salt
1½ cups sour cream
⅔ cup strawberry preserves
½ cup chopped walnuts

Preheat oven to 350°. Grease a 10 x 4 inch tube pan. In a large mixing bowl, combine sugar, butter, eggs, and vanilla. Beat on medium speed for 2 minutes. Combine flour, baking powder, baking soda, and salt. Blend into butter/sugar mixture, alternately with the sour cream. Combine preserves with the nuts. Pour ⅓ of the batter into prepared pan. Batter will be very thick. Spread gently with spoon or flexible knife. Spoon ½ of preserve mixture on top. Repeat process. Pour remaining batter over preserves. Bake 55-60 minutes. Cool slightly before removing from pan.

FROSTING:

⅓ cup strawberry preserves
½ cup chopped walnuts
1½ cups confectioner's sugar,
    sifted

1 tablespoon water

Combine ingredients and spread over top of cake.

NOTE: Raspberry preserves may also be used. Cake also looks wonderful in a bundt pan. Freezes well.

Yield: 12-16 servings.   Natalie Katz

 Slip your hand inside a sandwich bag to make a perfect mitt for greasing pans.

Raspberry Nut Torte

PASTRY:

½ cup unsalted butter, room
   temperature
⅓ cup sugar
1 egg

1¼ cups flour
1 cup finely chopped walnuts
1 (12-ounce) jar raspberry
   preserves

Cream butter with sugar in large bowl until fluffy. Beat in egg. Combine flour and walnuts. Stir into creamed mixture. Blend well. Do not overmix. Refrigerate 2 hours. Pat dough into bottom and sides of 9 inch springform pan. Spread 1 cup of preserves evenly over pastry.

FILLING:

4 eggs
¾ cup firmly packed brown
   sugar
2 cups chopped walnuts
½ cup flaked coconut

2 tablespoons flour
¼ teaspoon baking powder
Kirsch, optional
Powdered sugar, for dusting

Preheat oven to 350°. Beat eggs and brown sugar at high speed until light. Combine walnuts, coconut, flour, and baking powder in another bowl. Gently fold into egg mixture. Pour mixture over pastry. Bake 1 hour. Cool. Remove springform. Optional: Thin remaining preserves with Kirsch and decorate top. Dust with powdered sugar.

Margie Kurzmann

"Everything You've Always Wanted Pound Cake"

1 cup butter or margarine
3 cups sugar
1 cup sour cream
3 cups cake flour

¼ teaspoon baking soda
⅛ teaspoon salt
6 eggs
1 teaspoon vanilla

Cream butter and sugar. Add sour cream. Sift flour, baking soda, and salt. Add eggs, one at a time, alternately with flour. Add vanilla. Put in a greased bundt pan in a cold oven and bake for 1½ hours at 300°.

NOTE: This can be made with egg substitute and it is just as delicious.

Jackie Tepper

Superb Date Nut Chocolate Chip Cake

1 cup dates, cut into small
    pieces
1 teaspoon baking soda
1 cup boiling water
½ cup butter
½ cup margarine
1 cup sugar

2 eggs
1⅓ cups flour, sifted
¼ cup cocoa
¼ teaspoon salt
1 teaspoon vanilla
3 ounces pecans
3 ounces chocolate chips

Preheat oven to 350°. Combine date pieces, baking soda, and boiling water. Set aside. Cream butter and margarine. Add sugar and continue creaming. Add eggs. Sift flour, cocoa, and salt together. Add dry ingredients alternately with date mixture. Add vanilla. Pour into a greased 9 inch springform pan. Bake for 45 minutes. Sprinkle with pecans and chocolate chips and return to warm oven until chips are slightly melted.

Marise Levy

Chocolate Crème Torte

4 ounces bittersweet chocolate
1 cup milk
5 eggs, separated

2 cups sugar
1 cup pastry flour, sifted twice
1 teaspoon baking powder

Preheat oven to 325°. In a small saucepan, melt chocolate in milk and let cool. Cream egg yolks and sugar, then add flour and baking powder. Add chocolate mixture and fold in beaten egg whites. Pour batter into two non-stick 9 inch baking pans. Bake for 35 minutes. Remove from oven and let set for 5 minutes before inverting.

FROSTING:

4 ounces chocolate instant
    pudding (not sugar free)

1 cup milk
½ pint whipping cream

Whip ingredients together with electric mixer. Frost cake between layers and on top and sides.

NOTE: Can be frozen

Yield: 10-12 servings.

Vi Cohen

Hershey Bar Cake

1 (7-ounce) milk chocolate bar
1 (16-ounce) can chocolate
 syrup
½ pound butter
2 cups sugar
4 eggs

2 teaspoons vanilla
2½ cups flour
½ teaspoon baking soda
1 cup buttermilk
Confectioner's sugar, optional

Preheat oven to 300°. Melt chocolate bar and syrup over low heat. Let cool. Cream butter and sugar. Add eggs and vanilla to creamed mixture. Sift flour and baking soda together. Alternately add flour and buttermilk to creamed mixture, a little at a time. Add melted chocolate mixture. Pour into greased tube pan or 12 cup bundt pan. Bake for 1½ - 1¾ hours. Place a pan on lower rack, as batter may spill over. Cool before removing from pan. Dust with confectioner's sugar on top, if desired.

NOTE: Non-stick spray may be used in pan to prevent sticking.

Robin Attard

Plum Torte

1 cup sugar
½ cup sweet butter
1 cup unbleached flour, sifted
1 teaspoon baking powder
Pinch of salt

2 eggs
24 halves of pitted purple plums
Sugar
Lemon juice
1 teaspoon cinnamon

Preheat oven to 350°. Cream sugar and butter. Add flour, baking powder, salt, and eggs and beat well. Spoon batter into 9 inch springform pan. Place plum halves, skin side up, on top of batter. Sprinkle lightly with sugar and lemon juice (depending on sweetness of fruit). Sprinkle with cinnamon. Bake for 1 hour. Remove and cool. Refrigerate or freeze. May be served warm or cold, plain or topped with ice cream or whipped cream.

NOTE: If frozen, defrost and reheat briefly at 300°. Other fruits may be used such as tart apples or peaches. If peaches are used, sprinkle flour on them also.

Yield: 8 servings.

Helen Shevin

Sour Cream Nectarine Tart

SHELL:

1⅓ cups flour
2 tablespoons sugar
½ teaspoon salt
¼ teaspoon cinnamon

½ cup cold, unsalted butter, cut
   into bits
1½ tablespoons ice water

In a bowl, stir together the flour, sugar, salt, and cinnamon; add butter and blend. Add enough ice water to form mixture into a soft dough. Press the dough evenly onto the bottom and up the sides of a 9 inch tart pan with removable fluted rim and chill the shell for 30 minutes.

FILLING:

5 cups peeled and thinly sliced
   ripe nectarines
2 tablespoons fresh lemon juice
¾ cup sour cream
½ cup firmly packed brown
   sugar

1 large egg
½ teaspoon salt
1 teaspoon vanilla
2 tablespoons flour

In a large bowl, toss together the nectarines and lemon juice. In small bowl, whisk the sour cream and brown sugar until smooth. Whisk in the egg, salt, vanilla, and flour until combined well. Add to the nectarine and lemon mixture and blend just prior to filling the shell.

TOPPING:

2 tablespoons softened,
   unsalted butter
2 tablespoons brown sugar
2 tablespoons flour

½ teaspoon cinnamon
½ cup chopped nuts (pecans,
   almonds or walnuts)

Cream together the butter and brown sugar. Add flour, cinnamon, and nuts. Set aside.

Transfer the filling to the shell, sprinkle with the topping and bake in lower third of a preheated 425° oven for 25 minutes. Reduce heat to 350° and bake for 20-30 more minutes or until the top is golden. Let tart cool on a rack.

Yield: Serves 10.   Abbey Brasch Nathan

Brandy Alexander Pie

1 envelope unflavored gelatin
½ cup cold water
⅔ cup sugar, divided
⅛ teaspoon salt
3 eggs, separated
¼ cup cognac

¼ cup créme de cacao
2 cups heavy cream, whipped,
   divided
1 (9 inch) graham cracker crust
Chocolate for garnish

Sprinkle gelatin over cold water in a 2-quart saucepan. Add ⅓ cup sugar, salt, and egg yolks. Stir to blend. Heat gelatin mixture over a low heat, stirring until gelatin dissolves and mixture thickens. DO NOT BOIL. Remove from heat and stir in cognac and créme de cacao. Chill until mixture starts to mound slightly. Beat egg whites until stiff. Gradually beat in the remaining sugar and fold into thickened mixture. Fold 1 cup whipped cream into mixture. Pour into crust and chill several hours or overnight. Garnish with remaining whipped cream. Top with chocolate curls, if desired.

Yield: 8-10 servings.

Freddy Shiffman

Caribbean Fudge Pie

¼ cup butter or margarine
¾ cup brown sugar, packed
3 eggs
1 (12-ounce) package semi-
   sweet chocolate pieces,
   melted
2 teaspoons instant coffee

1 teaspoon rum extract
¼ cup all-purpose flour
1 cup walnuts, coarsely
   chopped
1 (9 inch) unbaked pie shell
½ cup walnut halves, for
   decoration

Preheat oven at 375°.

Cream butter with sugar. Beat in eggs, one at a time. Add melted chocolate, instant coffee, and rum extract. Stir in flour and chopped walnuts and turn into unbaked pie shell. Top with remaining walnut halves. Bake for 25 minutes. Cool. Top with vanilla ice cream, if desired.

Yield: 8 servings.

Sheila Brown

Cheesy Peach Pie

8-9 graham crackers, crushed
2 tablespoons butter, melted
1 (20-ounce) can peach halves,
    drained

2 eggs, beaten
1 cup sugar
1 pint sour cream

Crush graham crackers. Add butter and mix until completely moistened. Line a 10 inch pie plate with graham cracker mixture. Save a small amount for top. Drain peaches and put into pie shell. Beat eggs with sugar until light in color. Add sour cream and pour over peaches. Sprinkle remaining graham crackers over peaches. Bake at 350° for 35 minutes, until browned and high.

Variations: Use a 9 inch deep dish pie plate. Sliced peaches can be used.

NOTE: Place pie plate on a cookie sheet to catch any overflow or spillage.

Yield: 6-8 servings.

Rose Green

Pecan Pie

1 cup sugar
1 cup light corn syrup
⅓ cup butter or margarine
4 eggs, beaten

1 teaspoon vanilla extract
¼ teaspoon salt
1 (9 inch) unbaked pastry shell
1-1¼ cups pecan halves

Preheat oven to 325°.

Combine first 3 ingredients in a medium saucepan. Cook over low heat, stirring constantly, until sugar dissolves and butter melts; let cool slightly. Add eggs, vanilla, and salt to mixture, stirring well. Pour filling into pastry shell, top with pecan halves, arranging them in concentric circles. Bake for 50-55 minutes.

Esther Becker

 Pies will be brown and glossy if crust is brushed with milk before baking.

Pecan Tarts

CREAM CHEESE PASTRY:

¼ pound cream cheese,
    softened

¼ pound butter, softened
1 cup flour

Mix all ingredients together and refrigerate overnight. Divide pastry into 24 small balls (walnut size). Press each into small muffin tins, or roll out pastry on scantly floured board. Cut into small circles and place in muffin tins.

FILLING:

1 egg
½ cup plus 2 tablespoons
    brown sugar, firmly packed
1 teaspoon vanilla

1 tablespoon butter, melted
Dash of salt
⅛ cup corn syrup (light or dark)
1 cup chopped pecans

Combine all ingredients except pecans and beat until smooth. Add chopped pecans. Pour mixture evenly into pastry shells. Bake at 325° for 20-25 minutes, until pastry is golden brown.

NOTE: Freezes well.

Yield: 24 small tarts.

Charlotte Edelheit

Never-Fail Pie Crust

1½ cups sifted flour
¼ teaspoon baking powder
⅛ teaspoon salt
¾ cup shortening

1 egg, slightly beaten
1 tablespoon cream or pareve
    equivalent

Sift together flour, baking powder, and salt. Cut shortening into sifted ingredients, add beaten egg and cream. Mix lightly until dough holds its shape. Divide in two. Press dough with heel of hand, spreading evenly on bottom and up sides of pie plates.

Baking time and degree varies with whatever is used as filling.

NOTE: In spreading dough in pie pans, work it up over the rim and you will have enough to crimp the edges.

Yield: 2 pie shells.

Tillie Brandwine

Crisp Pecan Latke Cookies

1 cup firmly packed brown
   sugar
1 cup butter, melted
1 cup light corn syrup

2 cups flour
2 cups finely chopped pecans
3 teaspoons vanilla

Thoroughly grease cookie sheets. In a 2 quart saucepan, combine sugar, butter, and corn syrup. Cook over high heat, stirring constantly until mixture comes to a boil. Remove from heat, stir in flour and nuts until blended. Mix in vanilla. Drop batter by level teaspoons about 3 inches apart on cookie sheet. Bake at 350° for 8 minutes or until cookies are rich golden brown. Cool about one minute and remove to wire racks to cool. Store in covered can.

Yield: About 80 cookies.

Amalia Gold

Velma's Fashion Spree Cookies

2 cups brown sugar
1 cup margarine
2 eggs

3 cups flour
1 teaspoon cream of tartar

Preheat oven to 375°. Spray cookie sheet with vegetable spray. In electric mixer, cream brown sugar and margarine well. Add eggs and beat until blended. Add flour and cream of tartar; mix well. If dough seems too sticky, add a little more flour. Place ½ teaspoon of dough on prepared cookie sheet and pat out thinly (dip fingers in cold water to stop from becoming sticky). Bake 5-10 minutes—watch, as cookies brown quickly. When lightly brown, take from oven. Use spatula to remove cookies and let cool on wire rack.

Velma Friedman

 To soften brown sugar, store in a covered container overnight with a piece of fresh bread. To keep soft, keep in refrigerator or store tightly covered with a slice of fresh bread.

Mother-in-Law's Butter Cookies

1 cup margarine or butter
1 cup sugar, divided
1 egg yolk

2 cups flour
1 teaspoon vanilla
½ teaspoon cinnamon

Cream butter, ¾ cup sugar, and egg yolk. Stir in flour and vanilla. Roll into two logs (3 inch diameter). Refrigerate for a few hours, slice into ¼ inch sticks and place on greased cookie sheet. Mix remaining ¼ cup sugar and cinnamon together, then sprinkle on cookies. Bake at 350° for 10-12 minutes.

NOTE: Freezes well.

Ann Zousmer

Vinegar Cookies

1 cup margarine (no butter)
1 cup sugar
1½ cups flour
½ teaspoon baking soda

1 teaspoon cider vinegar
2 tablespoons milk, for
    decoration

Combine all the ingredients except the milk. Mix well until light and smooth, preferably in a food processor or electric mixer. Drop by ½ teaspoon about the size of a dime, press to no bigger than a quarter. Place 2 inches apart on an ungreased cookie sheet. Dip tines of small fork in milk, then press into cookies to flatten. Dip fork in milk frequently. Bake for 20 minutes at 300°. When golden brown, remove with spatula. Cool on rack.

NOTE: If using a food processor, pulse 3 times for 5 seconds to mix. Stir down, then mix until light and smooth, about 15-20 seconds.

Yield: 60-75 cookies.

Charlotte Harris

Jan's Big Soft Ginger Cookies

2¼ cups flour
2 teaspoons ground ginger
1 teaspoon baking soda
¾ teaspoon cinnamon
½ teaspoon ground cloves
¼ teaspoon salt

¾ cup margarine
1 cup sugar
1 egg
¼ cup dark molasses
2 tablespoons sugar

Combine and set aside the flour, ground ginger, baking soda, cinnamon, ground cloves, and salt. In a large mixing bowl, beat margarine with electric mixer on low speed for 30 seconds to soften. Add one cup sugar and beat until fluffy. Add egg and molasses, beat well. Stir dry ingredients into beaten mixture. Shape into 1½ inch balls (one heaping tablespoon dough each). Roll in two tablespoons sugar and place on ungreased cookie sheet, 2½ inches apart. Bake at 350° for 10-12 minutes. DO NOT OVERBAKE! Let stand 2 minutes before removing to wire rack.

Yield: 24 three inch cookies, or 48 two inch cookies.   Mary Schwartz

Oatmeal Chocolate Chip Raisin Cookies

¾ cup sweet butter
½ cup sugar
1 cup brown sugar
1 egg
2 tablespoons water
1 teaspoon vanilla
⅔ cup unbleached flour

½ teaspoon baking soda
½ teaspoon salt
1 teaspoon cinnamon
3 cups quick-cooking oatmeal
1 cup raisins
1 (12-ounce) package milk
   chocolate chips

Preheat oven to 350°. Grease cookie sheets with vegetables spray. Cream butter, sugar, and brown sugar until fluffy. Add egg and beat; add water and vanilla. Sift dry ingredients together, and add to egg mixture. Mix well. Add oatmeal, raisins, chocolate chips, and mix.

Keep your hands wet and form into walnut size balls. Put on cookie sheets two inches apart. Bake for 13-15 minutes. Cool slightly and then remove to rack and cool completely.

Yield: 60 cookies.   Wendy Wagenheim

Cookies from Art Class

1 cup solid vegetable
  shortening
¾ cup white sugar
¾ cup light brown sugar
2 eggs
1 teaspoon vanilla
1 teaspoon hot water
1½ cups flour
1 teaspoon salt
1 teaspoon baking soda

2 cups quick-cooking oatmeal
Optional ingredients, up to
  3 cups of the following:
Chocolate chips
Nuts
Coconut
Dates
Raisins
Butterscotch chips

Cream vegetable shortening, white sugar, and brown sugar. Add eggs, vanilla, hot water. Stir in flour, salt, and baking soda; add oatmeal. At this point you can add optional ingredients. Place heaping teaspoon of dough on cookie sheet that is covered with aluminum foil. Bake at 375°. Place on bottom shelf in oven for 4 minutes, then move to shelf above the middle of the oven for another 4 minutes. The cookies will appear light at this point. If you take them out they will be chewy. If you like them crunchier, leave them in for 5 more minutes. Remove and place on waxed paper to cool.

Yield: 36 large cookies.   Geraldine Palmer

Oatmeal-Raspberry Bars

1 cup butter or margarine
1 cup brown sugar, packed
2 cups quick cooking oatmeal
1¾ cups flour
1½ teaspoons cinnamon

½ teaspoon salt (optional)
½ teaspoon baking soda
½ cup chopped walnuts
¾ cup raspberry jam

Cream butter and sugar until smooth. Add all other ingredients except jam. Mix until well blended—mixture will be coarse. Reserve 2 cups of mixture. Spread the rest of mixture onto the bottom of a 9 x 13 x 2 inch ungreased baking pan. Cover with jam and sprinkle reserve mixture over the top. Bake in 400° oven for 18-22 minutes, until brown. Cool before cutting.

Variation: Any flavor of jam can be used.

NOTE: Texture will be fine if food processor is used.

                                                    Sharon Leider

Pumpkin Cookies

½ cup vegetable shortening
1 cup sugar
1 cup pumpkin
1 teaspoon vanilla
½ teaspoon baking soda

1 teaspoon cinnamon
1 teaspoon baking powder
2 cups sifted flour
1 cup chocolate chips or raisins
  (optional)

Cream shortening, sugar, pumpkin, and vanilla until smooth. Stir together baking soda, cinnamon, baking powder, and flour, then add to pumpkin mixture. At this point you can add chocolate chips or raisins. Drop by teaspoonful on greased cookie sheet and bake at 350° for 10-12 minutes until brown on bottom.

NOTE: Recipe may be tripled as 3 cups of pumpkin in large can of pumpkin.

Yield: 2½ dozen.   Geraldine Palmer

Mandel Bread

¾ cup vegetable oil
3 eggs
1 cup sugar
1 teaspoon baking powder
1 teaspoon vanilla

2½ cups flour
Optional: Semi-sweet chocolate
  bits, nuts, or cinnamon and
  sugar, to taste

In the following order, combine: oil, eggs, sugar, baking powder, vanilla, and flour, mixing well after each addition. The batter will be very heavy and hard to mix. This recipe works well in a food processor or electric mixer. Spread half of the batter in two or three metal ice cube trays, cover with any of the optional items. Chocolate bits may be melted and spread over batter. Cover with remaining batter and marbleize mixture by pulling a knife through the center of the batter. You may cover batter with additional topping as well. Bake at 350° for 30 minutes. Cut into bars immediately and place on a cookie sheet. Bake another 15 minutes. They should be hard but moist.

Yield: 2-2½ dozen.   Robin Gold

Mandelbrot

3 eggs
1 cup sugar
½ cup margarine
½ cup cooking oil
1 teaspoon vanilla
Juice of ½ lemon

Dash of salt
3 cups flour
2 teaspoons baking powder
1 cup pecans, chopped
Cinnamon-sugar mix, to taste

Preheat oven to 350°. Beat eggs; add sugar, margarine, oil, vanilla, and lemon juice. Sift dry ingredients and blend into mixture. Add nuts. Shape dough into three equal loaves and put on cookie sheet. Bake for 45 minutes. Remove from oven and cut in thin slices. Sprinkle with cinnamon-sugar mix. Return to oven for 5-8 minutes to brown.

Gloria Siegel

Peanut Butter-Chocolate Bars

1 (12-ounce) jar peanut butter,
    smooth or crunchy
2 cups graham cracker crumbs
¾ cup margarine, melted

1 cup confectioner's sugar
1 (12-ounce) bag semi-sweet
    chocolate chips

Combine first four ingredients. Spread into 13 x 9 x 2 inch pan sprayed with non-stick vegetable spray. Bake 5-7 minutes at 375°. Remove from oven. Sprinkle chocolate chips over hot mixture. Place sheet of aluminum foil over top. When chips melt, spread evenly. Cool and refrigerate about ½ hour, cutting into squares before totally solid.

Yield: 36 cookies.

Geri Pasternak

Honey Butter Balls

1 cup butter or shortening
¼ cup honey
2¼ cups unsifted flour

2 teaspoons vanilla
2 cups finely chopped nuts
½ cup confectioner's sugar

Blend butter and honey together. Add flour and vanilla. Blend well. Mix in nuts. Roll into small balls and place on greased cookie sheet, 2 inches apart. Bake at 325° for 20 minutes. Allow to cool and roll in confectioner's sugar.

NOTE: Freezes well.

Yield: 60 balls.

Goldie Adler

Nut Fingers

Graham crackers (enough to
cover pan)
1 cup margarine

1 cup brown sugar
1½ cups chopped pecans

Break crackers on perforations into fingers. Pack fingers tightly on a 10 x 15 inch jelly roll pan. Melt margarine, add brown sugar, mix until dissolved. Bring to an active boil, stirring constantly. Remove from stove and add nuts. Pour evenly over graham crackers. Bake at 350° for 10 minutes. Remove and cool for about 5 minutes. Remove from pan, separating fingers, and put on wax paper to continue cooling. Keep in tin when completely cool.

NOTE: Freezes well.

Yield: 54 fingers.

Goldie Adler

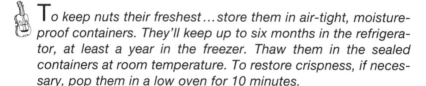 To keep nuts their freshest…store them in air-tight, moisture-proof containers. They'll keep up to six months in the refrigerator, at least a year in the freezer. Thaw them in the sealed containers at room temperature. To restore crispness, if necessary, pop them in a low oven for 10 minutes.

Date-Nut Torte Bars

2⅓ cups graham cracker
    crumbs
1 teaspoon baking powder
¼ teaspoon salt
3 eggs
1 cup sugar
1 teaspoon vanilla

1 cup pitted sliced dates
1 cup chopped walnuts
Optional:
    ½ cup coconut
    Whipped cream
    ½ cup confectioner's sugar

Combine graham cracker crumbs, baking powder, and salt. Beat eggs until light, gradually adding sugar, and continue beating. Stir in crumb mixture, vanilla, dates, walnuts, and coconut. Mix well. Spread batter evenly into greased 9 inch square pan. Bake in preheated 350° oven for 30 minutes. Cut into squares and serve warm with whipped cream or cut into bars and roll in confectioner's sugar and serve as cookies.

Yield: 3 dozen bars.   Fran Penskar

Ice Cream Strudel

1 pound margarine or butter
4 cups flour
1 pint vanilla ice cream
Fruit preserves, about 18-24
    ounces, or enough to cover
    dough

1 cup chopped nuts
1 cup sugar
1 tablespoon cinnamon
1 cup raisins

Soften margarine and ice cream. Blend. Gradually add flour and mix well. Refrigerate dough for several hours. On floured board, roll dough into 3-4 long rectangles. Spread with the preserves, covering the dough. Sprinkle with nuts, sugar, cinnamon, and raisins. Roll up jelly roll style. Sprinkle the tops with sugar and cinnamon. Bake at 350° for 30-40 minutes on a greased cookie sheet. Slice when cool.

Ann Zousmer

Crescent Cookies

3 cups flour
¼ cup sugar
Pinch of salt
1 package dry yeast
½ pound butter or margarine
3 egg yolks
1 small (6-ounce) can
   evaporated milk

2 teaspoons cinnamon
¾ cup sugar
Apricot jam (can be
   unsweetened)
3 egg whites, stiffly beaten
1 cup chopped walnuts or
   pecans

In processor, combine flour, sugar, salt, and yeast. Cut butter into small pieces. Add to processor. Pulse until dough is crumbly. Add yolks and evaporated milk. Process until well mixed. Flatten dough into disk. Cover with plastic wrap and refrigerate overnight.

Combine cinnamon and sugar. Sprinkle ¼ on wax paper. Divide dough into 4 equal pieces. Place on top of mixture. Roll out into circle, 9 to 10 inches in diameter, lifting dough as you roll and pushing sugar back underneath. Spread lightly with apricot jam.

Cut circle into 16 wedges. Roll each triangle from outside edge to point and bend to form crescent. Dip crescents into egg whites and then into ground nuts. Place on lightly greased cookie sheets. Bake at 350° oven until golden, 15 to 20 minutes.

Gerry Palmer

Good and Gooey Brownies

4 ounces bittersweet chocolate
½ cup butter or margarine
4 eggs
¼ teaspoon salt
2 cups sugar
1 teaspoon vanilla

1 cup flour
1 cup semisweet chocolate
   chips
Optional:
   1 cup chopped nuts

Melt bittersweet chocolate and butter, let cool. Beat eggs and salt until lemon colored. Add sugar and continue beating until light and fluffy. Stir in melted mixture and vanilla. Add flour, beat until batter is smooth. Add chocolate chips and nuts. Pour into greased 9 x 13 x 2 inch glass baking pan. Bake for 30 minutes, or until firm, at 325°.

NOTE: This is a moist brownie and freezes well.

Trudy Weiss

Apricot Strudel

2 cups flour
1 cup butter or margarine
1 (8-ounce) package cream
  cheese
½ cup plus 2 tablespoons
  sugar, divided

1 (12-ounce) jar apricot
  preserves
1 cup pecans, chopped
1½ teaspoons cinnamon
1 cup shredded coconut

Combine flour, butter, cream cheese, and 2 tablespoons sugar and mix thoroughly in an electric mixer or food processor. Form dough into three balls and refrigerate overnight. Roll dough thinly on floured board. Mix remaining ½ cup sugar and cinnamon together. Spread preserves, nuts, cinnamon, sugar, and coconut over surface. Roll up like jelly roll and bake on a greased cookie sheet for about one hour at 350°. Cut while hot. Let cool and dust with confectioner's sugar.

Yield: 12-16 servings.   Jackie Tepper

Butterscotch Brownies

4 tablespoons butter, melted
1 cup dark brown sugar
1 egg
¾ cup flour
½ teaspoon salt

1 teaspoon baking powder
½ teaspoon vanilla
½ cup broken nut meats
¼ cup coconut

Mix butter and brown sugar together, add egg and mix. Then mix in flour, salt, and baking powder. Stir in vanilla, then add nuts and coconut. Spread into buttered 8 x 8 x 2 inch square baking pan. Bake at 350° for 25 minutes. Cool and frost.

FROSTING:

¼ cup butter
½ cup brown sugar
⅛ cup half and half or milk

1 scant cup confectioner's
  sugar
½ teaspoon vanilla

Melt butter until brown and add brown sugar, cook, stirring, until sugar melts (should be dark brown). Pour in milk and stir. Let cool, add confectioner's sugar and vanilla and beat well. Spread onto cooled brownies.

Yield: 20 squares.   Sally Green

Palm Beach Brownies

8 ounces (8 squares)
  unsweetened chocolate
1 cup unsalted butter
5 eggs
1 tablespoon vanilla extract
1 teaspoon almond extract
¼ teaspoon salt

2½ tablespoon dry instant
  espresso or powdered
  instant coffee (not granular)
3¾ cups sugar
1⅔ cups sifted flour
2 cups walnut halves or large
  pieces

Preheat oven to 425°. Line a 9 x 13 x 2 inch baking pan with aluminum foil, grease, and set aside. Melt chocolate and butter in double boiler or heavy saucepan over low heat. Stir occasionally until smooth. Remove from heat and set aside. In large mixer bowl, beat eggs, vanilla, almond extract, salt, dry instant espresso, and sugar at high speed for 10 minutes. On low speed, add chocolate mixture, beat until mixed. Then beat in flour until just combined. Stir in nuts. Spread batter into prepared pan and smooth top.

Bake for 35 minutes. After 15 minutes, reverse pan from back to front to insure even baking. There will be a thick, crisp crust over the top. Remove from oven and cool at room temperature.

Cover with a cookie sheet and invert. Remove pan and foil lining. Cover with another cookie sheet and invert again. Let stand 6-8 hours or refrigerate for a few hours before cutting. Cut with serrated bread knife.

Yield: 16 huge or 24 large brownies.   Barbara Kuhlik

Lenora's Delightful-Sugarless Cookies

DOUGH:

4 egg whites or egg substitute
About ⅔ cup water or orange
   juice
1 cup corn oil

4 teaspoons sugar substitute
4 cups flour
2 teaspoons baking powder
½ teaspoon baking soda

Measure egg substitute or 4 egg whites in measuring cup and enough water or orange juice to equal 1 cup. Combine egg mixture, oil, and sugar substitute in a large bowl. Add dry ingredients. Knead until manageable. Divide dough into four parts. Roll out one portion of the dough and fill with the filling of your choice.

FILLING VARIATIONS:

¼ pound dried apricots or
   3 ounces unsweetened
   chocolate

1 tablespoons margarine
1 tablespoons water or ½ cup
   chopped nuts

For apricots: Cover apricots with water and cook until soft. Put them through a processor or blender. Spread apricots on dough and roll up jelly roll fashion.

For chocolate filling: Melt unsweetened chocolate in top of double boiler. Add margarine and water. Mix well. Spread on another portion of the dough. Roll up jelly roll fashion.

For nut filling: Roll out another portion of the dough and spread with the chopped nuts. Cut rounds with a cookie cutter or use a glass.

Bake at 325° for 20-25 minutes.

Lenora Noler

 Low-Fat Substitute for Whipped Cream… Make a tasty but low-fat substitute for whipped cream by beating a banana and the white of one egg together until stiff.

KITCHEN MATH
(Size of Pans and Baking Dishes)

4 CUP BAKING DISH:
> 9 inch pie plate
> 8 x 1¼ inch layer cake pan
> 7⅜ x 3⅝ x 2¼ inch loaf pan

6 CUP BAKING DISH:
> 8 or 9 x 1½ inch layer cake pan
> 10 inch pie plate
> 8½ x 3⅝ x 2⅝ inch loaf pan

8 CUP BAKING DISH:
> 8 x 8 x 2 inch square pan
> 11 x 7 x 1½ inch baking pan
> 9 x 5 x 3 inch jelly-roll pan

12 CUP BAKING DISH AND OVER:

13½ x 8½ x 2 inch glass baking pan	12 cups
13 x 9 x 2 inch metal baking pan	15 cups
14 x 10½ x 2½ inch roasting pan	19 cups

(Total Volume of Various Special Baking Pans)

TUBE PANS:

7½ x 3 inch "bundt" tube pan	6 cups
9 x 3½ inch fancy tube or "bundt" pan	9 cups
9 x 3½ inch angel cake pan	12 cups
10 x 3¾ inch "bundt" or "Crownburst" pan	12 cups
9 x 3½ inch fancy tube mold	12 cups
10 x 4 inch fancy tube mold (Kugelhupf)	16 cups
10 x 4 inch angel cake pan	18 cups

MELON MOLD:

7 x 5½ x 4 inch mold	6 cups

SPRINGFORM PANS:

8 x 3 inch pan	12 cups
9 x 3 inch pan	16 cups

RING MOLDS:

8½ x 2¼ inch mold	4½ cups
9¼ x 2¾ inch mold	8 cups

CHARLOTTE MOLD:

6 x 4¼ inch mold	7½ cups

BRIOCHE PAN:

9½ x 3¼ inch pan	8 cups

TABLE OF EQUIVALENTS

Almonds	1 pound in shell	= 1-1¾ cups shelled
	1 pound, shelled	= 3½ cups
Apples	1 pound (3 medium)	= 3 cups sliced
Bananas	1 pound	= 3 medium
Butter or margarine	1 pound	= 2 cups
Cheese	½ pound	= 2 cups shredded
Chocolate, unsweetened	1 square	= 1 ounce
Cottage cheese	1 pound	= 2 cups
Crackers, graham	12-14	= 1 cup crumbs
Crackers, saltines	28	= 1 cup fine crumbs
Cream, whipping	½ pint	= 2 cups whipped
Dates, pitted	1 pound	= 2½ cups cut up
Eggs, whites	8-10	= 1 cup
Eggs, yolks	12-14	= 1 cup
Flour, all-purpose	1 pound	= 4 cups
Flour, cake	1 pound	= about 4¾ cups sifted
Lemon	1 medium	= 3 tablespoons juice plus 1-1½ teaspoons rind
Marshmallows	¼ pound	= 16
Onion	1 medium	= ¾ cup chopped
Orange	1 medium	= ⅓ cup juice plus 1 tablespoon rind
Peaches or Pears	1 pound	= 4 medium
Peas in the pod	1 pound	= 1 cup shelled
Pecans	1 pound unshelled	= 2¼ cups shelled
	1 pound shelled	= 4 cups
Potatoes, white	1 pound (3 medium)	= 2⅓ cups diced or sliced
Raisins, seedless	1 pound	= 3 cups
Rice	1 cup raw	= 3½-4 cups cooked
Sugar, brown	1 pound	= 2⅓-3 cups packed
Sugar, confectioner's	1 pound	= 4 cups sifted
Sugar, granulated	1 pound	= 2⅓ cups
Tomatoes	1 pound	= 4 small
Walnuts	1 pound unshelled	= 1⅔ cups chopped
	1 pound shelled	= 4 cups

Fruit Products

TO MAKE	USE
4 cups sliced apples	4 medium
2 cups sliced strawberries	1 pint
2 cups pitted cherries	4 cups unpitted
4 cups sliced fresh peaches	2 pounds or 8 medium
1 cup orange juice	3 medium oranges
1 teaspoon grated orange rind	½ orange
3 tablespoons lemon juice	1 lemon
1½ teaspoon grated lemon rind	1 lemon
1 cup mashed banana	3 medium

Dairy Products

TO MAKE	USE
8 tablespoons butter or margarine	¼ pound or 1 stick
2 cups butter or margarine	1 pound
1 cup freshly grated cheese	¼ pound
1 cup cottage cheese	8 ounce carton
1 cup whipped cream	½ cup cream for whipping
1 cup sour cream	8 ounce carton
⅔ cup evaporated milk	1 small can
2 large eggs	3 small eggs

Macaroni-Rice Products

TO MAKE	USE
4 cups cooked spaghetti	8 ounce package
2 cups cooked elbow macaroni	1 cup uncooked or half an 8 ounce package
4 cups cooked rice	1 cup uncooked
5 cups cooked noodles	3½ cups uncooked or an 8 ounce package

INDEX

INDEX

REORDER FORM

STILL FIDDLING IN THE KITCHEN

NCJW - Greater Detroit Section, 30233 Southfield Road
Southfield, MI 48076

Please send _____ copies of **STILL FIDDLING IN THE KITCHEN**

$15.00 each _____

Postage and handling $ 3.00 each _____

Total Enclosed $ _____

Name _____

Address _____

City _____ State _____ Zip _____

$ _____ Check or money order enclosed

Make checks payable to **National Council of Jewish Women**
The profits received will be used to support the
many community projects of **NCJW**.

STILL FIDDLING IN THE KITCHEN

NCJW - Greater Detroit Section, 30233 Southfield Road
Southfield, MI 48076

Please send _____ copies of **STILL FIDDLING IN THE KITCHEN**

$15.00 each _____

Postage and handling $ 3.00 each _____

Total Enclosed $ _____

Name _____

Address _____

City _____ State _____ Zip _____

$ _____ Check or money order enclosed

Make checks payable to **National Council of Jewish Women**
The profits received will be used to support the
many community projects of **NCJW**.

RE-ORDER FORM